better
is not so far
away

DECIDE TO RECOVER FROM
BINGEING, STARVING, OR CUTTING

Melissa Groman, LCSW

Mc
Graw
Hill
Education

New York   Chicago   San Francisco   Athens   London   Madrid
Mexico City   Milan   New Delhi   Singapore   Sydney   Toronto

1 2 3 4 5 6 7 8 9 10 DOC/DOC 1 0 9 8 7 6 5 4

ISBN 978-0-07-184084-2
MHID 0-07-184084-2

e-ISBN 978-0-07-184085-9
e-MHID 0-07-184085-0

Library of Congress Cataloging-in-Publication Data
Groman, Melissa.
Better is not so far away : decide to recover from bingeing, starving, or cutting / by Melissa Groman, LCSW.
pages cm
ISBN 978-0-07-184084-2
1. Self-mutilation—Popular works. 2. Eating disorders in women—Popular works. 3. Women—Mental health—Popular works. I. Title.
RC552.S4G76 2014
616.85′82—dc23

2014020119

Interior design by Monica Baziuk

McGraw-Hill Education products are available at special quantity discounts to use as premiums and sales promotions or for use in corporate training programs. To contact a representative, please visit the Contact Us pages at www.mhprofessional.com.

For all of the young women who have braved

and do brave my couch.

Yes you can. And you are.

Contents

Part One

HURTING

Part Two

HEALING

Part Three

TOOLS FOR LIFE

Part Four

A BETTER PLACE TO BE

ACKNOWLEDGMENTS

THE WRITING of this book has been a gift. Though the writing journey was mine alone, as with most good projects, I could not possibly have kept at it without the love, work, support, and/or ideas of the following people. My deepest thanks:

To Lynne Klippel for your good advice, encouragement, and enthusiasm for publishing.

To Charlotte Friedlander, Madeleine Eno, and Gwen Hoffnagle, for your expert assistance in shaping the manuscript.

To my advance readers for your spot-on feedback and for your enthusiasm, fast work, and dedication to the field of eating disorder work.

To eating disorder, addiction, and self-injury therapists, nutritionists, physicians, mentors, and sponsors for all the work that you do day in and day out, for staying the course, advocating for wellness, spreading the message, and being part of a strong, collective effort to transform lives.

To all of the young women who have shared their pain and their stories with me and braved my couch. Thank you for showing up, opening up, and forging forward with me.

To those who have recovered and those who are in recovery who continue to tell your stories. For your hope, your strength, and your courage and for being unarguable living proof that recovery is possible.

To SG for your art and your artistic input, perseverance, and enthusiasm.

To Esther Zlotnik for being the first to see my words and offering your candid and gentle feedback. Thank you for being you and for being on this and many other journeys with me.

To Janet Rosen for your good agenting, good humor, and belief in this project.

To Kathy Keil, for your expert editing and for believing in the message and in my voice and for taking on this project. And to Nancy Hall for your good guidance and for making the journey so smooth.

To Amy Lipsey, Miriam Lemerman, and Susan Saunders for showing up again and again and for your encouragement, candid feedback, and emotional honesty. And to all the good folks at The Academy of Clinical and Applied Psychoanalysis (ACAP) in Livingston, New Jersey, for your unwavering dedication to the study and betterment of emotional health and relationships and for your expert training.

To Dr. Vicki Semel, Dr. Roger Lope, Rosanna Murray, and Marcia Pumilia for your wisdom, professionalism, integrity, and staying power, as well as your support, direction, and good ideas. And for modeling patience for process and for helping me to clear away the clutter and learn to hear and trust my good instincts.

To my Friday morning women's group for sharing your stories, your foibles, your humor, and your willingness to work on yourselves with gentle but rigorous honesty and for helping me to do the same. I am continuously awed by the power of togetherness, acceptance, recovery, and love as well as by your wisdom. And for being a constant reminder that there is most always relief when we live in the solution.

To Liz Diamond, Priscilla Mahr, Chaya Sora Mendlowitz, Lori P., Sarah Schiffman, Fran Schumer, and Yael Zoldan for your wisdom, candor, always good ears, good humor, and good hearts and for bringing me back to God, to myself, and to what's real and what's not real—time and time again.

To T., once known as Calamity Jane. For your inspiration, insights, bravery, consistency, honesty, and persistence. Not to mention your loveliness, ideas, good humor, art, and countless hours of effort on all fronts. It's really your book too.

To my mom, Brenda Weintrob, and my father, James Weintrob, may his memory be for a blessing, and my father-in-law, Philip Groman, and my mother-in-law, Hadele Groman, may her memory be for a blessing. For your constancy and constant kindness and your enthusiasm. For always believing in me and for so much more.

To my five "very ones," Chani, Moshe, Leah, Yosef, and Gitty for pitching in and your inspiring spirit, integrity, love, and amazing good humor. May God bring you the joy that you bring me.

To Elchonon for being by and on my side always. For your steadiness, your integrity, your love, making it fun, and getting me through many different episodes of "Hour of Doubt." And for telling me over and over and over again to "just keep writing."

I am endlessly grateful to God for all of the above and so much more, and for the balance, the beauty, and the serenity that comes with a recovered and recovering life.

Landing on Life

FOR THE past 15 years I have been sitting in my brown suede chair listening to the stories of teenagers and young adults who starve, binge, cut and burn their flesh, drink, take pills, and have sex with people they don't love and sometimes don't even know. They spend endless hours exercising, criticizing their bodies, and contemplating death and suicide. I listen to young women who shoplift, lie, pull pranks, want to sleep for days, or can't sleep at all.

Because you opened this book, you are most likely suffering. Maybe you are caught in the deepest part of the darkness, or maybe you are on and off the edge. I want you to know that I hear you. I hear you in the silence when you sit saying nothing in a therapist's office like mine, in protest at being told you have to be there or in fear of saying the wrong thing or of being judged, questioned, misunderstood, ordered about, lied to, corrected, or betrayed.

I hear you when you cry in frustration, pain, panic, despair, and confusion. I hear that you hate your body, don't understand your parents (and how they haven't got a clue about you), don't know who you are, don't know where you want to be, or don't know how to live when you feel like dying, are overwhelmed, under pressure, and have no idea what is normal, possible, or pleasurable in life.

I hear you when the seemingly unstoppable urge to binge has you by the throat. I hear you when you are frozen in fear of gaining weight and when you must get the number on the scale lower and lower. I hear you when you cannot, will not, must not eat at all. I hear you when you have no idea what you feel, when you do not want to feel, when you believe that you are a failure, when you are not sure you want anything different, and when you are not sure you are even remotely capable of attaining anything different. I hear you when you feel urgently capable of everything and deserving of nothing all at the same time.

Your pain is deep and powerful. It is woven into your identity like laces in an old shoe. Your pain and the rituals of relief that tie together your body and soul have you walking through life with secrets, anger, shame, and fear.

Perhaps you were hurt physically, perhaps emotionally—or both. The road to relief usually seems way too long and lonely and paved with sharp objects. You have learned to breathe, speak, and search for answers by attacking your body. The difference between *can't* recover and *won't* recover is blurred with the blood from your arms, the vomit in the toilet, the endlessness of dealing with food, and the tears from your frustrated eyes. You are holding on to hope by collecting razor blades and laxatives and trying to quiet the voice in your head that tells you that you are out of control, under a spell, and alone in the woods.

My work with young women who are hurting and hurting themselves—caught up in the throes of eating and self-injury disorders and addiction—has taught me much about emotional pain, self-attack, what it takes to get better, what it takes to *want* to recover, what's in the way, and how to progress to a far better way of life.

Along with personal experience and my own journey of recovery, my work has taught me that there is often more than one truth when it comes to understanding yourself, others, and life. While eating disorders are about the food and about your body, to a great degree they are also about emotional pain and relationships—the same with cutting, burning, and any other forms of self-abuse. Whether you have an eating disorder or you cut yourself, harm yourself, or steal from the local mini-mart, I think you will find a home in these pages and hopefully find some truths that soothe you, help you move forward, and help you feel less alone and more ready to heal and find a better way to live.

One thing I know for sure is that not everyone wants to get better, though I think everyone can. Another thing I know is that the definition of *better* is different depending on whom you ask. I know that these years when you are going from girl to woman are hard enough to begin with. Being a slave to your eating or self-injury disorder is going through life without living (which sometimes is precisely the point). Millions of young women like you are well seated on the merry-go-round of emotional pain, self-attack, and ambivalence about recovery. Whatever your pain is, here are a few more things I believe to be true:

- ◆ You cannot go any faster than you can go, but you can take good care of yourself along the way even though you might not want to or know how to.
- ◆ If you are open to discovering *what's in the way* of your willingness and your progress, you can make progress.
- ◆ Underneath all the pain lies a jumble of anger and mixed-up thoughts and beliefs. And underneath those is fear. And underneath the fear is desire. You can tap into that desire and create a good life.

Over the years and many thousands of hours I have spent listening to young women like you, a few themes have emerged about this struggle toward recovery:

- ◆ You might be caught in the stretch toward independence from your parents, which often extends well into your twenties and emotionally, for many, even longer. You are unsure what *growing up* means exactly—especially if your parents are difficult, hurtful, or absent. (If you grew up with someone other than your parents, please take into account that whenever I say "parents" in this book, I mean whomever you grew up with.)

◆ Your identity is probably wrapped up in your behavior. Your
behavior is how you cope with both the good and the bad
things in your life. To give it up would mean the absence of
something that seems to work on some level. And you're not
at all sure what, if anything, could fill the void that healing
would create. But at least some part of you is probably interested in getting out from under your behavior.

Progress requires getting to know your hungers as well as your
hang-ups. It might mean giving up on the idea that there's a prover-
bial knight who will whisk you away to the land of love and safety
(though more on this soon!).

It might mean acknowledging that it is helpful to understand
what brought you to this point in life, but that alone won't set
you free—there is other work to do. And this: No matter what or
who contributed to your problems, you are the only one who can
do anything about them—with some help. And this will most likely
turn out to be a good thing.

There are many different roads to recovery. There is good stuff
to be learned from all the approaches to getting better. I'm giving
you what I know to be the best and most fundamental ideas from
all the sources out there that I've encountered on recovery and
surviving and thriving through emotional pain and some notions
about how to do what it takes—even when you are not sure you
can or even want to.

A life well lived means more than just a lessening of symptoms;
it means a true shift in how you think and how you relate to and
tend to your own thoughts and feelings and the feelings of others.
It means being willing to believe that somewhere deep inside you is
a vibrant, unique, instinctively healthy core that if given the chance,
can emerge. It means finding yourself, or at least looking in earnest.

It's hard to even imagine a better way of life, and there is a big
part of you dedicated to maintaining your status quo—even if it's
killing you. There is some kind of delicious comfort in being holed

up alone with your food. There is some kind of perfect peace in starving the pain. There is some kind of relief in shutting the bathroom door and downing a box of ex-lax. And there is some kind of buzz-like out-of-body, float-above-the-floor feeling—from slicing deep into the top of your soft, white-pink, jiggly thigh; from it being no one's business; from being in a place where no one can come close.

There is the stubborn, steadfast, grip-it-like-your-life-depends-on-it stance of refusal that part of your psyche takes when it comes to recovery and to leaving the underworld of secret pain, power, drama, and denial of your body and soul.

And then there is the other part of you that hurts—that *really* hurts. The part that wants to stop, do it better, to *feel* better, get off the train, and be OK. At some point, when it hurts more to keep going than it might to stop, you are ready to set sail. It can seem impossible to give up dangerous or self-harming behavior, an eating disorder, or drugs of any variety and get into recovery, when you are up against swells of emotional pain, the vice of habit, addiction, or mental obsession, sometimes coupled with physical cravings. Moving toward *better* can seem like trying to turn back the ocean with a spoon, as part of your brain commands you to engage in acts to protect yourself and get relief—but those acts actually hurt you.

Are You Asking?

In some ways I am a slow mover when it comes to helping young women stop hurting themselves and give up what they are doing—I don't want them to replace it with doing something worse. And it rarely helps to tell someone what to do if she is not asking. Sometimes it takes you a while to ask, even when you want to.

But maybe, since you are reading this now, you are asking. Getting better when you don't want to, are not sure if you want to, or want to and don't know how is like walking through water looking for sunshine. You can catch some glimmers of light, but mostly your sight is blurry, and you move slowly, not sure where you will end up or what the point is.

But I am hopeful. Even if there is a small part of you that does not want to be eating until you are ill and aching, sticking your fingers down your throat *again*, taking extra pills, denying yourself food, exercising for hours on end, or straining for the number on the scale to hit low enough to keep you out of the hospital but still in your safe zone—then you are on your way to something better.

When you tell me that the eating disorder, cutting disorder, pain, drug addiction, or whatever you're dealing with is such a big part of you that you don't know if you even want to live without it, or if you could even if you did want to, I know hope has found a foothold. Maybe you think you want to be left alone, but really you are aching to be understood. Just listening to all the parts of you is the beginning of something better. And telling it to someone who won't argue, but will really hear you, is one next right step.

This Is Not a "How to Recover" Book

This book is not a "how to recover" book. It's more of a "whether to, why to, do you want to, and what's in the way?" kind of book. It is not a book of philosophy or theory or research. It's written from my experience and from my heart—to yours. There are lots of great books about how to recover from eating disorders and self-injury, with solid and specific ideas, exercises, suggestions, and directions (you will find some here too). There are resources listed at the back of this book.

This book is about emotional pain, recovery, and progress. It's for anyone who is hurting, but especially for those of you who do not want to recover, are not sure if you want to recover, are being told you should recover, are being forced into treatment, think you might want to recover but doubt it's possible, or think that everyone ought just to leave you alone.

It is also for you if you are not sure you are worth anything or think you are unappreciated, misunderstood, or mistreated by some, most, or many people in your life. It is for you if you have parents who don't act like parents, or who try too hard and keep on missing the mark and making you want to slice your thigh with a steak knife.

It is also for you if you are a cynic, a skeptic, a sneak, and/or a liar. Thieves are welcome too—especially if you know it and hate yourself for it.

It is for you if you are scared, angry, hopeless, stubborn, suspicious, and live alone in your own head—a place you both revere and fear.

And it is for you if you think there is a part of you somewhere that thinks you might just dare to be hopeful if only you had a little grace and a few more ideas about how to survive and make a place for yourself.

I see lots of "refusers" in my office—young women who are afraid to talk because they are used to being dismissed, criticized, or told to take action they are not ready to take, or of saying too much too soon about secrets they keep.

When you start to open up, you tell me you have yielded your identity to the disorder; that thoughts of death are the default setting in your psyche; that you are attached to your self-destructive behavior in an oddly protective way. You like what you do. It works. You hate what you do. It scares you. It's a civil war of the psyche.

A Word About Therapy

The most important element of therapy or treatment is to be able to say everything and anything you want to even if you are not sure of it; even if you change your mind, your opinion, your mood.

We all need consultants in life. Whatever else your therapy might be, is supposed to be, or you might like it to be, you should be able to say it all to your therapist if you wish to. You should not be judged, reprimanded, corrected, or dictated to. But if you are, or feel that you are, you should be able to say so and work it out from there.

If you have been cycling through therapy and treatment centers for years, maybe you have picked up some new friends, a few good ideas, and some other useful stuff. Some of the young women I work with have been helped greatly by rehabilitation, intensive outpatient programs (IOPs), and treatment centers. Others have learned how to get sicker, angrier, and more entrenched than ever before. For those of you in the latter group, I hope you will find something in these pages to help you move forward in a better direction.

It may very well be that you must take life as it is for a while—in and out of treatment programs and battles with your parents, friends, partners, and yourself. You might think you have no choice. If so, I ask that you keep an open mind. Hurting yourself, for all its reasons, can seem like good company at times—sometimes better than no company at all. And sometimes you believe that you just need it. But I know that there are other options.

Since I do a lot of listening, this book is my turn to share what I have learned, heard, observed, experienced, and felt over the years as I have worked with girls growing into women who are in emotional pain, with eating and self-injury disorders, and all kinds of mad, sad, scared, and stuck.

My references in the book are to young women. This is by no means meant to exclude the boys and men who share the same pain and struggles. Simply, my experience both personally and professionally has been mostly with girls and women, so it is to them that I most relate. I most certainly hope that anyone, male or female, young or older, who is hurting or searching for themselves, for a better life, better feelings, for meaning and recovery, will find something of comfort and value in these pages. And although different eating disorders, addictions, and self-injury can have very different nuances and symptoms, this book is written to the common themes that they all share: emotional pain, obsession and compulsion, self-attack, the physical body and psychic self.

Though there are millions of young women who suffer, millions have recovered or are recovering. My experience both personally and professionally is a testimony to this. The women whose stories are in these pages have gone on to lead healthy, productive, satisfying—but by no means perfect—lives. Some have gone on to successful careers, marriages, parenthood, or artistic accomplishment. Most importantly, they have come to a personalized recovery in which they feel safe, progressive, and willing and able to live life. They are able to see—and feel—what they never thought possible while in the deepest years of their pain and disorders. They no longer think that recovery is for everyone except for them. I hope that in their stories you will hear parts of your own story or recognize parts of yourself or your struggle and use them as a way of reflecting on and enhancing your own journey.

I hope as well that you will come to view emotional pain as a means to opening your mind and heart—not closing them.

While life is life, and difficult thoughts and feelings are part of the ride, I have seen recovery take hold, creativity launch, and joy and serenity find its footing—what I call "landing on life."

And I do really and truly believe that the work it takes to get to a better place is worth it.

Part One

HURTING

CHAPTER 1

Inside Emotional Pain

*I found that words like **hope** and **faith** were only
letters, randomly put together into something
meaningless—words only for fairy tales.*

—DAVE PELZER, *A Child Called "It"*

THERE IS a space somewhere deep inside of us that seems absolutely untouchable. It is where we feel the pain of being misunderstood, the isolation of being mistreated, and the frustration of being unable to act, feel, or be different from who are at any given moment. It is the place where loneliness vibrates, and emptiness seems sharp and clear.

It is also where hope, love, faith, and courage are born. It is both the deep end of despair and the wellspring of real inner strength.

The Deep End of Despair

Perhaps you know this space well, where your feelings and thoughts are a jumbled mess; where the voices of love and recovery are drowned out by the thunder of self-criticism, rejection, hurt, obsession, and fear. Where the despair can be so deep at times that hope would seem cruel.

So this book begins in darkness. The first few chapters discuss intense emotional pain, hopelessness, anger, and worthlessness. I have had much feedback about this, usually encouraging me to move faster into the solution, the better feelings, hope, relief, wellness, and light. (They are here too!)

But just like in life and in recovery, I think that the hard stuff can't be hurried, left out, or glossed over. It needs to be well acknowledged. The pacing of this book reflects this idea.

The grim truth about emotional pain is that many who struggle with an eating disorder, addiction, or self-harm get stuck in it (just like so many get stuck in the tricky darkness, harshness, and pain of the disorder) and have a tough time forging on toward the better stuff that's coming. This book reflects pain that I believe is worthy of at least a few chapters so that you know that I know how it is to hurt, not only how it is to be *totally* consumed with food and body, and to reflect that we can't just skip the pain, but that we can move through it to much better feelings.

Your emotional pain may make it difficult to read certain parts of this book, or it may help you to relate. I hope you will stay with me through the early chapters. But if you are finding these first parts too dark, I want you to feel free to skip ahead to what's most useful to you. Because, like recovery, the better stuff is there if you keep turning the pages.

When you are caught in the struggle with food, body, and self, like I was, and are coping with all the pressures of growing up in a world where expectations are high and genuine emotional support is often low, recovering, *wanting* to recover even, from an eating or self-injury disorder can seem impossible. There is most likely a circle of craziness that you are somehow managing to survive in, maybe even feeling righteous about at times. But things are fundamentally out of control, and somewhere inside of yourself, you know it.

In this place, you might believe that you deserve the pain you are in. Or that you have caused or invited it. This belief alone can stop you in your tracks.

So many young women are deeply resistant to getting well; so deeply grooved are the paths of self-harm, self-deprivation, neglect, unhealthy attachments, and patterns that to dig new ones can seem not only impossible, but undesirable. Many young women are subconsciously compelled to repeat the abuse of their childhoods, reenacting it over and over again with their own bodies. Many are compelled to obey strict self-imposed rules and an inner critic that they believe to be the only way to survive in a world full of difficult and confusing feelings, people, and circumstances, and in a culture that promotes physical beauty with distorted, unrealistic, competitive messages.

And pressure abounds—in your home, social life, school, work, and love. You're trying to map out a future and understand the past. And there is the quiet—and sometimes not so quiet—drama in the bathroom bent over the toilet, or with weapons that cut skin, or in the hours upon hours during which you deny yourself food or have to eat so much and then get rid of it, and where these self-imposed rules seem to both save and singe.

For a long time, I did not know that my emotional pain was connected to my eating disorder or how to pull the pain apart into feelings and thoughts that I could name and deal with. I did not know how to feel my feelings safely or how to bear discomfort without hurting myself and sinking into the disorder. I did not know how to stop hating myself and nurture each tender part of myself in a way that left me feeling well and steady and whole.

I did not know how to stop eating. I did not know how to start. I did not know how to want to recover. I could not find my voice, forgive mistakes (either mine or others'), or figure out how to swim up from the deep end to a warm and sandy shore.

I do now.

In the deep end of despair you believe you cannot get better, that you don't want to get better, and that if you do venture out, you will most likely regret it. And you will most certainly not be safe. All you will be is fat.

You are not the only one in the darkness. Many young women are teetering on the edge of self-hate, self-deprivation, and self-harm. Many lead double lives and skate by doing just enough to stay in school or hold down a job, and function around people. Others overachieve in a relentless pursuit of perfection and accomplishment. And some slip under the radar and live only in the space of their pain and in the company of their disorder.

Maybe you believe hunger is dangerous or that your cravings can and will never be satisfied. Instead of expecting good things, despair rules, and you operate on the default setting that reliable people and good things are not available. You believe that if it takes work to create a good life, you might not be capable of the work; if it takes love or money, you don't have enough; and if it takes luck, yours ran out a long time ago. You might feel entitled and worthless at the same time, stuck in what seems like an endless cycle of pain and escape from pain. And all of these beliefs are masked by the daily reality of dealing with your food and your body.

Life in the deep end of despair is exhausting at best and deadly at worst.

Tired All the Time

If all of this sounds depressing, that's because it is—right now. But hang in there with me as we wade through the muck and the dark parts. We'll get to the light soon.

But first, let's talk about exhaustion. Physical and emotional exhaustion are part of eating and self-injury disorders and the early stages of recovery from them. What adds to that exhaustion is:

- Being overwhelmed by all the decisions you have to make about recovery and about life. As the tide of adulthood comes rushing forward, there are decisions to make. Decisions are often coupled with the fear of having to make them—of making the wrong choice. Having too many options can seem overwhelming and not having enough can seem stifling. When you are exhausted you may not want to, or feel able to, even look at the possibilities. When you feel so dark, options and choices tend to seem dark as well.

- Your long, private list of all that is wrong with you and with your life. Knowing precisely and constantly what is flawed in your body, your character, and your whole person generates exhaustion like nothing else. And it's intensified by the impending work of recovery—of waking up to the idea that even though you did not knowingly sign up for your issues, you are the lead player in your recovery story. Others can have supporting roles, but you are the lead.

- Attempting not to feel—or not to feel the way you feel. When you are continually fighting the fact that a life wrapped up in an eating or self-injury disorder is not actually living, exhaustion settles into your bones. Yet the idea of getting better and finding and having a body and a life you actually feel good about can also leave you feeling drained and wasted.

- Denying food, hating your body, and endlessly pursuing thinner while being a slave to food and self-injury.

- Wearing the heavy armor of perfectionism and constantly striving to control the uncontrollable.

I get that you are exhausted. And I don't believe that you can walk toward a better place or even want to walk toward a better place if you think the effort is more than you can bear, given how tired you already feel.

It is remarkable how many young women *do* manage to function, though exhausted, while walking through the day-to-day chores of living. And how utterly isolated and alone you can feel in your own internal universe of emotional pain, often with no other human having a clue about what's going on inside you.

Together with my clients, I have been to exhaustion. I have been to defeat, and to that place where perpetual wipeout seems like all there can ever be. But I have learned that this kind of *tired* is temporary. And that when you decide to recover, you can find energy that you didn't know you had.

Killing the Pain

Many of the young women I work with tell me that they would not at all mind dying. They tell me—at least when they first come into treatment—that while they are not actively suicidal, they really don't care if they die. Many have funeral fantasies, death wishes, and thoughts of how others would react if they killed themselves. There is a frightening mingling of self-injury, starvation, bingeing, recklessness, tiredness, and dangerous behavior—all with great urgency to kill the pain and get relief. There is sometimes, as well, a clueless carelessness around danger that gives off a message of "who cares anyway, so what if I die."

Though you might contemplate dying as a way out—to end the hurts, demands, expectations, and doubts, or to punish the offenders—a part of you dares to hope that there really is a future for you. On some level you know that your focus on your body and your food is a slow road to actual death as well as the immediate daily death of your precious time, talent, creativity, energy, and soul.

But what if you have it all backward? What if focusing on your body and obsessing about food does not bring about a better anything, but rather focusing on recovery brings a better everything, including a better body and a better relationship with food?

Slicing your arms for relief, shoving fingers down your throat, or refusing to eat can kill the pain for a while. There are indeed some brief and glorious moments of exquisite escape—piles of food, scarcely any food, or rabid, hateful focus on your rebellious thighs—on your whole body, in fact—as a battleground can seem like the only safe ways to kill the pain, control the craziness, and find your equilibrium. Being immersed in your own private world of victory by deprivation, frenzy, punishment, control, or pain provides the believable illusion that you are safe and OK. And for just a moment, the dread is gone.

The theory that many young women live by goes like this: *If it hurts on* my body, it will hurt less *in* my body; if I pinch hard enough on the outside, I will relieve the pinch inside. And you know what? It works. If it did not work, you would not do it. The fact that it can become an addiction, an obsession, a way of life, does not matter. What matters is survival—survival from pain by pain, causing pain to kill pain, and trying to cure the eating or self-injury disorder, the self-hate by diving straight into it. If you are hurting and in the thick of it, this, nonsensical as it is, makes perfect sense.

The Edge of the Ledge (Where Does It Stop?)

There is a stopping point. The "edge of the ledge" is an image that comes up often in my work with young women. Mary, a young client of mine, told me, "I am sitting, emotionally, at the edge of the ledge. I do not really want to jump, but I cannot get up and run back to safety. I just sit there, numb, lonely, thinking about nothing and everything all at the same time, hating myself, not caring, not believing that there is any life for me."

Together Mary and I imagine me sitting down beside her on the ledge, both of us dangling our feet over the side, taking in the vast expanse of blue sky above us and the jagged rocks below us. In my own mind the edge of the ledge is above something that resembles the Grand Canyon.

You can sit at the edge for a long, long while and think about your life. You can hate your body, yourself, your shame, and your life. You can believe that no one will ever understand, no one will ever help, and no one really knows what it's like to be you. You can continue to believe that the eating or self-injury disorder has nothing to do with emotional pain. You can believe that recovery is just about as doable as flying over the canyon with wings you don't have.

Or you can consider getting up and backing away from the edge, step by small step, toward help and life and possibility.

There comes a time at the edge when you decide that you are not going to heal your pain by punishing your body and that you are willing to look elsewhere for ways out; when you decide that hating yourself is no longer helping you; when you get that there will never be a low enough number on the scale, enough food in the fridge, or enough room on your skin to relieve your pain; when you are willing to consider for real that the obsessions are not saving you. There comes a time when you can let hope in without it hurting so much that it pushes you back down into the pain and punishment again and again and again.

The ironic thing about emotional pain—anger, shame, grief, self-pity, self-hate, frustration, loneliness (to name a few)—is that dealing with it can seem like a free-fall into the canyon. And backing away from the edge of the ledge can seem like a way to avoid emotions. That's what's so crazy about recovery when you are in deep emotional pain—it's a jester's paradise. What seems safe can be dangerous; what seems most dangerous can be safe. Confusion abounds.

Though you can get to the edge of the ledge because you are so lost, it can very well be the place where you find yourself.

CHAPTER 2

Alone in the Woods

No matter how far into my flesh I push the pin,
I can't seem to hit the pain.

—CALLIE, *age nineteen*

THERE ARE six feelings that can bring us to our knees: anger, fear, worthlessness, self-pity, loneliness, and grief. (Do any of these sound familiar?) It can seem impossible to identify and begin to walk through these feelings while deciding to recover, but not doing so will bring you down faster than anything.

Your Angry Heart

Let's start with anger. For a long time I had no idea that underneath my anger was the fear of not being safe, of not getting something I believed I needed for my self-worth, wellness, and survival, and my feeling that I had been betrayed or maligned or that I was worthless, failing, and stupid.

Anger has a way of making us think the worst of ourselves and of others. And often, we don't even know that we are angry.

Writer and therapist Dusty Miller says in her book *Women Who Hurt Themselves*, "What makes anger so deceptive and destructive is that it is often disguised as something else. Anger can easily masquerade as sadness, reluctance, aloofness, or even overcompliance."

When we don't have a way to deal with anger that's safe, freeing, and effective, we go to what we know. And if the eating or self-injury disorder has you by the throat, what you know is how to binge, purge, starve, or cut.

Most, if not all of the young women I work with have a ton of anger. Some have no idea that they are angry, and others know it all too well. Most believe that anger is "bad" or at the very least frightening and overwhelming. Some are ashamed of it.

We glean most of our ideas about anger from our families. Maybe your family exploded with anger or suppressed it. Some of us have families who drink, drug, eat, or gamble to waylay their anger. Some young women have been hit, kicked, tickled, or screamed at in anger. Some have been left in anger or blamed, frightened, or denied by anger. Very few of us have been exposed to ways to deal with anger productively and safely. So without any real rubric for dealing with our own anger and the anger of others (whether it's directed at us or not), we turn to our bodies to both quiet the rage and release it. We turn toward hurt in the name of safety.

There are studies that suggest that anger actually causes people to want more pain, think more painful thoughts, feel more painful feelings, and choose more painful actions. It seems that we humans, based on a combination of biology, culture, and character, use pain to relieve our pain. We don't know how to comfort, relieve, or act with responsible compassion toward ourselves. And we often believe that if a person is angry with us, the anger is justified, or he or she is better than we are just because he or she sounds so angry or certain. We learn to repeat the anger of others inside ourselves and to ourselves, adding it to our own anger and directing our physical bodies to bear the burden of our emotional pain. Perhaps this is one reason why we hold on so tightly to our disorders—because we know of no other way. Anger is part of what drives us to harm ourselves, even—and perhaps especially—when we don't know we are angry.

It hurts like crazy to feel angry with people we love or need, or who are supposed to be taking care of us. On one level, you don't want to be angry, especially when anger has you scared that you will do something crazy to yourself or someone else. And when you are angry it can seem like you will never be "un-angry" again. Like a headache, when your head is pounding it's hard to imagine what it feels like not to have one.

Many people with eating or self-injury disorders believe that being angry with yourself is synonymous with self-hate. But—contrary to this popular belief—you can be angry with yourself and still like yourself.

Some studies have shown that people who have eating or self-injury disorders get angry more often than people who don't. It seems that we hear things through the ears of the disorder that make us more sensitive, irritable, critical, bothered, and afraid.

Think about it. If you are starving, stuffed, sugar-crazed, or high from purging, how can you possibly process anything clearly, especially if you filter things through your own poor sense of self? And since anger is also physical, it lights up your brain and you can feel it in all parts of your body, running through your blood, throbbing in your chest, pounding at your head, and straining your limbs. Even if you don't know that's what it is, it happens, and you need relief.

Think for a moment about the angriest you have ever been. At whom? Why? What happened to that anger? Where did it go? What happens to your body when you are angry? If you were not, just for a minute, tied up in the disorder—if you did not cut or binge or restrict—what might you learn about your anger? What do you think would really happen?

Think also about what your parents are like when they are angry. Was there—is there—yelling, hitting, threatening, name-calling, leaving, or denying in your house? Or silence—hard, cold, you-do-not-exist silence? Was it OK to express anger in your house? What happened when you sounded or acted angry? What kind of response did you get?

Getting to know your anger and how to deal with it is key to wanting recovery for a few reasons:

- **Acknowledging your anger actually calms down your amygdala, the part of your brain that holds emotions.** Even if feelings, especially anger, take a long time to pass, recognizing, naming, and allowing your anger is like putting a cold compress on your overcharged, throbbing brain so it can decompress.

- **While it hurts to be angry, it hurts you more to try not to be angry when you are angry; eventually it catches up with you.** Even if you don't know yet how to be angry and survive it, or how to survive others' anger toward you, trying not to be angry when you are angry is like not having enough air when you're swimming up to the surface of the pool.

- **Ignoring anger causes us to rebel.** We cut off our noses to spite our faces. Maybe you can go to college, but you don't because it would make a difficult parent happy. Maybe you hang out with a bad crowd when you might otherwise walk away. Maybe you get into drugs, violence, or bad sex to get relief, but also, deep down, to punish yourself, your parents, or your boyfriend. Or maybe you are willing to begin to recover but you don't because someone with whom you are angry is pushing for it—because it seems like recovering will make all the things that person is angry about seem relevant and all the things that you are angry about seem irrelevent.

- **Anger causes severe cases of the "forget-its" and the "screw-its."** It gets in the way of wanting recovery. When you are angry you are more likely to sink into worthlessness, self-pity, hopelessness, and self-sabotage. You start thinking things like

"Who cares anyway," "I may as well just do it," "Nothing matters anyway," and "Why bother?"

◆ **You can't deal with something you believe does not exist.** I'm not saying that anger is the only block to wanting recovery, but if you really think that you are not angry at anything or with anybody and that the obsession with food and body is only about food and body, what then do you believe is keeping you in it?

◆ **Feeling healthy anger can help you clarify what you believe in and what you stand for.** Processing your anger properly can allow you to act sanely and safely in response to the things you believe are worth your time and energy. It can help you stand up for justice, for humanity, and for compassion.

Despite the pull to get relief by hurting yourself, rebelling against others at your own expense, or continuing to believe that the disorder will solve your issues, you can do it differently. And in fact, you must. Somewhere deep inside you know this, too.

When You Feel Worthless, Pitiful, and Lonely

I once heard a story about a young man in his thirties who was dying of cancer. As he was facing his final days, he asked his brother to help him plan his funeral. He made his brother promise to locate his fifth-grade teacher and ask him to deliver the eulogy.

When his brother asked why, the man explained that as a young boy he felt very bad about himself. He was awkward looking, not good at sports, and not especially good academically, either. One day, as part of a class project, the fifth-grade teacher asked each student to write down one good quality about each of the other students in the class.

One by one, the teacher read out loud what had been written. The boy heard that he was a loyal friend, lent a helping hand, told funny jokes, and had a nice smile. The man told his brother that it was the first time he thought he was worth something. From that point on he tried harder in school and his grades improved. He never became good at sports, but he discovered that he could draw well and felt good about that. He stopped thinking the worst of himself, and when he started to slip backward he always recalled not just the good words that were written about him but the warm smile and kind look the teacher had on his face as he read them. He remembered feeling like he mattered, and he carried that feeling with him from that day on.

"That teacher changed my life by helping me to change how I saw myself," he told his brother, "and even though my life is ending sooner than I had hoped for, it has been a life well lived because of that teacher."

Here is the definition of *worthless*: Having no real value or use. Having no good qualities. Deserving contempt. Useless. Good for nothing.

If you do not believe you are worth anything, how can you believe that recovery is worth the effort? How can you believe that you are worth the effort? Here's the conundrum: You are wrapped up in the disorder because you feel worthless, and you feel worthless—in part—because you are wrapped up in the disorder. I know this because feelings of worthlessness, and its followers, self-pity and profound loneliness, are no strangers in my office and in my own emotional life. It's a tough trio.

I am a recovered bulimic and a recovering food addict, and I am well acquainted with emotional pain. I used to be convinced that every feeling I had was a fact. If I felt like trash, I was trash. If I felt fat, I was fat. If I felt ashamed, I was shameful. I believed, too, that if people sounded angry or sure of themselves, they were right, better than me, or more worthy than me. Even if part of me was frightened or in disagreement,

I felt "less than." And since feelings were facts to me, that meant that I *was* less than. I remember believing that not knowing what I wanted to do or could do with my life meant that I really was nothing, and that the feelings I had—when I could name them—would last forever. I believed that my pain was permanent.

But feelings are not facts; even when they seem to be, they are only feelings—overwhelming, unrelenting, out of control sometimes, but still just feelings. It took me many years to stop believing that what I felt in any given moment was the gospel truth. It took even longer to come to know *what* I was feeling, or even *that* I was feeling. And then even longer to understand that my feelings—while guideposts to my desires, instincts, beliefs, and morals—were human and survivable and OK.

Finding healthy relief, however, was a whole other level. For years I simply ate till it hurt and then threw it back up. I vacillated between the grip of the eating disorder, the issues of life, and the legitimate pain of both. Either way, I knew hurt, confusion, escape, being overwhelmed, and self-attack. I knew the call of food, the fear and hatred of fat, and the pursuit of thinness. I know all about ordering takeout for five, telling the cashier (as if she cared) that you hope your family isn't too hungry waiting for you to come home with their dinner, and then eating it in the car and throwing it up when you get home. I know about saving all your calories for ten o'clock at night and then turning on the TV and eating through boxes, bags, and bottles. I counted the calories in a box, not a single serving. Unless I was restricting, I never ate a single serving of anything. I knew how to hide food, dump food, and put what looked like forkfuls into my mouth that actually went into my napkin.

I never knew where my eating disorder started and stopped and where my life issues started and stopped. They were separate, equal, and overlapping. It was often a lonely, desolate place to be. Emotional pain has so many folds and bumps, and worthlessness is a thread that often runs through them all.

I don't believe it's possible to recover from eating and self-injury disorders, even when you want to, without taking a serious look at your self-worth. To move forward toward a lasting recovery, you have to be willing to find at least enough self-worth to make it worth your while to get started—not a simple matter when you are in the thick of it all.

I want you to get curious about why you feel worthless. If you could whittle it down to one or two things, what would they be? Or is it a combination of stuff? Were you hit? Ignored? Belittled? Were your basic human needs seen as too much or too burdensome? Were you hurt by caregivers, teachers, mentors, peers, or siblings? Can you think of any one event that made you feel bad about yourself? Did media messages, images, and cultural expectations influence your thinking and skew your idea of what is beautiful, valuable, and worthy? Are you under the impression that you must be competitive with your looks and your accomplishments in order to matter? Do you distrust those who reassure and support you?

What kind of messages did you get about your feelings, your ideas, and your place in the world? Do you actually believe you are worthless, or do you just seem worthless to yourself sometimes?

And finally, is it in some way better to be worthless? Does that work for you somehow? If so, how? If you could feel different, would you? Are you willing to decide that you do matter just because you do? Or is it a question of experiences, accomplishments, and achievements? Are some of us worth more than others? And if so, how much, and why? If you are in fact worth something, does that mean that you should decide to recover in earnest?

You Can Find Self-Worth

Finding real self-worth requires us to face our fears and learn about what we believe, what we truly value and why. As painful as worthlessness is, when we are hurting it can seem better than its flip side: self-worth. Self-worth brings with it the notion that we and our actions matter, and that we have substance and responsibility. Self-worth means having a place in the world; but that place in the world can seem far too demanding and overwhelming at times.

Self-pity follows closely on the heels of worthlessness. It's not easy to admit feeling pathetic. But on some level—before you are well into recovery—you likely feel sorry for yourself for your troubles and for not being able or willing to do things differently. You might even turn that pity into a defiant stance of indignant worthlessness.

Worthlessness and loneliness give you a certain power. You can isolate yourself and stay hidden from all the people who hurt, neglect, or fail to understand you. You can duck under the anger and frustration and keep hurting your body in ways that steer you just slightly clear of all the pain you know you are in and cannot face head-on.

Since we tend to think that what we feel in any given moment is what we will always feel, our motivation to find real self-worth can be sketchy. We need to be open to believing that worthlessness, self-pity, and loneliness—however valid those feelings are—are obstacles to deciding to recover.

If you are thinking at this point that I have forgotten how important the food is, or how important your weight is, or how important your cutting is, I have not. Just for now, I want to talk to you about the hurting.

Some of us have been hurt so often or for so long that we are simply, unconsciously, used to being hurt. You might gravitate toward hurtful people, hurtful situations, and hurtful scenarios simply because your mind seeks a familiar, even if painful, status quo or a chance to somehow right the wrongs. Your mind can make you gravitate toward situations that result in familiar feelings, even painful ones, in an effort to try to work them through to different outcomes. We are not usually aware that we do this. But no matter how overpowering your emotions might seem, it is ultimately you who must decide to claim yourself and your life.

In the pit of loneliness, you most likely feel the totally human ache to be understood, to be connected, to be soothed and loved. But when you are in the pit, you do not believe these longings are normal, and getting them satisfied seems like a very remote possibility.

When you agree, even a little, to move out of the pit of lone-liness and surround yourself with the voices of recovery, the voices of healing, and the voices of comfort, you will see that leaving the loneliness is not leaving safety, but rather traveling toward it.

I've heard it said that recovery is not a team sport, and I could not disagree more. There is no way to travel this road alone. It is too long and scary. While you can learn to nourish yourself, the fact that you need nourishment from others is indisputable. You might not know how to achieve either, even when you know you want to, but if you are still reading, you have begun—because part of the solution to self-pity, worthlessness, and loneliness comes from our own willingness to take a look at ourselves and be open to *self-reflection*, not self-attack, early in our journey. Even though it sounds hard, we have to learn how to give to ourselves in ways that heal, not hurt. Some of the solution comes from outside. We do need love, valida-tion, acceptance, and acknowledgment of our good traits. We need connection and emotional sustenance from others.

We have to be willing to seek out people who can offer us healthy relationships—the voices of comfort I mentioned above. Positive feedback and reassurance are part of your recovery, even if this flies in the face of your self-protective loneliness. Being open to other points of view and different ideas can help us adjust our sometimes skewed (disordered) version of reality. You need people to believe in you when you don't believe in yourself and to help you see when you are blind. Validation from others does not replace your own efforts, internal sustenance, and validation, but it does help you access them.

In your struggle to understand if and how to begin the journey of recovery, concede to a journey of discovery as well. As part of that journey you have to regard the eating or self-injury disorder as your current voice of legitimacy. If you believe your feelings don't matter or are foolish, silly, or unacceptable, the disorder you have serves the function of legitimizing them. You and your feelings are taken far more seriously when they are under the umbrella of the disorder. The disorder seems to put a "For Real" stamp on feelings that also reads: "She means business and you can no longer dismiss her or her feelings." People have to notice. They have to acknowledge that you are real, that you have feelings, and that you have to be taken seriously even if you are not sure you want them to notice you at all. In emotional pain, and with an eating or self-injury disorder, you often scream for both.

Your feelings matter, disorder or not. But there are, you will see, better ways to establish your credibility than through the disorder. Finding self-worth starts here. It starts now. It starts with you reading these pages. Because some part of you is open to a steadier truth than the one you are operating on now.

Fear and "What If I'm Empty Inside?"

"I could choke on the emptiness," Wendy tells me. "I can feel its nothingness slide up into my throat and swallow me."

No one can understand this who has not experienced it, I think as I listen to her. No one.

"I am alone in the woods. There is no path, no direction, no way out," she tells me.

Wendy came to see me last year after she had been caught shoplifting. She was five-foot-nine by the time she was fourteen.

Nineteen now, she has been cutting since she was fifteen and vomiting since she was sixteen. It has been a slow and steady war against her feelings, on the battlefield of her body. Her long, dark hair is always neatly pulled back in a nondescript pony, which makes her dark brown eyes look like huge frying pans.

"I took eighty dollars out of my parents' dresser one time," she tells me. "I bought laxatives, gum, and chocolate. And I thought about how good my family is to me. And how bad, too, sometimes. I thought about how upset they'd be if they found out that not only am I not who they think I am or want me to be, but I'm also a thief. And no matter how much I chew, spew, or poop, I can't seem to get rid of the emptiness."

Wendy describes walking through the woods in her mind, sometimes seeing blue skies through green leaves towering above her. She feels a strange comfort in her own solitude. But then comes the choking. The leaves shrivel and turn brown, the sky darkens, the trees seem to tower and lean in and out, and she is small and frightened and cold. Way too cold.

She tells me that fear seeps into her veins like warm milk, only it is not soothing. It runs up and down her limbs and through her body, takes over like a harness, and squeezes around her. There is no difference between what she feels and who she is. Her feelings are a huge jumbled mess, an unidentifiable black knot somewhere inside of her.

Wendy is terrified of the emptiness. She is afraid, too, of being hurt, caught, humiliated. She is afraid that she is not safe, not valuable, not capable. She is afraid of people, of food, of her own body. She is afraid of not having, not doing, not being, and just as afraid of having, doing, and being.

Sometimes a frightening darkness washes over her that we identify as dread—the feeling that something awful, unidentifiable, and uncontrollable is about to happen. Fear and emptiness collide into a sickening, unbearable pain.

Fear-filled questions come like missiles: "What's the point?" "What if I'm empty inside?" "What do I want to do with my life?" "What's wrong with me?" "Why are my parents the way they are?" "Why doesn't anyone understand?" "What if my body is really awful?" "Who am I?" "What if I can't do it?" (Whatever "it" is.)

There are more fears, so many more. But instead of presenting themselves as guideposts to insight and better feelings, they attack. They sit heavily on our hearts, spurring on emotional pain and pushing us further and further into unrelenting battles with scales and food and razors. Our own fingers become both our enemies and our saviors as they inflict pain on our bodies yet bring relief, however temporary, to our minds. We are left sitting clueless in a cyclone of questions and feelings without any safe route to relief or answers.

In the *Big Book* of Alcoholics Anonymous, the narrator of one story says that for him "not drinking was not an option, but drinking didn't help." When we are in intense emotional pain from fear in its many forms, along with all the other pain, and the pain seems unbearable, we cannot see any options. Eating, starving, cutting, bingeing, (plug in your own) is not *not* an option, even with all its complications.

When our feelings do not get taken care of properly we get stuck, and we do not want to be told that we cannot have what we want—what we believe we need to survive. We do not want to be told that what we believe is truth is not necessarily truth, or that our solutions are not working, or are not the path to relief. We might not be able to hear more objective truths or different realities. We do not want to have to figure things out or change what works, even if it doesn't really work. And we don't really know how to do that anyway, nor do we want to have to learn. It's almost impossible to believe that there is anything better out there anyway.

We are understandably, intrinsically skeptical. As one young woman I work with put it: "I don't feel comfortable having a basic conversation with anyone. How can I ask any questions *of* myself *for* myself? I'm not comfortable eating. I dread getting dressed. It makes me want to sleep. I hate my body. I'm mentally obese, and I feel physically larger with every meal. I'm uncomfortable in my skin, my mind, my lack of understanding of my purpose. I shudder when I see my reflection because I see the wrinkled waste of everything I could have been. I'm practically settling for hating myself—in advance—for whatever it is I'm missing, and I dread having to find that missing piece. It's not as easy as figuring out 'what I'm missing' in my life; I need to determine the shape of the missing puzzle piece. Can an unsatisfied, unhealthy person ever have a life? I want to be myself, not another layer of this broken shell. I just have no idea what to do."

We are afraid of knowing ourselves—what we were, what we are, and what we are not. And we are afraid of what we will be and what we think we will be. We are afraid of a future we have not even encountered yet, one that we have not even attempted.

We are not dead, but we are afraid to live. Even when there is a hint of hope, we are afraid it will be fleeting.

Often young women tell me, "I can't do this. I do not have the energy, strength, or ability to do this or anything else. It is too much. I am too scared." They are afraid that if they try and fail, there will be nothing left to try. Even hope can be scary.

Deciding to recover means that though you have not yet learned how to take mindful good care of your inner world and your fears, you agree early on to be open to the new thought that it *is* possible to work with and through your fear and not be stopped by it. It means realizing that though you have not yet had enough positive experiences or been able to hold on to the ones you've had—to fill up the space inside of you—that you are open to new possibilities.

Deciding to recover means that you are willing to believe that many of the answers will come from living life and opening up the vault inside of you to allow new ways of thinking and new voices of recovery to settle in and stay. It means being open to the idea that often thoughts are just thoughts and can come and go like trains at a train station. And that you do not have to get on and ride every one, especially the negative, fear-based, self-attacking ones. You can let them pull in and let them pull back out all on their own.

It means acknowledging that while you are busy bingeing and purging out all the bad stuff, the good stuff often gets washed away with it.

It means that emptiness, while sometimes painful, also creates a space for new and better ideas and feelings to move in.

It means bearing in mind that you have an unconscious mind that has been shaped by genetics and biology and culture and spirit; that tending to the emptiness means tending to the parts of yourself that are not always obvious or sitting out in the open.

You cannot stop the pain from presenting itself. But you can survive it, survive it well, and use it for good, growth, a safe fullness, and a good life that you cannot—just yet—imagine.

Good Grief

Grief is the emotional suffering we feel over loss—loss of people, relationships, hope, control, opportunities, faith, direction, knowledge; loss of things that comfort us, soothe us, nurture us, and make us feel safe; loss of our sense of self. It is wanting what we don't have, and having what we don't want.

There are so many different kinds of grief. There is grief over not having sober parents. Grief over having good parents who drive us crazy. Grief over fat. Grief that there is not enough food in the world for us. Grief that we cannot eat all we think we want and not get fat. Grief that we have to eat to live. Grief that we have to brush our teeth, wash our clothes, do our homework. Grief that we have an eating disorder. Even grief that it can get better, because that too seems to come with a cost. Grief that we are going to have to take care of ourselves. Grief that we don't really know how. Grief that we make mistakes; that life is unpredictable; that we don't always know who we are or what we want.

There is grief over our own shortcomings and flaws. There is grief when you have nothing to look forward to and when you see only burdens, obstacles, and expectations looming ahead. There is grief over what you have done, what you continue to do, what you want to do but believe you cannot. There is grief when you have been well loved and cared for but are still so sick. There is even grief over what you don't know; grief that you have been hurt, mistreated, or neglected; and grief that there exists in this world beautiful music, stunning sunsets, kindness to strangers, innocent children, and oceans so blue they hardly seem real—and here you are in so much turmoil.

"I can't do this anymore. It's too hard," is the voice of defeat. And of grief. But this kind of grief is a beginning. When you say this, it is the beginning of the end of the part of you that is hiding out. It's like saying, "OK, I give up. I've got this disorder, this family, this body, this life—whatever this is. I've got it; I get it. I'm tired, but there has to be a better way. I'm willing to look."

There is a certain amount of grief that comes up naturally as part of recovery itself; yes, on top of all the other things you are grieving. This is the grief of reckoning with and acknowledging that there is loss involved in recovery itself—the loss of ideas and behaviors that used to protect you but that in fact hurt you, or don't work well enough anymore. It's the grief that you cannot go on not knowing you are angry and believing that you and your feelings don't matter, or that they only matter in the context of the disorder. It's the grief that we have to give up using food the way we do and give up the idea that we are helpless, hopeless, and worthless. Losing the disorder and all the parts of ourselves that believe in it is a loss. Even necessary losses can still make us grieve.

The point at which you decide to recover is where, despite your grief—or perhaps because of it—and despite the seeming impossibility of it all, you can accept your willingness. It's where you cross some invisible line inside your psyche even though you are grieving; even though you are terrified.

I know that you are afraid that the grief will kill you, and that sometimes you hope it does. And what if you do get better? Who around you will change? How will they feel, or be, or act toward you? Will they be jealous or distant or angry with you for your progress? Will they feel left behind or left out if you move forward? Will you have to grieve that, too? Haven't you felt left back when others seemingly moved forward and made progress when you could not? So how can your grief work for you? Is there any such thing as good grief?

I believe there is. Recovery is not about undoing the grief or slamming up against it again and again in your heart. It is about allowing it and working on your willingness to expand, grow, and believe in a better way to live *because* of your grief. It is about honoring all the truths of your grief enough that you become willing to exist both despite those truths and because of them. It is about agreeing to begin even when you do not yet know a better way; even though you are skeptical and scared, heartbroken and hurt.

We do this slowly, tenderly, and with a new attention to what is possible. We ride on the wings and words of those who have done it. We remember that what we feel in any given moment *matters*, but it does not have to dictate our actions. We embark on the idea that we are more than our pain, but because of it, we are open to discovering ourselves.

CHAPTER 3

If You've Been Hurt or Abused

Although the world is full of suffering, it is full also of the overcoming of it.

—HELEN KELLER

WHEN SHE was seventeen, my client Kasey was mildly sexually assaulted on a cable car in San Francisco. I say "mildly" because she was not harmed physically, nor did the stranger succeed in touching her other than on her knee. It was a mild incident in her own mind (though it might not be mild to someone else), but then again, she has never forgotten it.

Kasey was sitting on a bench facing the outside of the cable car, and the man was riding standing up, holding on to a pole, facing her. Her mother and aunt were on a bench a few spots away. At first she thought she must be imagining things or it must be an accident. And then she realized something very awkward was happening. She remembers feeling nothing but frozen and out of her own body.

The assault "only" lasted ten minutes or so, with the beautiful San Francisco Bay lapping in the background. The man positioned himself so that he was rubbing himself against her leg. He stared at her the whole time, a smirk on his face. And Kasey did not move.

She's often wondered, as did her mother and aunt, why she did not move or call out or do *something*. Later she felt shame and repulsion. Only years later did Kasey actually feel anger. But ultimately Kasey has been able to forgive herself for not doing what she was not able to do in that moment.

I have listened to many stories of sexual assault far more invasive than that, and some that were less invasive but resulted in bad feelings or trauma nonetheless. While many young women who have been hurt or abused, sexually or otherwise, develop eating disorders or self-injure, many don't. And while many women with eating or self-injury disorders have been abused in some way, many have not. Emotional pain has many provocateurs, and though the sources of pain differ, we can share the many tools for and paths to healing. Kasey's eating disorder was in full swing well before she got on that cable car.

It is also important to note that not all experiences of sexual abuse are obvious. Many people experience feelings of shame, repulsion, discomfort, fear, helplessness, and confusion from more subtle experiences such as being kissed on the lips, tickled, massaged, or spoken to in an inappropriate way. If it resonates somewhere in your psyche, it's worthy of attention.

Clients of all ages have come to my office to begin the slow and tedious trek toward talking about what has happened to them, how they have responded, how to heal, and how to live safely, freely, and emotionally well. Many have connected the dots between unwanted touch and starvation, between violence and vomit, between repulsion and ripping skin.

With tender care—not insisting that someone talk too soon or too much about events that were or are deeply wounding—I help them sort through the maze of feelings, thoughts, and patterns.

If you have been hurt or abused and you are sifting through incidents, large or small, wondering what was your fault and what was not (abuse is *never* a child's fault); what you do or don't have control over; how to stay safe; how to release painful thoughts, memories, or feelings and unlock the shame, the fear, the blame, and the secrets you carry—or you are pushing it all away—you should know that you are not alone.

Since this book is about *wanting* to get better—about feeling safe while feeling and being well—it is not my intention to discuss in detail the specifics of healing from abuse except to say that healing these wounds is most likely a necessary part of getting better. Sometimes staying in the eating or self-injury disorder seems like the only way to push away the pain of those traumas. It often feels better to be deeply involved in cutting your arms up or throwing your guts up than to face and deal with all the trauma and awfulness of being abused and all the feelings that go along with it.

I do not think that injuring yourself or sinking deeply into anorexia or bulimia or food compulsion is a conscious choice. But recovery is. It requires pulling yourself forward in the right direction again and again and again. The pull to protect yourself, escape the pain, and release it on yourself has a power all its own. Your task is to uncover what gets in the way of your being able and willing to get relief without hurting yourself.

Recovering from the trauma of sexual abuse is its own journey, and if you are also suffering from an eating or self-injury disorder, the journey is intricately connected with your recovery from the disorder.

Paula, a lovely woman in her midforties with whom I have been working for close to a year, asks me why she is not worth protecting. Her big green eyes fill with tears as her soft brown hair falls lightly over her shaking shoulders. We talk about how she loves her father though he hit her frequently and tickled her beyond fair play. He gave her baths until she was eleven, and still insists on kissing her full on the mouth. Paula does not want to feel anything about this, but she does. She feels angry and repulsed, guilty and ashamed. She has feelings about her feelings, one on top of the other.

Paula's mother used to call her fat, insist she play sports, and tell her that no man wants a sack of potatoes. Her parents were good providers of her physical needs and at times loving, and they have mellowed out over the years. She does not want to be angry with them, to distrust them, or to see them as people who have faults, made mistakes, or acted abusively or without thinking, especially when it came to parenting her.

When Paula was a teenager, she cut and threw up. Cutting brought so much relief. It got rid of all that anger and shame and confusion, at least for a while. As an adult she started bungee jumping, never knowing whether she would slam into the earth or bounce back up. Paula has become so used to hurting herself to protect others from her rage and to protect herself from her rage, her sorrow, and her shame (and in a way, to carry on the cycle of being banged up that she learned from her parents), that protecting herself in a healthy way seems about as doable as a flight to Pluto.

She does not have even a small clue about *how* she could protect herself in a healthy way. No one taught her, and deep down Paula does not want to have to protect herself. **She wants to *be* protected. She wants her parents to have protected her and to have had her back. And she doesn't want to have needed protection in the first place.**

Healthy protection is a faraway concept for a multitude of reasons. So much has to shift. So many feelings have to be felt and worked through in order to heal and be well. Paula and I wonder together if there is a faster, easier way, but we don't think so.

If we could look at a map of the journey, the destination would seem so far away—so high up on the mountain—that we would think it hardly possible to reach. Why even set out? We will never get to Pluto, it seems. Maybe it's no better there anyway, even if we knew what Pluto would mean. Paula and I marvel together that hopelessness, self-hate, sadness, rage, and resentment are not reasons not to try for better. They merit as feelings to be acknowledged and reckoned with but cannot be employed as excuses not to recover, much as we might like them to be. And it's hard to fathom peace and happiness if you've never really felt them.

So in recovery, we go step by step. We take breaks along the way. We rest. We breathe. We keep on keeping on even when we are not so sure we can. We gather nuggets of wisdom from those who know the pain and have traveled the path, and we gather ideas about life and love and possibilities that make the journey easier, that clear the way a bit and bring comfort. What those things are specifically follows later on in the book.

The destination is not finite or final. There is no finish line, but rather many milestones. There are always more places to go. But there will be accomplishments, victories, and periods of true relief, joy, and insights along the way that will form pillows under your psyche so that when the bad feelings need to be let loose, you can land softly. And as you go (and I hope you will decide to go), you will see that you can.

Bit by bit, you can.

CHAPTER 4

Who Are You?

I was reminded again of why I was anorectic: fear.
Of my needs, for food, for sleep, for touch, for simple
conversation, for human contact, for love. I was
anorectic because I was afraid of being human.

—MARYA HORNBACHER, *Wasted*

You Are Not Nothing. Really.

This book was written from the inside out. I started, somehow, to write the middle parts of the book before I wrote the beginning and the end. The only way I could let my ideas come together was to start from where I was, not where I wanted to go, because I was not entirely sure where I wanted to go. And I could not start where I've been, because the beginning was way too difficult and confusing. So I started with Chapter 5 and worked my way forward and backward according to how I was feeling—a little this way and a little that way, until it started to take shape. I had to do it this way because I did not really know if this book could be something. I thought perhaps it was nothing.

A lot of the young women I work with believe they are nothing. I've been told many convincing stories of nothingness and invisibility. While worthlessness is about value, and emptiness is about sense of self, nothingness is about existence and self-respect. I've come to understand that while painful, believing you are nothing has certain advantages. When talking about eating and self-injury disorders, the idea of *nothing* is really something, and it is still more of something when it comes to recovery.

If you are scared of what you are supposed to be, what you want to be, or what other people expect you to be, or have no idea what being something would be like, being something can seem pretty daunting, not to mention that it can feel like too much of a burden. It's almost easier to stay nothing.

Many of us who have a knack for self-attack walk around with a lot of shame and blame and anger turned inward, and being nothing seems like the obvious conclusion. Being nothing is better than trying and failing and becoming a pathetic loser.

Being something comes with responsibility that you are probably not sure you want or are ready for. If there is no set standard, then there is no bar to raise. If you keep your self-worth low in the midst of all the pain of body-hate, starvation, endless food, and self-disgust, you don't have to join the aggressive, competitive world trying to be good, better, and best—trying to really be something.

At an age when you don't know yet where you are headed, what kind of life you want, or how you will move into the next stage of life, being nothing can actually feel safer than being something. Besides, being something implies that you could recover—if you exist, if you matter, if you have substance, it could mean that you can do this; that you are not so broken that you are unfixable. Being something means that you matter, that you take up space, that you have a voice. And existing means that you have some responsibility for your life.

On top of that, we can get so good at being nothing—at believing that we are nothing—that our comfort meter gets set on nothing. Believing we are nothing becomes the set point in our psyches, so much so that even when it seems like being something could be better, we hedge. We are still more at ease being nothing—at least we know what we are.

Author and teacher Geneen Roth says that the most difficult part of teaching people to respect and listen to their bodies is overcoming their convictions that there is nothing to respect. For most young women in the tornado of self-harm, finding self-respect, dignity, and grace is pretty far off. Even though we can learn so much about who we really are by feeling our feelings and respecting our bodies, we are held back by the urgency of the disorder and our enslavement to it. We do not respect ourselves nearly as much as we respect the disorder. We have no idea that respecting our feelings won't kill us, but will rather light the way to learning about who we are and what we need, believe, and want.

Anger, for example, teaches us what we are passionate about, what we believe is just and unjust in the world, and where our sore spots are. Fear teaches us what we hope for and yearn for, and what we believe about what we need in life to feel safe. Sadness informs us about what we long for, stand for, and hope for. And joy?—about what we desire, what lifts us, and what we value.

When you take every measure possible to distance yourself from your feelings—even when you are trying to save yourself—and from your hunger and your pain, you miss out not only on the experience of learning that you can survive, but the experience of finding out who you are. In protecting yourself from what you believe are unbearable feelings, you shut off the flow of learning that being something is not as bad as it seems. When you attack yourself by starving, bingeing, cutting, or running into walls headfirst, you are practicing staying nothing; you are reinforcing again and again the idea that nothing is better than something—because you believe it is.

And we are tired just thinking about it. The whole process of recovery is as confusing as the disorder itself: where to start, how to start, if to start, why to start. If you are nothing, then why bother?

And if you are not nothing, then what are you? Can you dare to believe that you are something when you are not sure what something is; when you've been told that you are nothing; when you are—or think you are—the sum total of your thighs, your stomach, and your rear end?

This is why becoming something is like this book. You probably will have to start right in the middle—right where you are right now—and then work your way backward and forward in little bits and pieces—one small next right thing after another, with mistakes and repeats and rewrites—in order to get from nothing to something. Starting with not knowing what can be is the only way to start. You will not have to make your debut in some grand fashion on the stage of life. Just by virtue of your eyes being able to read these words, you have at least one respectable body part. You have started.

Sitting quietly alongside the enormous mountain of nothing inside you is a tiny little hill of aching to be something. I don't want to take away your nothingness if you still need it, but while I have heard many convincing stories and arguments about the virtues of being nothing (yours is likely among them), I am still unconvinced that being nothing is better or easier or more sensible than becoming something. And I think you actually don't want to convince me that you are nothing.

I have heard the mantras of the negative voice; the disorder voice; the voice of fear, conviction, and certainty; the messages that seem like poured-concrete evidence of nothingness:

If I were something my parents would treat me better. If I were something they would listen to me, not drink, not fight, not yell, not criticize me. If I were something they would trust me, love me better, pay more attention. If I were something I would not have this problem, this addiction, this behavior. If I were something I would be smarter, prettier, funnier, more likeable. If I were something I would have more friends.

And I have heard the cattle call of perfectionism—the myth that to be something means being perfect; that perfection is the goal; that anything less is nothing—the whipping voice of self-pity:

If I were something I would not hurt like this, feel like this, act like this. I don't deserve happiness because my parents are not happy, because I am fat, because I am slow, because I am stuck in my own confusion about life, because I am not perfect, because of a hundred thousand things. As long as I am nothing, nothing can really hurt me, nothing is expected from me, I need nothing, I can say nothing, I can feel nothing, I don't have to know, to answer, to perform, to please—even though I both long to please and long to rebel. The only solution to this is nothing.

Nothingness is one of the great fears, and sometimes the great desires, of many who struggle and suffer with overwhelming feelings, eating disorders, and self-injury. You are afraid of being nothing, having nothing, and wanting everything, yet being satisfied by nothing except nothing because it is familiar and because it seems safe. It seems easier than unjamming all the thoughts and questions and seemingly crazy stuff that goes on in your head.

But you are not nothing. You are in the middle, right where you are now. You can wander toward the beginning, toward your history, toward what has shaped you, and you can wander toward the future, toward what awaits you. Or you can stay put. You can meander back and forth over the blurry line between *can't recover* and *won't recover* under the blanket of different moods and around the blockades of different obstacles. And you can listen in while your mind argues between the stubbornness to stay nothing and the knowledge that you are not nothing.

You can let out deep, gulping sighs of grief as you are letting go of being nothing. You can know that it is possible to stop punishing yourself for being nothing—or for being something; it works both ways. You can begin to let go of the idea that you don't want anything. You can be afraid to want, and still want. Staying nothing and wanting nothing (even though deep down you want so much but are afraid) will not protect you from being disappointed or burdened or having to rise to new levels of responsibility. It will only keep you starved for true nourishment and deprived of the tools that can give you better feelings and a good life.

The fragmented pieces of your life, your body, the past, the future, your hurt, your mind, school, friends, parents, love, and food are all fluid and free-floating. You don't have to have answers. You don't have to have things all sorted out in order to live. You can be in the here and now, not knowing exactly which direction to go, not sure about what being something will mean or how it will feel to be something, inch by inch. You can be safe and still be something. You can say, "No," "I don't know," and "I'll let you know," and still be something. You can be unsure, unfinished, and unglued and still be something. You can be right here in the middle of your own book.

Don't Tell Me I'm Not Cold

Like many of the young women I work with, Hanna, dark-eyed, black-haired, and bubble-wrapped in her oversized black sweat-shirt, sits on my couch and tells me that she does not deserve to recover. Her nutritionist told her last week that if she is not going to make an effort to reach her goals, she should stop coming. The nutritionist was not being mean, just honest, Hanna tells me. Her psychiatrist told her she was doing a great job and to keep up the good work. But her friends tell her she really seems out of it lately. When I ask for her thoughts, she simply says, "I can't." And then, "I can't do my food journals; I can't meet these goals; my world is dark." It seems to Hanna that recovery is something *everyone else* wants for her or from her. She has no idea what she really wants at all.

Hanna's eyes are full, and then the tears just spill over and drip down onto her lap. After a few minutes she covers her face with her hands and begins taking deep, heaving breaths. She is sobbing. She is suffering. As I sit with her, I think about something her psychiatrist said to me last week when we spoke—that Hanna seems to be fundamentally opposed to wellness. I roll this idea around in my head as if it is putty between my finger and thumb.

Every so often, Hanna's treatment team touches base to figure out how best to work with her. We discovered that we all share a similar feeling: that Hanna can get better, but that though we feel uncomfortable saying it out loud, she does not really want to. She wants, we think, to go back to the hospital. Her best friend has just been readmitted, and Hanna seems to envy her. We all also feel somewhat guilty for thinking this. We know Hannah is hurting. We know that recovery is often like pushing a truck uphill in the mud. We know that no one chooses this pain or this path. We have great respect for the unconscious mind, biology, brain chemistry, genetics, and socialization. We know that there is a canyon of confusion beneath wanting to recover and being able to recover, and a fine and slippery line between *can't* and *won't*.

I have been thinking about *can't* and *won't* quite a bit. I think about all those pro-ana and pro-mia blogs ("ana" for anorexia, and "mia" for bulimia) and about all the young women I know who really do choose to live their lives in the presumed protection of self-harm and under self-hate disguised as self-love. I think about everyone I know who is enslaved to the pursuit of thinness and committed to body-hate, and I wonder if I have any business wanting something different for them. How sure am I that living with progress and gentleness and being able to deal with emotional pain is a better life than living with self-hate and body-hate and being in service to self-harm, deprivation, obsession, and compulsion? Very sure. Actually, very, very sure.

At the beginning of our work together, Hanna's parents and sister came to a session with her. Since I am always cold, I keep my office heat piped up; some of my clients have been known to come in wearing T-shirts in the middle of a New Jersey January. I always invite people to let me know if they are too warm so that I can adjust the temperature. I don't mind setting it to the comfort level of my clients.

When I inquired whether the temperature in the office was OK, Hanna said she was cold. Instantly Hanna's mother said, "No you're not. It's not cold in here." Hanna shrugged and sank deeper into my couch. Hanna's sister, who was sitting quietly next to Hanna on my couch, spoke up rather suddenly and said, "Well, I'm cold, too. Could you turn up the heat?"

I often think about that moment, and Hanna and I talk about it every now and again. It symbolizes so many things we think. We wonder at how Hanna shrank, and at how her sister spoke up. Hanna tells me that her sister argues with her mother all the time, but that Hanna just accepts these directives. Hanna tells me she is like tofu; whatever the flavor of the moment is, she will just absorb it. It's easier that way. If her shrink thinks she's doing great, she's doing great. If her nutritionist thinks she's a loser, she's a loser. If her mother says she's not cold, she's not cold. Best not to argue. She's not really sure what she thinks anyway, so why not just go along with everyone else's ideas? She tells me that she is just taking up space; that she has no real substance.

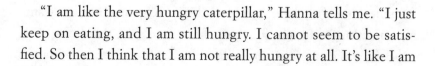

"I am like the very hungry caterpillar," Hanna tells me. "I just keep on eating, and I am still hungry. I cannot seem to be satisfied. So then I think that I am not really hungry at all. It's like I am drawing a picture with markers and crayons and lines and circles.

When I finish, I show it to my mom who hangs it on the fridge and oohs and ahs over it, but it's not really mine. I like that she likes it. But I feel completely unattached to it."

This detachment from her own sense of self, her accomplishment, and her effectiveness is one reason Hanna (and many young women) struggle to get started in recovery. It's hard to recover without a strong and deeply confident sense of self, but you don't develop one until you are further along the road to maturity. Living in the definitions of others only leaves you more confused and angry, because somewhere deep inside you know that time will keep moving on and you will travel anyway, and that walking in the shoes of others is worse than walking in your own. Somewhere deep down, you know this is true.

As the weeks pass, Hanna and I talk about the story of her picture. We wonder about the difference between being tired and being stubborn; between being nothing and being something; between being her mother and being herself. If Hanna is cold and her mother is not, then Hanna will be different from her mother. She will be separate. Hanna's sister does not seem to mind this, but for Hanna it's too confusing. It's even risky. Her mother is supposed to be right. Hanna has the idea that her life—not just her recovery—is about getting praise from her parents, not just because some part of her wants acknowledgment or positive feelings, but because she feels enslaved to the idea that pleasing them and making them happy is really what her life is supposed to be about. They are something, and Hanna is nothing.

Though there is a deep feeling of rebelliousness somewhere in Hanna's soul, she does not want to go up against her parents, her nutritionist, her psychiatrist, or me. The kind of dependence Hanna feels is very confusing. She has not yet learned that it's possible to depend on people for support without having to wear their feelings as her own or be responsible for their happiness. She has no idea that she can ask for ideas from others and then filter them through her own instincts; that just because someone is angry, sounds certain or confident, or looks good does not necessarily mean that person is right; that comparing your insides to other people's outsides is often False Evidence Appearing Real (FEAR). And that in fact, even in the darkest moments of her depression and the thickest immersion in her body-hate, there is a part of her that is clear and whole and unbroken; a part that can live in connection and in healthy reliance on those who are generally trustworthy, despite their character defects and personality quirks.

Being told you do not feel how you feel, or that you should not feel how you feel, is like living in a straitjacket. But you get used to it as a way to survive. Sometimes it seems impossible to tolerate all the messages you get from everyone around you and to filter out their own fears and claim only what rings deeply true for you. It can be altogether too difficult to figure out what is fear, what is survival and protection, and what is the voice of the disorder—sometimes all of the above, and then to find, amid it all, your own voice—the voice that knows when you really are too cold.

We do need reassurance, positive feedback, and good regard from others. We usually crave them from those closest to us. When we get them, we need to stockpile them inside to help us build our sense of self; to help us detach from our attack of our own soul and psyche. And we can be open to feedback at some point, if given safely, in the right tone, from those we trust. And we need reliable voices of recovery to help us reestablish our true voice and develop that strong, confident identity that is separate from the disorder. It is difficult to filter out the voices of others and their messages sometimes—to discern the supporters from the naysayers and advice-givers.

Sadie, a client of mine in her midfifties, tells me a story about her childhood. She came home from school one day very sad because she had learned that her best friend was moving away. When her mother asked what was wrong, Sadie said she was sad and told her mother why. Her mother responded by saying that Sadie had lots of other friends and shouldn't be so upset. Sadie remembers feeling angry, not wanting to be cheered up, and throwing her backpack on the floor. Then came the slap. Not terribly hard, but still. She was sent to her room and told to think about how disrespectful she had been to her mother.

Sadie tells me that she remembers sitting up in her room waiting and wishing for someone to come up and hold her, and wishing even more that she could disappear into nothing. Eventually her mother did come to get her. She said she hoped Sadie had learned her lesson about getting so upset. It was time for dinner. Sadie had no appetite.

It's been many years since that day, and Sadie has grown children of her own and has long since learned that it's OK to be sad and angry and long for loving arms around you when you are hurting. She has put her own loving arms around her own children and is grateful that over the years she has not treated herself or them the way she was treated growing up. She is in therapy now because she lost her husband to cancer last year and wants to talk about him as much as she possibly can because it makes her feel closer to him and it helps her continue to reject the idea that she will be slapped in the face for feeling how she feels. She went to therapy a long time ago as well and has had a thousand new life experiences that have helped her heal those wounds. But every now and again that memory surfaces to remind her that she is allowed to feel all her feelings without getting slapped. She and I marvel at how far she has come from feeling that she was nothing; from wanting to be nothing to being something. She is someone whole, and someone good, and someone brimming with life.

Hanna, like Sadie, has the idea that expressing feelings is quite dangerous. Getting slapped, physically or verbally, will do that to you. It is the colossal effort to suppress your feelings that keeps you grounded in the stubborn belief that how you live is how you have to live. It is hard to imagine that you can just feel whatever you feel. Many of us, as children, never get to experience that our feelings are valid and that they often pass if we are allowed to have them and express them without rejection or punishment.

The crushed and defeated experience of not being allowed to feel, of being afraid to feel, of others rejecting your feelings or criticizing or punishing you for having them, is like a sliding-board down into nothingness. And when those messages come from those closest to you—society, teachers, friends, or professionals, your confusion can be downright paralyzing. It's no wonder, then, that staying immersed, consciously or not, in physical pain, obsession, and compulsion, and sitting tightly on the can't /won't recover border, seems to make so much sense.

Whose Fault Is This?

Hanna thinks that if her mom would really own her own stuff Hanna would finally get some relief. She believes that if her mother were not so critical, and her father not so distant, and her sister not so competitive, that she, Hanna, would not be so sick.

At the same time she believes that it really is all her own fault. In our work together, and in my work with young women who battle food, weight, self-hate, and self-harm, the questions of "Why?" and "Whose fault is this?" lurk in the background.

Why do I have this? Why am I like this? Why can't I just stop this? Why does everyone have to pay so much attention to me? Why doesn't anyone really care? Why do they have to be the way they are? Why am I so much trouble? Why are they so much trouble? Why does what I do to myself matter so much to them? Why doesn't it matter more? Why don't they do more? Why don't they just leave me alone? If we don't register at Macy's for our troubles, who's to blame for them? And whose job is it to fix them? Who should pay for help? Who should arrange for help? Who should get help?

Hanna and I have talked a lot about how parents themselves are confused about whose fault things are, and that many parents become deeply defensive and self-critical in fear that they are to blame. Instead of looking at how they might have contributed or how they might help, they sometimes become angry, distant, or hurt. It often seems like we are all stuck in the dough of blame together. Conflicting feelings abound. On the one hand we know that how we are raised shapes us. On the other hand we know that our family background cannot be the sole source of our challenges.

In our role as daughters, we look at how we were treated and what our experiences and our responses were. Parents understand that how they interact and behave shapes their children, but they also know that just like them, their daughters are born with their own genetic wiring and biological predispositions. Parents are often defensive because they have the same questions that their daughters have: "Did I do this?" "Did I cause this?" "Should I have prevented it?" "Could I have prevented it?"

Blame, shame, and frustration often get mixed up together. You don't know how to claim your own part without being or feeling damned and blamed. You long to be understood or to be let off the hook somehow, neither of which is easy or simple.

I have found over the years of my work with mothers and daughters that the fear of being separate is as great as the fear of being close. Feeling close seems to be filled with inoperable shame and burden, with confusion over your own identity and life. But staying at painful odds feels bad, too. It's hard to negotiate the years between late teens and early twenties without eating and self-injury issues, but all the more so when mothers and daughters are caught in these storms.

Growing up and figuring out who you are gets twisted up with recovery. It seems that *everyone's* well-being and success gets intertwined with yours and the pressure to make things better seems only to make things worse. Blaming each other seems to be a way to relieve the pressure, but instead it usually explodes into chaos.

Some parents invest oodles of time and money in their children's therapy because they feel obligated to help their children; because it's their job. Some do it because they feel responsible or guilty or believe that they have significantly contributed to the problem. Many help out of love, fear, and the longing to help their children progress in life.

Some parents don't help so much. They are unable, or even uninterested, or don't believe it's their role.

Most of the time it's a big mix of all of the above. But talking about it is tricky because feelings run deep. And the truth is that you don't really know whose fault it is. And another hard truth is that knowing whose fault it is won't cure you.

Your mother and father play a significant role in your body issues, but it is not a blame game. Your mother could be dealing with her own unresolved body and food issues. Maybe your father sends you confusing messages about attachment, sexuality, love, and intimacy. In the best of circumstances, parents often dance haltingly and awkwardly around issues of sexuality, closeness, emotional communication, achievement, and separation. You are bombarded with media images, cultural competitiveness, and an unachievable mandate for a perfect body. You are taught to ignore cravings, hide from feelings, and keep the peace.

There is no shortage of explanations for what contributes to the development of eating disorders in the more than ten million women in the United States who have them. It is not hard to understand why more than eight million young women self-injure. We share both a personal and a culture rage and deep confusion about what is good enough and how we know when good is good enough. There is a Grand Canyon–like deficit in our emotional education, and it's no wonder that it seems easier to cut and burn and binge and starve the pain.

Studying the problems, who contributes to them and how, does help. Everyone—daughters and parents—being willing to learn about what's going on and own their own stuff can go a long way toward everyone finding relief and life and relationships being much better. But it's not the whole cure. It's great to know what has shaped you, though, because it helps to know your patterns and tendencies and how they work for you or against you now.

Eating and self-injury disorders are the results of many factors. There are lots of correlations and cause-and-effect theories out there. But there is no one scientific fact and no combination of factors that always empirically draw a line from a particular event to a particular result. The hard fact for all of us, parents and daughters and professionals and humans—those of us who are suffering and struggling, is that while no one is to blame for the problem, we all, individually and collectively, must take part in being responsible for the solution.

Get Out of My Food and My Money—I Think

In an effort to be part of the solution, Hanna's mother is in Hanna's food. And her father and sister are in her money. Despite the various different messages that her parents get from the various different professionals in Hanna's life, her parents seem to land on more involvement rather than less. But the level of involvement is not the problem. It's how to be involved, and when.

Parents and families are given many conflicting messages from professionals about if, when, and how to be involved—and exactly what *involved* means. Some treatment methods advise deep involvement, others just the opposite. Parents and their daughters are left in the muck of confusion as to who wants what and with what motives.

"Are you sure you want that?" asks Hanna's mother when she sees Hanna reaching for another doughnut. "Did you finish your lunch?" is the question when Hanna is in a starving rotation. Despite Hanna's gift for skimming off just the outside of cakes, hiding and replacing empty ice cream containers, and putting her potatoes in her underpants, she still cringes every time her parents catch her and get in her food.

When Hanna and I talk it through, we decide that part of the bubbling fury she feels is actually desire. Some part of her wishes her parents could be helpful, but just not like this. Hanna herself does not know what she needs exactly, and when her parents start in with how much she is or is not eating, it feels suffocating, annoying, and attentive all at once. *Butt out. Butt in. Leave me alone. Don't leave me alone.*

If you are still living at home, your parents will most likely be in your food and in your money in the millions of day-to-day moments together. Part of the rage you might feel is because the real messages seem to be "You are weak. You cannot do this on your own. You need help. I am not happy with you. You are not doing a good job. You are failing. You are failing me. I am better than you. You are out of control. You can't have what you want and don't want what you have. You are so totally messed up." But for your parents, underneath is the quiet whisper of "I am failing you. And I am failing myself. I love you, and I am helpless." All of this from a simple "Did you have enough protein at lunch?"

The definition of a normal eater probably applies to one-tenth of the population. Everyone else is on the spectrum of crazy—at least that's how it seems. But when your food and your body are the front men for everything else in life, any little interference seems significant and packed with untold messages. You are not just fighting with your mother; you are fighting with yourself and society for some seemingly uncatchable spiritual prize. You are also fighting for your mother and for all the daughters and mothers who are elbowing their way through the maze of food and ambition and self-definition.

Hanna tells me that sometimes she has the most amazing fights with her mother. She herself does not understand them. It seems to her that she is her own Jekyll and Hyde. She cannot understand why her mother continues to buy ice cream when she knows it's a trigger for Hanna. She wants her mother to make reasonable, "safe" dinners and gets infuriated when her mother does not do this. She expects her mother to anticipate her food needs and work with them. And then, in the next breath, she fills with rage when her mother asks the wrong question or makes a suggestion.

It seems like a lose-lose for both of them. Hanna and her mother are both searching for a way to be known, understood, connected, and free; to be effective without having to be perfect; to be able to make mistakes without having to be condemned; to get and give help in some indescribable way that makes everyone feel better, not worse; to be fed and satisfied, and safe and good enough.

Money also brings up this tug of war. Most young people are in some way financially dependent on their parents well into their twenties, even those whose parents have little means or willingness to help. Many still live at home, return home after college, or are out of the house but still getting some kind of help from their parents.

You can find yourself stuck in the spiderweb of wanting to be financially independent but not being able to break free just yet—needing and wanting to stay, and needing and wanting to get out at the same time. It is possible, but not easy, to go to and finish college, get a job, and live independently without help. But the facts of needing food, transportation, housing, and time to either study or work all require support. Even when your family is not able to help, help is still needed.

The need for all these things can leave you in the position of having to negotiate with your parents while wanting to make decisions on your own. You do need guidance, ideas, support, and opinions from your parents. In some ways these needs mimic your food issues. You need nourishment but don't always know how much, at what cost, or from what source. Once again there are blurred boundaries and a sticky balance beam to walk between independence and dependence that makes daily life stressful.

Trying to make progress in life and recovery simultaneously gets all mushed up together. Part of staying immersed in the eating or self-injury disorder is as a way to stay close to home. Getting better might mean getting out. And strangely enough, both staying and going are equally powerful needs.

Standing firmly in the way of wanting to get better is the unconscious belief that as painful as the back-and-forth is, it is better than breaking free. Breaking free seems to mean forgoing any chance of being deeply loved, viscerally connected, and wholly known. Perhaps you have the idea that in recovery you will no longer be parented, even if it's not the parenting you need or want.

You can become so frustrated with the back-and-forth with your parents that you punish yourself. You don't realize that somewhere between a mentality of deprivation and a mentality of entitlement lies a peaceful meadow of calm and ease and "good enough." Learning how to negotiate the give-and-take with parents requires everyone to be bold, but humble. Traipsing through the land mines of feelings and expectations means understanding that no one can possibly get it right all the time. It means believing what you do not believe—that you can grow up and still be a kid; that you can leave home and stay close to home; that you can learn about your cravings and satisfy some of them in ways that are progressive and safe and good enough; that needing help is human and that wanting it and not wanting it at the same time is normal; that not knowing how to settle softly amid all this turmoil does not mean you should not take the next right step toward bowing out of the war on yourself.

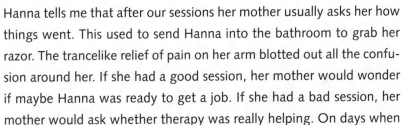

Hanna tells me that after our sessions her mother usually asks her how things went. This used to send Hanna into the bathroom to grab her razor. The trancelike relief of pain on her arm blotted out all the confusion around her. If she had a good session, her mother would wonder if maybe Hanna was ready to get a job. If she had a bad session, her mother would ask whether therapy was really helping. On days when Hanna seems to be doing better, her parents ask more and more of her. On days when she is not doing so well, their frustration is apparent.

Somewhere in the middle of the fog, Hanna herself is trying to figure out how to exist and whether to exist among everyone's expectations. It is difficult, in fact, for Hanna to even come up with her own ideas when she is surrounded by the intense personalities and feelings of everyone around her. It is hard to know whose dreams belong to whom, and who wants what and why.

Hanna was often told as a child that she brought sunshine into the lives of all who knew her. Though this was meant as a compliment, Hanna's unconscious heard it also as a message of responsibility. She has the idea that she is responsible for making everyone happy, and that she is capable of it. Her father often tells her that all he wants is for her to be happy. To Hanna's mind, this means that everyone else's satisfaction rests on her. She is, in some ways, way too important— and fearful. Not only do they want so much for her and from her, but when she succeeds, they seem to only want more. It is never clear to her whether they want success for her because they are her parents or because they believe that their own self-worth rides on her accomplishments. Most likely, it's some combination of both.

Great Expectations

Author and psychologist Mary Pipher writes in her bestseller *Reviving Ophelia* that girls "must figure out ways to be independent from their parents and stay emotionally connected to them. They must discover ways to achieve and still be loved." She explains how difficult it is for young women to find the balance between asserting themselves and pleasing others, and how tricky it is to find one's own identity in a critical, confusing culture.

The task is great, and girls becoming women have little real guidance about how to do this. Neither do most adults. We are all in a collective knot about how to grow up well, and a collective confusion about who is supposed to know what and how and how much accomplishment is enough.

You most likely have, hidden under your pain, expectations of your own. It's hard to know what's reasonable. Young women have deep expectations of their parents, even of parents who don't, won't, or can't provide. They have a longing not just for emotional connection and love, but for money, shelter, and all the things needed to live. Depending on how well parents provide these things, and with what attitudes, young women are often caught in the volley between guilt and resentment, entitlement and sacrifice, desire and denial.

Though it can seem impossible in the heat of your pain, focus on viewing others' expectations with curiosity in order to lighten the burden they put on you. You can look at your expectations of yourself, of becoming a woman, and of your parents, therapists, and educators the same way you look at your obsessions and feelings: as teachers and informants about your desires, wishes, and fears, and as guideposts leading the way step by step *out of* nothingness and self-hate rather than *into* it.

Deciding to turn your thinking toward recovery means taking a look at what is reasonable to expect—a ridiculous expectation in itself, really, because how do you know? You don't. You can only find out by taking at least one small step toward looking inside yourself, past the cuts, past the fat, under your rib cage, and into that part of yourself where you think nothing lives. Tunnel through all the voices, fear, and images of other people and what you think are their great and perfect lives, and have a look around in the dark.

Though it can seem daunting, when you let yourself slow down and hold gently in your hands everyone's expectations of you, and yours of them, you can relax a bit. Expectations can be seen as wishes with bowling balls attached to them. You do not have to make others' expectations your own. If you take off the bowling balls, they are free to float around and teach you about what you hope for, long for, and aspire to.

Still a Kid

Hanna tells me that she is afraid to tell her parents the truth some-times, not just because they might respond in a way that hurts, but also because they, too, are confused about whether she should keep growing up or not. They want her close and far away at the same time. Even at nineteen, she fears that her accomplishments will obligate her to doing more than she is ready to do and that every step forward is a step away from the safety and familiarity of her life as a kid. Her family's culture is confusing, rocky, and frustrating, but it is still her home culture.

It's not clear when Hanna will really have to take on more of the responsibility for her basic needs, and she fears that the better she takes care of herself, the more she will have to take care of herself. Instead of seeing this as the sun coming up, Hanna sees it as a destination of more loneliness, one that will trump even the worst places she already goes—in her mind.

One of the great unspoken obstacles to getting better is the idea that getting better will satisfy your parents. You think that as long as you are suffering, they will suffer. You believe that your ongoing pain and sickness is just reward for others who have hurt you. This is not the whole reason behind your refusal, but it is part of the picture. Those who have hurt or who are hurting you emotionally do not deserve to be let off the hook by your getting well. They do not deserve to have the satisfaction of your independence, success, or recovery.

While it can seem impossible not to keep meandering around the can't/won't fault line of recovery, you do have a choice. You can take the bold view that your recovery is not connected to granting others' wishes or holding on to your childhood. You can recover and still be a kid. Though recovery is about stepping into your own life, you do not have to leave your childhood behind if you don't want to.

The normal hormonal agitation and moodiness of these years of your life do not have to keep you stuck in the gap between childhood and adult life. Most adults I know still tumble back into that gap from time to time. The fear of being responsible for your own life is one that everyone feels from time to time no matter how old they are. And just like recovery, one more small step in the right direction is all that you ever need to take.

Our desire to hold on to the feelings of childhood—the fullness of deep golden summers, the calm of fresh falling snow, the endlessness of clear blue skies, and all the simplicity of the dreamy world of make-believe—is so precious, it's no wonder that we fear that growing up will mean losing touch with our own hearts. So much of what we long for seems to depend on being a kid.

You can stay safe in the cocoon of childhood, and hold on to the fantasies of childhood, and still grow. And you can take steps toward recovery without stepping away from the things that are precious to you. The sense that time is passing and you are moving forward does not have to mean relinquishing the places you retreat to that are whole and pure and hidden deep inside you.

Getting better does not mean that you will be thrust into an independence that you cannot handle or do not want. It does not mean that you will lose the parts of you that you know and love. It does not mean that you will lose your family. It means you will find more of you, and most likely a better family—more that is good and more that is well. You can get better and still be safe. You can get better and still be a kid. You can grow up and still stay connected to the parts of yourself that you treasure.

The work of recovery teaches you how to do this. The books you read, the journals you write, the pictures you draw, the conversations you have, the prayers you whisper, the quiet time you take—they all become part of you. They tie together the past and the future. Responsibility for your life becomes a blessing, not a burden. Dependency turns into reliance and reciprocity. Fear turns into safe hope. And refusal turns into relief.

Keep walking. You will see.

Part Two

HEALING

CHAPTER 5

Maybe I Don't
Want to Recover

The Best is the enemy of the good.

—VOLTAIRE

HOLLY, WHOSE dark brown hair falls loosely down to her waist, often comes to my office, sits down on the couch, looks up at me, sighs, and says, "I am really glad I have you today."

When Holly starts with this I know I am going to hear about how bad her latest binge was. I listen as she tells me all about the box of fat-free cookies, the half-gallon of sugar-free ice cream, the 12-pack of whole-grain muffins, and the four grilled cheese sandwiches that she stuffed herself silly with while watching reruns of "30 Rock" and "Grey's Anatomy."

There is something both resigned and resistant in her voice, as if she accepts her binges as givens and does not really want to do anything to stop them.

Sometimes, though, when her eyes are red and swollen and her face is pale and puffy, there is desperation in her voice. And frustration. And the raspy aftermath that comes from vomiting hard until it all comes back up. But the pain of these moments fades into the lull of her life, and they don't seem so bad a few days post-binge—until the next time.

Holly and I have been working together for about two years—since she graduated from college. A bright, beautiful, and talented singer Holly is unsure what to do with her degree, and she jokingly refers to this time in her life as her "quarter-life crisis." Her boyfriend landed a hot finance job in the city, her best friend is teaching kindergarten, and her parents are about ready to throw her out.

Except that they won't. Holly's older brother went off to do a missionary stint in Africa, and they like having her at home. However, they are sick and tired of her crazy self-hating binge-a-thons, her staying up most of the night, sleeping until noon or later, and then spending hours online searching for singing gigs and job ideas without really pursuing any. But they keep giving Holly money, food, and love. And while they also give her the idea that they want her better yesterday, they seem to rally together best around her craziness.

Seriously Stuck and Stubborn

Holly's dad is on a mission to "cure" her. He has led her around the wide world of eating disorder healing options, which Holly rejects, rails against, and then gives in to. None, so far, has made much of a dent in Holly's disordered behavior. I am Holly's fourth therapist in as many years. She has seen three hypnotists and more than a handful of nutritionists; she has done two residential programs and a smattering of recovery groups, and has attempted one or two Overeaters Anonymous meetings. Holly is now working with a new naturopath who gives her mineral waters, herbs, vitamins, and adjustments, along with acupressure, which is sort of helping but not really. She has tried intuitive eating and gluten-free and vegan food plans.

Holly tells me she is suffering from dangerously high levels of self-hate this week. She tells me that she is desperate to recover, but when she won't crack open a workbook more than once or stay with a program, I know there is something deeper in her way. Her desperation is fleeting.

I have a whole library in my office with most of the old and new eating disorder, body-image, and foodie books ever to grace the universe. Reading is food for the soul, food for thought, and often a gateway to new ideas. I always welcome book-inspired conversations in my office. So when every now and then Holly insists that we *do* something—not just talk (I do not ask yet again what Holly would like to do or what she is willing to do), I look lovingly over at my bookshelves.

But in Holly's case, I am more of a reluctant passenger than a copilot or guide when it comes to books. While they do not always trigger her, they do make her furious, mostly because at some point the message is always: "No one can do it for you; you have to do it yourself—with help, with love, with persistence, but you're the one who has to do the legwork. Doesn't matter who caused it, who deserves it, how impossible it seems, how much work it might be, how much it hurts, how sorry you feel for yourself or how entitled to your actions and methods you think you are, you are the one who has to do the work. You can get lots of help. And it will be a better life inside and out once you do it. But you are the muscle, whether you like or not." And with Holly, it's mostly not.

It's been a big accomplishment for Holly to stay with me these past few years. She believes that there is some kind of cure out there—some way for her to have her binges and her dazed life but not feel so bummed about it. Or at least not get fat. Holly, like many of us, yearns for a way to have her food and her weapons (I am using the word *weapon* to mean all the actions and things that you use for relief and control that actually hurt you physically, emotionally, or spiritually) but not suffer from the not-so-side-effects of weight gain, shame, frustration, and self-pity—or the physical damage. But it's hard to know which comes first—the feelings or the weapons; it seems like an endless circle indeed.

Holly and I know a lot about her binges, but that in itself does not stop them. We plotted the anatomy of a binge from the first semiconscious thought to wiping up the toilet and walking out of the bathroom. We know that she binges to punish herself and to punish herself for punishing herself. We know that she yells at her dad with each gag; that with each finger crammed down her throat she is digging out all the frustration of not knowing what to do with herself; that each clump of ice cream or chunk of cheese that comes choking back up leaves her drained and empty and clean. And victorious. And defeated.

And we know that the food will call again and again and again. The craving monster will wake up, out of nowhere, and drag her along. She will be mesmerized and anesthetized and then dropped on her head all over again. Even though we know a lot about the meaning behind Holly's bingeing, still and all the food itself calls and calls. And Holly can't imagine being willing to stop or being able to stay stopped.

Holly and I leave no stone unturned in our search for her answer. Countless books, family therapy, dialectical behavior therapy (DBT), cognitive behavioral therapy (CBT), and psychoanalysis are all on the list. We explore them all, but Holly won't give credence to any of these paths or ideas, thus proving to herself—in her own mind—that they won't work for her. She has been on and off medication. Her depression ebbs and flows, and when it flows, she wants the world to leave her alone. She won't kill herself, but she would not mind getting hit by a bus.

Sometimes Holly and I wonder if she is, in fact, one of those rare individuals whom the Alcoholics Anonymous *Big Book* calls "constitutionally incapable" of getting better.

But we think not. We talk about longing for a cure—for anything but having to push the truck up the hill herself. We wonder too, if it has to be that hard. And we think that maybe, just maybe, it doesn't always have to be. And while we have talked about her past, her present, her parents, and her pain, we have not talked enough about her future or what life might look like without the constant call of the food and the scale and fear of being fat. We know that recovery does not mean that she will always feel good; sometimes it just means that she will feel. And Holly is not sure she wants this just yet.

Gathering Your Personal Truths

So we start to gather truths—the things we know to be true for Holly, at this moment in time, about what is getting in the way of her making progress.

Truth 1: Holly wants to think she can have a little sugar, here and there; except that she has never been able to have a little without going nuts. Sugar and sugar substitutes make Holly want more sugar. If, for her, sugar is addictive, it is also a weapon. If it sets up the physical cravings, it has to be out of her food plan for now. It's almost impossible to imagine life without sugar; it seems so drastic and counterculture. It seems like one more gimmick. But after years of evidence, a physical addiction to sugar—the fact that sugar wakes up the craving monster—is a fact, for now, for Holly. Thinking about getting better means getting off sugar to help ease the cravings and compulsion, and to help clear her mind and stabilize her moods and her food.

As much as she wants to go with her body's natural hunger signals, the compulsion takes over more often than not. Intuitive eating seems to go on and on into intuitive bingeing. Intuitive eating is not for her just yet, just now. For now she is more stable with a reasonable food plan in place. Even if she has difficulty following it. That is Truth Number 2.

Holly also wants to believe she can recover on her own. The idea of relationships replacing disorders seems corny and weird to her, though doing it on her own never led to progress, either. She does not like the idea of needing ongoing support. There really isn't any way around it, though, I reason. Mentor relationships and support from others are necessities in recovery work. Twelve-step programs are cornerstoned by having sponsors and forging a relationship with the God of one's understanding. Traditional therapies encourage group work, too—relationship-based and ongoing. No one thinks recovery happens in isolation, though isolation is as central to emotional pain and disorders as ink is to pens. Isolation is a subtle weapon that denies access to people, to necessary healthy messages of recovery, and deprives one of comfort and company— especially for Holly, who avoids people like the plague. She can't stand their successes, their shortcomings, their insensitiveness, and their idiosyncrasies. "People are annoying," she often tells me. "I either hate them, hate me, or think they hate me." Even her boyfriend and best friend are on her blacklist most of the time. Truth Number 3 is that Holly needs regular support, like it or not.

Holly tells me that she thinks people in recovery are often worse than civilians. They are either full of annoying, know-it-all advice or they are real sickos. We wonder if she might have to tolerate other people's awfulness in order to join a wider community of wellness—in order to make a better life. At her own insistence, this is not something she is willing to do yet, though the notion of it goes on the truth list as well.

It's not this way for everyone: sugar addiction, needing more support, a food plan. These are Holly's own combination of facts. And she is not done wishing they were different. She still hopes for emotional healing first, and letting go of bingeing and purging second.

It has to be the other way around sometimes for recovery to get some wheels under it, just like when you are starving you have to be fed first in order to get better because your brain cannot grab hold of healing ideas when it's depleted of nourishment. The coping weapon of starvation usually has to be put down first so your brain can think right again. The folks in AA will tell you this about alcohol.

If sugar, isolation, and lack of structure around her meals are weapons—ways that Holly copes and gets relief—she may have to put them down in order to get better. Sometimes putting down the coping weapons has to come before—or at least alongside—the emotional healing, not after, especially if your weapons are addicting. We don't know if this is an absolute truth for Holly, but we put it on our list things to consider anyway.

Most of the people Holly knows who are recovering or recovered have some sort of serious motivation—a deep and solid love relationship, a passionate career, the desire for a family of their own, a wish to move forward in life, a sense of purpose or meaning, or a sense of self. As much as we have talked over these ideas, Holly thinks that maybe a part of her really does not want to recover because she thinks that recovery will not be as good, as safe, or as predictable as her eating disorder is. She has no idea how her parents will treat her if she is not constantly in drama and pain. Perhaps she will have to face the empty space inside of her that has no definable location. Perhaps she will have to face her quarter-life crisis head on then and find something to do with her life.

When being boldly honest, Holly is not sure she wants recovery yet. She is not really interested in moving out or on with life. In many ways, she is comfortable right where she is, eating disorder and all. And she is afraid that recovery will force her to move away from the things she finds comfortable and familiar. Holly is stuck somewhere between rock bottom and rock top. Nothing really bad is happening to motivate her, but neither is anything really good. We wonder together if it is possible to choose to recover when there are no big motivations—if it's worth quitting sugar (in Holly's case, to ease her cravings); getting into a recovery group, mentor relationship, or 12-step program; and agreeing to the idea of a food plan, if it will mean having to face life without any notion of what it would really be like.

So we start exploring passions and possibilities. We talk about finding something temporary until a passion presents itself. We decide that she does not have to embark on the world's most worthwhile career in order to recover. We also decide that she does not have to be a professional singer if she does not want to. She is not sure whose dream that really is anyway. We will have to talk it out some more. What she wants matters, even if she is uncertain. More truth.

Life without the disorder seems empty, impossible, and unimaginable. As hard as it is to think back to a time when food was just food and her body was just her body (was it ever?), or when the high of control and starvation and the free-for-all of bingeing didn't rule, thinking ahead is like staring at a blank screen. It's like wandering around empty city streets with absolutely no noise. It's like trying to imagine life without your feet. You just can't.

For now, for Holly, these truths are a start. They are on the table, in the light and what we know to be true at this point in her recovery. We know that truths can change. As recovery takes hold and new insights and abilities come, truths can shift and can blend into new ones that meet you where you are at different places on your path. Even though Holly might not yet be ready or willing to take the next step, it helps us to know what's what.

Imagine If

For the most seriously stuck and stubborn, considering what recovery might look like—what you'd like it to be like—is a good place to begin. Contemplate a moment in time when just for a few tiny seconds you are free. What would that feel like? What would you do? Wear? Say? Feel? Eat? What in the world would you think about if you were not busy trying to make safety margins between you and 200 pounds; if the food were not calling all the time; if you didn't have to eat the whole thing; if you didn't *want* to eat the whole thing; if your relief did not come from a bag, a box, or a bottle—or a razor blade; if you didn't have to get on the scale again; if it didn't dictate your day, your mood, or your safety, self-worth, or identity? What if sad was sad and mad was mad? What if you slept when you were tired, ate when you were hungry, and graced yourself with some slack when you screwed up? What if you showed up for work even if your jeans were tight, your parents were beastly, and your best friend showed her underwear to your boyfriend? What if showing up meant something to *you*, not them?

Can you imagine life with joy? Feeling high from fresh air and bright sunshine? A good ballgame or a starry night? How about a long walk with a good friend or a decent grade on a paper you put some, but not a lot of, effort into? Or maybe a moment or two of real understanding from your mom or total comfort from your father. Or just a break in the hate and a sliver of grace?

What if recovery were fine? What if for a while you had to keep an eye on your food, or stay in group, or go to OA meetings because many healthy people do? What if you still had to check in with your shrink or pull out one of the ED books from your closet and skim it over a bit? What if you didn't hate your body with such conviction anymore and could still feel safe? What if your thighs were just your thighs, large or small, and your stomach was fleshy and that was just how yours was—a creation of God and not the lightning rod for all of life's evils—just your soft belly with its sweet skin and tender rolls? What if recovery meant that sometimes you had to be a bitch and sometimes you had to be too nice; that you didn't get the assertiveness thing down pat all the time, but you kept at it until you could say what you meant, mean what you said, and not say it mean? What if recovery meant being able to say "I don't know," "I'll let you know," or "No thanks"? What if recovery meant that you didn't get to please everyone all the time, nor did you get to tick them off?

What would it be like if people sometimes disappointed you and sometimes pleased you, but they were just people? What if recovery was just life un-drugged, on its own terms, with no givens other than no using? What if it really was better than what you have right now?

What if you could actually take part in the world? And if you didn't feel like it, you got to hide out, without injury and shame but with choice and dignity and serenity?

What if you slept well, ate well, felt well, most of the time? What if you could look in the mirror and really smile at yourself? What if you felt resilient, peaceful, resourceful, and productive? What if you could laugh and really mean it . . . at jokes, at yourself, at life?

What if you could concentrate and create and connect and love? What if you liked what you saw in the mirror, felt good about your decisions, forgave your mistakes, and felt OK with life on this planet? What if the dread, the panic, the shame, and the deep loneliness faded away? What if you felt *good*?

What if you could sit quietly and know that you were good, unique, and wholly entitled to nourishment, freedom, and love? What if you could trust your instincts, feel comfortable in your own skin, and be able to deal well with difficult people and feel well through difficult situations?

What if you had to get really clear about the personal truths of your disorder and why you might or might not want to recover? What if you had to get some idea of what you would like recovery to be, even if you didn't yet want it or believe it was possible? If you could do this, you would be on your way to a more honest life, which is worth a lot even if you are not ready to move forward just yet.

Recovery is no straight line anyway, but the circles go deeper and deeper. Can you start imagining it, even if you don't want to?

Can you create your own idea of what you would be like if you were out from under? Can you dream a little and wonder, "What if?"

Holly and I are willing to think that perhaps she is not actually doomed until science catches up with her; that she does not have to wait for a biogenetic breakthrough in order to make progress.

Why Am I Here?

What's the point? What's my point? Does anything really matter? Do I even exist? These are the questions that give us headaches. Here are my answers, even if you don't believe me:

Yes, you exist. You are here because you are here. We are all here. You can hate your body, fear your mind, and resist your spirit, but you are still here. You can be enraged with your soul and feel undeserving and unworthy and at odds with the world, but you are still here. Self-hatred does not mean that you do not exist; it just means that you do not yet know who you really are. And shame does not mean that you should not exist; it just means that you have hurts that have yet to heal.

My friend Liz tells me that you don't have to feel grateful to be grateful, you just have to "act as if." You can apply "act as if" to many things, including existence and meaning. You can use it as a pathway to the real thing or until the real feeling settles into your bones. You can feel alive by taking a deep breath, holding it in, and letting yourself feel the amazing feeling of being full of life-giving oxygen, free and fresh and available all the time. You can let yourself exhale slowly and think for a few seconds that in this moment—even if it's only for a moment—you can relax. You can put your hand over your heart and feel it beating and pulsating inside your chest. You do not have to draw blood and watch it run down your arm to verify your existence.

Maybe you are here to help someone else. Maybe you are here to send some money to Haiti to help them clean up the horror. Maybe you are here to add your energy to the spirit of the universe, and maybe that's good enough. Maybe you will write something that makes someone's life better or say something that eases someone's pain. Maybe you are here to just do your best with what life gives you.

Maybe you are here to practice grace and model resiliency. Maybe you are here to clear up some past life problem, to collect good deeds, or to serve humanity in some way. Maybe you are here to give birth to the woman who will discover the pill that takes away food obsession. Maybe you will never know why you are here or maybe you will only find out 50 years from now when you have the wisdom of age and experience and can see a bigger picture. Maybe you don't have to know exactly why just now, just yet.

Sometimes a deeper clarity of meaning comes much later in life, after you have survived your suffering and stockpiled experiences and collected insights like pebbles from the beach.

One thing I do know about questioning your existence is that sometimes it's the honest beginning of a sincere spiritual journey and sometimes it's a pretty good indicator that you are dipping your toe in the quicksand of self-pity—the latter being fine so long as you know it. If you are on a genuine spiritual quest, that's wonderful. Truly. And it will take you far in life and in finding satisfaction and joy and holy peace. You might end up studying ancient texts or philosophy or learning yoga or art or just finding that place deep inside you where peace dwells.

When people ask me about why they exist it is usually to tell me that they wish they didn't, not that they are going to embark on the wonderful journey of spiritual exploration. Most of the time questions like "What's the point?" are depression, emotional pain, and hopelessness speaking. And they mean the person needs care and attention and love.

If you are asking these questions, find out. Make this the beginning and take yourself seriously, but from the angle of curiosity and quest, not defeat. Inside the depression may actually lurk desire, all cloaked up in black but wanting to shed the garb and breathe free.

It might seem like too big a jump. I'm not suggesting you pack off to India or Israel. But pay attention. In the midst of your eating and body issues there lives someone who asks good questions about life and purpose and meaning. You deserve to look for meaningful answers. It's part of tunneling out when you are ready.

My father died at age 63, when I was 30 years old. Some people I know never had a father at all. Others had very difficult fathers. Some had fathers who lived until they were 92. My father was by no means perfect, but he was my hero, my biggest fan, my confidante, my port in any storm. I could not imagine life without him. With his death, my fantasies of his knowing my children and sharing the next stages of our lives together—with all the joys and markers of time and progress—died, too.

I did not ask why. There was, there is, simply no "why." I accepted it then, in quiet outrage and grief. I accept it now. I did not agree. I did not like it. I was not consulted.

In the years since his passing, my mother and I have forged a new and lovely connection. She is close to my children, a regular guest in my home, and a source of comfort and companionship. I am deeply grateful for this relationship. I suspect, however, that it would not be what it is if my father were here.

The relationship with my mom is by no means an explanation of my father's death, or a consolation. It does not make his death meaningful or right to me, either. It does, however, help me to know that there is a long view.

There are trade-offs and outcomes that I have no say in. I cannot predict them, control them, or make sense of them. There are things

I don't know and don't get to choose. I don't run the show. I don't always have to, or get to, know "why." I just need to be quiet sometimes and open up to new ideas and possibilities and blessings. I need to accept life on life's terms—no fighting, no complaining, no trying to survive by pushing my own will on others or slipping down into that quicksand of self-pity.

I do have some choices about how I live my life, but no amount of lamenting my existence brings on better days, gets me out of pain when I'm in it, or explains with conviction the reason I'm here. I don't have to like it all the time, but I still exist. And so do you.

You do, however, have to come up with some things that have meaning in life and mean something to you. Write out a list of what matters in this world and what matters to you specifically. You can put chocolate and flat abs on the list, but you cannot stop there, and you know it. I give you my full-out permission to "fake it 'til you make it." Start to know what you want from life and where you might maybe contribute that is separate from the galaxy of food and body. Guess if you are not sure. Make it up. But start thinking.

I will start you off with a few answers from my clients and from me:

A family of my own
To be a writer, a dancer, a high school teacher, a librarian
Charity
Generosity
Helping kids
Garbage collectors (seriously, where would we be without
   them?)
Serving God
A green conscious culture
A good laugh

A long kiss
A day of sobriety
Good art
Good music
Good friends
Good deeds
Honor
Dignity
Grace
Integrity
Gardening
Fighting for the underdog
Amnesty
Fighting for human rights
Rescuing animals
Getting through the day
Sharing my life
Privacy
Making it as an actress
Kindness to animals
Organic agriculture
Deep listening to another's pain
Being an example to others trying to recover

I don't mean to mix up motivation and values. They are separate. But they do hold hands sometimes. If you are escaping life or protesting it, you should know what you stand for or against. If you think about what your parents value, you can get a clue as to the origins of your psyche. Do they value time? Money? Honesty? Body? Family? Peace? Fairness? Censorship? Freedom? Respect? Love? Grace? Religion? Work?

Do you agree? Disagree? Don't know? Don't care? Care some though, because it will shed some light on what has shaped you, what continues to shape you, and why you think the way you do; or why you prefer not to think. And it will help you sort out your own ideas and existence.

When your disorder has you by the throat—especially if it's being cheered on by depression and you are not sure if you even want to, or let alone could, loosen its grip—agreeing to think about something, anything bigger is yanking your toe out of that pit of self-pity and putting it into the pool of possibility—even if it's for a millisecond. It will help pave the way. It will help you know that you exist. And that your existence does matter in the universe.

The Great Wait Debate (Decisions, Decisions)

My friend Liz says getting better is about giving up a thousand promises and making one decision—a decision to recover. It's always a bad time to recover. There is always competition in life—phases and stages and stuff going on. There is always a reason why you should wait to decide. But life keeps rolling forward. Time passes and you will still be slipping further and further down the rabbit hole into your eating-disordered way of life—a world where you practice deprivation and control and punishment and denial of your hungers. A world where you keep signing on to this being what you believe most about existence.

Before recovery we don't know what to do with our hungers. We don't know what to do with having. We don't know how to practice satisfaction. Enough is just too scary. We don't know that it's OK to be OK.

Why is it so terrible to face ordinary days, pleasure, and contentment? Why can't we allow the good feelings? When we are pre-decision to recover, we cannot imagine not craving and not wanting food or skinniness or deep slices into flesh—what will you want if you don't want those? What will you do if you are not busy wanting? We are taught to want. Are we not an insatiable society? When you get what you want, what will you want then?

I recall watching the last game of the World Series last year, and immediately after the win, a reporter was interviewing the winning pitcher, as champagne was pouring down over his face. "Congratulations on a great series," she said to him. And then, "So what do you think you'll do next season?" To his credit he said straight to her, "How about we just enjoy the moment."

I am telling you this, lest you think that we do not live often in a culture of impatience and dissatisfaction. Maybe, even you could add "enjoying the good moments of life" to your list of things that have meaning to you, that you believe in, and that give purpose to your existence.

We are caught between the legitimacy of desire and the legitimacy of satisfaction. It's hard to know how to balance them. So we wait. We linger in the confusion caused by an overly indulgent society that's obsessed with women's bodies at the same time as it's growing more spiritually aware. Writer Courtney Martin says in *Perfect Girls, Starving Daughters* that "Our bodies, our needs, our cravings, our sadness, our weakness, our stillness inevitably become our own worst enemies." We are given little guidance toward emotional intelligence, wellness, and how to negotiate our way through the fog.

When I was a kid, I heard two comments repeatedly from other people about myself. (Do they sound familiar to you? Because I'm fairly certain that I am *not* the only one who heard these!) One was that I had "*such a pretty face.*" This was, of course, said to offset what I imagined to be people's disappointment in my fat body. Or maybe to encourage me somehow. Or perhaps just to make conversation. Or maybe they meant it. I do, actually, have a pretty face; I just always assumed the worst.

And the other was, "*She does not work up to the best of her ability*." This one was particularly painful because I did not know what my abilities were, so how could anyone else? Who really knew what I was capable of? And who knew that if I was doing great work in English, but bombing in chemistry, that wasn't the best of my ability? The constancy of this comment helped shape the idea that I had to keep having more in order to have any value. I felt as if I should read every book in the library, do every job, play every sport, be everyone's friend, and make everyone feel great. The idea drove me and made me feel awful for years. Coupled with my pretty face (such as it was—a pity, a waste, or a consolation prize—because of my otherwise unappealing body), the idea made me believe that I must be rather pathetic. Somewhere in the mix, when my eating disorder became not just a habit, but who I was to boot, I realized that I was stuck.

I now know that it's great to have goals and aspirations and to want to excel and achieve but not at the expense of having a balanced and reasonable life. There will always be something you cannot do, have, accomplish, or finish. More is never-ending.

We even want more recovery—which is OK, as long as we don't lose sight of how far we've come. Recovery healers often caution about replacing one addiction for another, one obsession for another. Disorder symptoms may lift, but those of us inclined toward obsessions are well-advised to stay alert for the call of more, the call of perfectionism and other kinds of self-attack when we are feeling hurt or low. We know that even when we are making progress, the tendencies of our unconscious minds can continue to pull at us if we leave them untended.

Holly's parents are fond of sending me little e-mail ditties thanking me for all I am doing for her, and then hinting that I need to be doing more. I am not at all unaware or insensitive to the suffering of parents. Whatever problems they might have, parents suffer when their child suffers. And their suffering is real. But that does not mean that we can hurry up and have more before "more is possible." Sometimes we just have to wait. Sometimes my job is to help everyone wait safely.

I have never found pushing someone into more recovery than that person was ready for or interested in to be successful. I have found that an arm around the shoulder works better. That has always been a reliable formula—unless of course you are in grave danger.

If your weight is dangerously low, or low and losing; or your bingeing is violent; or your cutting is too deep and too risky, you can be overtaken by society's support system and protected until you can recommit to getting better. You might be fed if you cannot feed yourself. Your food might be monitored. If your weapons are killing you quickly, they will be taken away.

But somewhere along the line you have to decide for yourself that it's time to get better—time to decide. It has to come from you and you alone. You might need help, nourishment, or protection along the way, but the decision to get better has to come from somewhere deep inside of you and stay long enough to get a foothold. And then you will have to re-decide over and over and over again, a thousand times a day—sometimes a thousand times an hour. You will have to remind yourself that you decided. You will have to tolerate putting down your weapons of self-destruction—the ones that are parading around dressed up as self-protection—and decide again.

You will have to put a crowbar into that teensy tiny miniscule space where doubt and resistance have their stronghold, and insert the word *decided*.

Even if you are not quite there yet, or do not yet have the tools or the knowledge to put these decisions into action, you can decide to get interested in finding out how you might go forward. You can decide to feed yourself when you need nourishment and let go of extra food when it's not for nourishment. You can decide to tolerate the number on the scale being higher than you want and closer to scary so that you can live. You can figure out a food plan that works and do whatever it takes to follow it in order to be free of cravings and compulsions and restrictions. You can decide that hating your body does not protect you from life's troubles or spare you bad feelings. You can decide that your body is OK in all its fleshy, mushy, soft, pimply way. It will have to do because it's the only one you are going to have in this lifetime. You can learn to live with, tend to, and maybe even appreciate a disorder that tells you that you don't have it, can't live without it, and don't really want to anyway. You can negotiate the mind-bending panic and righteous indignation at having to do this.

Decide to learn what to do with all that emotional pain that does not involve war on your body and spirit. Be the one to decide for yourself that it's time to start living; that the wait is over. Decide this when you are calm and have a breather from the insanity. Or decide this in moments of utter disgust over your last binge or in unbending shame over your last bout of cutting; decide this on the heels of being hooked up to an IV, poked by yet another doc, or hearing yet another threat from someone who loves you but is more sick and tired of your crazy head than you are. Decide this when you are malnourished, high from sugar, revved up from the adrenaline of barfing, or burning, or in the other-world trance of the disorder. Decide to become sane while your mind is stuck on crazy.

You may have to wait until the pain is just so very bad that it really is enough; that dropping your weapons is better than yielding them. Tune in to the ongoing wait debate in your mind even if you are deep in treatment: Maybe it's better to wait until summer. Or until you move out. Or until you lose five more pounds. Or until after the holidays. Or . . .

Somewhere in your head is this debate, and until the side of you that wants to move on is bigger than the side of you that does not, you will wait. You will debate. And you will maybe take in some of what the recovery world has to offer. Maybe you will be influenced by it, but you will not really get better until you decide to—until you decide that even though some parts of you want to hold on, and you respect that, it is time to turn the corner now and do whatever it takes.

I never know the answer to this: How much pain is enough to push me around the corner? I never know when the analysis, the right food plan, the nourishment, the tools, the rethinking, the love, will kick in, kick out the ED voice, and take over. When the decide is really the decision. I don't know if the switch gets flipped all of a sudden or over time. It's about as unique as each person, but I have seen it happen. I have seen the decision rise and shine and take over. I have seen refusal fade into ready, and fear give way to freedom, and obstinacy bow to acceptance. I see decisions being made all the time.

You can hang around for a while with no answers and just wait until something clicks or until more motivation comes along. Or you can decide that you will do whatever it takes to get well and live free. But it has to come from you. This does not mean just following the directions of your team, if you have one, or getting a team if you don't, but saying that enough is really enough; that living your life at the mercy of food and fat, punishment and deprivation, pasted-over feelings, fear, worthlessness, and self-attack is going to end. You might not know exactly how. You might not know exactly when. But you can know *that* it is going to end. You can let a seed of hope and recognition start to grow, knowing that you can push things along or wait until your psyche and spirit are walking arm-in-arm and telling you that the time is now. Either way, you can take care of yourself while the debate rages, and you can consider dropping some of your weapons.

Drop Your Weapons

Weapons come in many forms—glass shards for cutting, fingers for gagging, food for stuffing, hands for slapping, nails for scratching, pencils, cars, walls, noise, treadmills, mirrors, scales, forks, laxatives, pills, mean voices, scissors, Ipecac syrup, laundry detergent, matches. Bingeing, starving, and cutting. Isolating. And I am going to take the liberty of adding the Internet to this list because though it is a conduit of many good things, it can also be a source of pain and weaponry. Checking up on your ex-best friend's Facebook page, seeing all the fabulous pictures she just posted of her evening out, and comparing your horrible aching insides to her stunning and presumably happy-looking, thin, glowing outsides can feel like a thousand knives to your gut. Looking again and again at other people's seeming success, or reading posts on the web that seem either glib, hollow, competitive, condescending, or mean, also count as tools of torture. Pummeling yourself psychically, emotionally, or verbally is still pummeling. Pummeling yourself for relief, escape, punishment, protection, protest, or to prove a point is, on some level, a choice. Compulsive, repulsive, impulsive, or planned, in some way you are choosing your weapon and your target. (How to help yourself not do this is coming soon.)

Holly tells me she likes her bad moods and is annoyed with me for pathologizing her. When I ask her how I do this, she says, "See, you are doing it now." I ask her what about my questions feel like that to her. She tells me that all my questions feel like that; that she is a normal person with normal moods that go up and down; that sometimes she can pull herself out of them and sometimes she needs to barf her brains out. She tells me that she would like help with these low, low moods and very bad feelings, especially the self-loathing, but that I should stop being so understanding and just tell her what to do once and for all. She does not want to want to hurt herself or help herself with food. She does not want to feel so much self-hatred and frustration that she wants to jump out of her skin and die. But on our list of current truths is that she does not really want to drop her weapons. Not yet.

It seems like all my questions are bad ones sometimes. My attempts to understand are inadequate, and my advice is lacking. Somewhere in her mind are these thoughts:

*I am confused, frustrated, full of self-doubt, and thinking that
there is no way to please you or anyone else. Help me maybe,
but don't help me. I don't want your help. Tell me how to get
better, but I won't listen. Just make me thin, but don't tell me
what to eat. You are not helping. I will only tell you bits and
pieces. You should know what to do. And stop staring at me
like I am some nutcase. Maybe I am a nutcase. I'm fine. I just
blow through bags of cookies and then stick pencils down my
throat. It's normal. Stop staring and stop pathologizing me.*

Holly and I are still on the road together. We feel the stubbornness of her disorder and the deep longing of being attached
to your weapons, to the food itself, and to the terror and the thrill
and the dive into oblivion. We share a deep respect for the power
of obsession.

And we know that voluntarily putting down your weapons, even
for a minute, even if you could, does not seem like the starting point
at all. It's not even clear that putting them down is the right thing
to do. Sometimes putting down weapons without the safety net of
other good tools—a solid, reliable healing relationship; a place to
talk; a feeling, overall, of being willing to forge forward and bear
the pain—is not any safer than using the weapons to begin with.
Sometimes it seems that using the weapons is better than what
would happen if you did not have them.

But maybe it's time to drop your weapons. Maybe it's time to
give a little; to try to put down the sharp objects and turn to other
sources; to decide to just stop and then do whatever it takes to beat
the urge, to weather the fear of fat and fullness and frustration, for
a minute at a time. Maybe it's time to slowly, tentatively, lay down
the scissors and pick up the phone; to close the fridge and open
your journal; to walk and talk and cry; to start to feed your staving
body, gently, bravely. Maybe it's time to experiment with dropping
your weapons.

I have seen the seed of "perhaps" start to grow. Perhaps you don't have to hurt yourself to heal yourself. Perhaps you can be in your own skin without puncturing it to prove you are alive, to release the pain. Perhaps, when the food calls, you can answer without a raging binge. Perhaps you can rant and rave and rail and rally without violence, without shame, without losing yourself.

Recently Holly told me, "If you help me, I will leave." She said that even though she knows some truths about herself now—about food, her parents, her compulsions, about what it will take to take the next right small step—she has grown tired of my trying to heal her. I have become, we discover, just like her father. I have an agenda. I want to see her well. I want to stop her suffering. I want her to get a life. I know I have gone too far. I tell Holly she is right; I have crossed the line and have wanted to stop her suffering. Holly tells me that honestly, she gets this. She likes it even, in some way. But she would really prefer to come to things on her own. She wants to be the one to want the recovery, not me, not her parents.

Part of me thinks this is baloney. It's just Holly being afraid and not wanting to take responsibility. It's Holly wanting to have her food, her way, and her parents' support no matter what she is doing to herself. And then I think: *So what? It's my job to tolerate my feelings and Holly's feelings and not act on my own agenda. It's my job to wait with her until she is ready and not act on the urge I feel to push her or to stop her suffering, the way her parents do.* It sounds crazy. I want to intervene again and again and again. It is progress, after all, for Holly to speak her mind to me. I know, though, that part of my urgency is really Holly's urgency. It is the part of herself that she is not yet ready to admit to, know fully about, and feel. So I am feeling it for her. I tell her that I will work on checking in with her before launching into suggestion mode again. And that I will wait.

Holly is slowly but surely connecting the dots between her feelings and her food, and lets me know what it's like to be her. She will make me wait. So I will wait. It's not as bad as I think it will be.

The waiting is OK. It's like saying to the whole world, "We will do it when we are good and ready and not a minute sooner." It's like saying, "As soon as you stop asking, I will start recovering. As long as you are trying to get me to do what you think I should do, I will hold out. I am a fortress of holding out."

I can live in a fortress, I think. After many more months of talking, listening, and not putting forth my agenda of recovery, Holly edges forward. I see little signs, little hope markers. With a nutritionist she creates a food plan that is low on sugar and feels safe to her. She listens to some phone-in 12-step meetings, hears some new ideas, and finds a mentor through mentorconnect-ed.org. And she asks her dad to take a step back.

She has not been on the scale for more than two months and journals regularly. After combing the web for a part-time job in theater, she lands one answering phones for an agent in the city. And that's good enough for now. Her binges are fewer, and her days are not as dark as often.

Holly starts to want more life and less food. She continues to tell me all the things she does not like about how I work and what I say and do. I continue to hear them, appreciate them, and own them. Sometimes I disagree, and then we talk about it. Recently those big green eyes spilled over again. She put her face in her hands and shook with sobs for the better part of a session. I felt no urge to stop her suffering. It did not seem like suffering to me. It felt like the aching grief, frustration, and joy of life and progress that it was, and I was just glad to be there.

CHAPTER 6

Finding the Willingness

*Alice: Would you tell me, please, which
way I ought to go from here?*

*The Cheshire Cat: That depends a good
deal on where you want to get to.*

Alice: I don't much care where.

The Cheshire Cat: Then it doesn't much matter which way you go.

Alice: . . . So long as I get somewhere.

*The Cheshire Cat: Oh, you're sure to do that,
if only you walk long enough.*

—LEWIS CARROLL, *Alice in Wonderland*

I KNOW the look. I have come to love the look. I look for the look. From Robin, I get the look halfway into her first session. At twenty-one, she sports a long black pony, torn jeans, and a short-sleeved tee, so I easily notice the silver duct tape over gauze on the outside of her right forearm. Her wandering eyes focus abruptly on me when I ask her what kind of help she might like.

The look says, *Been here, done this, and you're supposed to be the expert, Lady.* And it says, *I want help, but I don't want help. And easy on the psychobabble. I want you to believe I am very sick and need serious attention, but I am afraid that you will think I am making all this up. I might even believe I am making all this up. I have no idea what I really need, and please don't tell me that my behavior is either the problem or the solution. And please know that I am praying to God that you will not turn out to be some kind of self-righteous know-it-all or patronizing do-gooder or someone else who doesn't understand or know what to do with me.*

I know it's a lot for one look, but it's a big look. She stares at me dead-on again and says, "Tell me something I don't already know."

When I ask Robin what she specifically wants to know, she shrugs and sinks deeper into my beige leather couch. Does she want to know things about herself? About me? About why it is that she is sitting on yet another shrink's couch and still feeling lost, angry, and alone? Does she want to know why she won't recover? Or can't?

"Of course you are skeptical," I tell her. Then I get the next look—my favorite look actually—the look of *interest*. I don't always get this look next, but it's good when I do.

Rebel with a Cause

In the search for self and recovery, if what you are doing is still working for you, and if somewhere, deep down, you still believe that whatever else you might try will not yield you anything better than what you've got now, then you won't really want recovery no matter how much you might need it. So of course Robin is skeptical. Good to put that on the table first thing.

Robin, I will soon learn, is in my office now because her parents are tired of her not being in school, not having a job, and not coop-erating in general. In fact, the more her parents push her to get a life and be (their version of) productive, the more she cuts and the sicker she becomes. Robin had successful therapy before and has some relief from her binge/starve cycle. She has encountered more than one good path to recovery, and yet her cutting persists. When I wonder with her about what *she* wants from me, she tells me that she really does not know. That blunt, honest, and very welcome statement hangs in the air all by itself. The rest of the session is silent.

In fact, Robin and I sit quietly for many sessions. One day, out of the blue, she tells me that she is tired of everyone giving her suggestions about what to do, how to fix this, and how to fix *her*, as if she is broken. Advice often seems like criticism. She does not feel able to *stay* better. Some days she does not have the energy to walk up steps, let alone get a job or finish school. Lately she has been having trouble breathing deeply, and after clearing her medically and talking with her parents, her medical doctor sent her to me. Robin is all at once sure, annoyed, and hopeful that her doctor is wrong and that something absolutely physical is wrong with her. With cash-register honesty she admits that she would like this for a variety of reasons, not the least of which is a "screw you" to the implication that her "issues" are fixable with a change in attitude. If only it were that simple.

Robin likes the idea of being sick even though it seems mental to her to admit it. It would feel like she could get some good, honest attention for once without all the nods of frustration she is used to getting.

One day Robin looks at me and says, "I just feel fat. And this is stupid."

"What is?" I ask. "This life? This therapy? This session?"

"Talking, therapy, this session—all of it."

The day this comes up is the same day Robin had seen her medical doctor who told her she looked better than she had a few months before when she weighed more. And the day before, her psychiatrist had told her that she could not lose any more weight. And after dinner her mother had told her that she could not possibly be full and should just try the pasta primavera that she had made for dinner. So many opinions on her food and her body!

So I do not tell her for the umpteenth time that fat is not a feeling. Because maybe it is after all. Besides the obvious of feeling bloated or hormonal, fat is the new horrible. It's the catchall code word for about a thousand feelings and thoughts; for feeling too noticeable or too important to people you both love and hate. Sometimes fat is code for feeling stupid, sad, left out, empty, or afraid. Or for being ticked off beyond words, frustrated, and having had more than enough of something (besides food). Fat is fear, outrage, disgust, protest, distraction, and rebellion.

Sometimes feeling fat is a distraction from feeling everything else. Sometimes your unconscious mind sends you fat feelings because it thinks that feeling fat is better than feeling regret or owning up to a character flaw, especially when you have the idea that character flaws and mistakes are unforgivable, or quickly changeable, or punishable.

(When you feel fat, take a second to figure out what else is bothering you in the moment. I know fat is fat—and maybe you are hormonal or feel bloated, but *what else*?)

Robin and I unpack it some and figure out that there are just too many advice pigeons and commentators cued up around her at the moment and she'd like a little space. We are working hard on decoding fat with respect to fat itself, with a big nod to fat as a code for all kinds of other feelings including frustration with being told what to do.

Directives often send Robin in the opposite direction. She is a rebel with a very good cause: safety.

But as we toss it around a bit, we think that you can feel rebellious and still take suggestions. You can feel fat and not be fat. You can be a rebel in a thousand ways and still decide to recover. You can feel fat and still make progress. And if you think that perhaps there is a bit of rebel in you, you can take the time to figure out what your own private rebellion is about or against, or who you are rebelling for or against.

One day Robin yells at me. I am pointing out to her how loud her eating disorder is at the moment, and ask her what the purpose of all the self-attack is, when she shouts, "God, can't you just let me attack myself if I want to? Stop helping me, damn it."

OK. And yes. I suppose I can. It is my job to help Robin talk, but sometimes my bias against her joy-stealing disorder gets in the way. I can get pretty caught up in helping you swim, but if you are not ready to put your toes in the recovery pool, then I am not doing you any good. Sometimes I need to be reminded to just hang out on the shore with you until you are interested. Pushing you in often doesn't work, though I do suggest testing the waters now and then.

Some months into our work together, Robin tells me that she thinks she needs to lose weight in her brain, not in her rear end. She says she has stopped cutting, but that I should not get too happy about that. And that she is thinking of going back to school, but maybe not just yet. And she has decided to go to a support group once a week and start seeing a nutritionist. She is thinking about what she is willing to do and what she is ready for. She thinks that having given some real airtime to her suffering has given her the idea that she might just be willing to do the next right small thing toward recovery after all.

OK, I'm Listening

A few years ago I became preoccupied with a certain problem of my own. It had caused quite a lot of painful feelings (anger, self-pity, and big, sad, frustration and grief and fear), and I had become addicted to thinking about it almost all the time. At some point I realized that the thinking had become an obsession and the obsession had become a way of life for me. And I needed help.

I went over all the possible ways that I might get rid of this problem and came up with quite a few ideas. I thought about which way might be the best—lots and lots (*way* too much!) of thinking.

Then I read a story in a magazine I was thumbing through that talked about going to the grave of a holy or righteous person and asking that person to pray on your behalf. The guy in the story—and he swears it is true—had his ailment healed after he prayed at the graveside of a holy rabbi.

Several years ago, a neighbor of mine died of cancer. She was a very pious woman and known to do kindnesses for many people. She is buried about half a mile from my house. It occurred to me that I could go to the cemetery and ask her to pray for me—to lift my bad feelings and help me move on. I had the idea that if I did this, my problem might very well be removed.

And I did actually believe in my gut that this would work. Even if I didn't really believe it totally, when you are really desperate you will try almost anything—some gesture of pure faith in something greater than yourself; a way to show the universe you're open to a miracle. And since going to pray at someone's grave was silly at worst and potentially relieving at best, and not even inconvenient, then I should just stop by one day, right?

It was six months before "one day" came along. So I must admit that some part of me did not actually want my obsession lifted. Not yet.

There I was, in exquisite pain. I believed that the prayer ritual might work (and it certainly couldn't hurt!), and it still took me six months to stop by her grave and pour my heart out. I passed that cemetery many times each week. It would have taken five minutes. Not even out of my way. Why did I wait?

Most of us get attached to our illnesses. We need them. Or we think we need them. Or someone needs us to have them. We are more afraid to let them go than we are to keep them. We have no idea what will be left if the pain goes away or the behavior does not consume us anymore. What will we be? What will we do? We imagine that there will be an abyss of emptiness too hard to bear; an emptiness that will actually be worse than whatever it is we've got now. Or maybe it will mean we have to get moving and do other things—things we are not so sure we can do or want to do.

I am not saying that we *like* our suffering, but, well, maybe I am saying that on some level we like our suffering. Or at least we are attached to it in some deep and important way. Certainly we do not like that very low, very real, very heavy darkness and dread that envelops our body and eclipses our soul. We do not like to feel so under that we don't or can't get out of bed or sometimes even roll over. There is a deep anguish that is so painful that we can want to just simply become null and void—dread mixed with darkness.

This, and pure fear, are the two things that folks are usually ready to give up to me on the spot, if only I had a magic wand. Everything else seems to have to stay around until either something really bad happens or the pain of being sick outweighs the pain of getting better. And that can take a while.

Why, as it says in the *Big Book*, do some folks have to be "pretty badly mangled before they are willing to take certain actions"? Why do many of us cling to the things that hurt us? Why do so many young women continue to burn their fingertips, skip breakfast and lunch and have an apple for dinner over and over again, or eat until it hurts and then throw it back up, until it becomes who they are, not just what they do?

Why keep driving toward the darkness? Why sit in the same? Why not plant yourself at a 12-step meeting, ask your therapist for more help, join a support group, or pick up a recovery book and read and follow one of the ideas it offers?

The answers to these questions are just as complex as why you have an eating or self-injury disorder in the first place. But if you can get interested in what's in the way of your willingness, you can make progress toward recovery. You might not be ready to be willing, or willing to be ready. Sometimes when you are all kinds of sad, mad, scared, or stubborn, you really do need to do what you do, at least until you know what else to do; until more of you wants to do something different; until more of you is less afraid, less stubborn, and more interested in taking suggestions and fighting the voice in your head that is telling you to screw it and take another swig, or just one more cut—the voice that tells you that you might as well because you are a fat, ugly, helpless, worthless witch. Or because you can't help it, or that this will be the last time, or you will try tomorrow, or no one will know or care, or whatever it is won't work anyway, is stupid, pointless, too difficult, not for you, never going to help, not worth the effort.

You do need relief. But to get relief without "getting" yourself physically—especially when getting yourself feels good, when it feels safe and better than whatever else it is you are feeling or will have to feel if you don't do it—*that* requires willingness. Deciding to recover means making the transition from getting yourself physically to understanding yourself emotionally and spiritually. A different kind of *getting*, if you will.

In the moment of madness and craving, unless you have a pretty good plan in place you will most likely fall right back into robotic compulsion or the same old, same old of trying to control the uncontrollable. But in the calmer moments—even as you tell yourself that what you do is not so bad—you know that the constant battle with food and your body is not exactly a place to call home, even if it works for now. Even if you believe it is who and how you are. Even if you do not want to be without your food or your restricting.

It may not seem like it is yet time to be willing, but then again, really, do you know why not?

———————◆———————

Sandi, whose mom died when she was fourteen, and who still, at twenty-one, throws up dinner (and lunch too, most days), does not really want to plow through the homework her therapist gives her. She stalls and doesn't do it. That the throwing up has become a full-on eating disorder is beside the point. The point is that she *could* unpack what's behind the eating disorder; she *could* start down one of the many good roads to recovery; she *could* just do what her fine therapist tells her to do after she listens to her pain for a while; but she does not.

She just goes back to the bathroom. No pushing the truck uphill. Too hard. All wheels spinning in the mud. And besides, the part of her that does not want to deal is still bigger than the part of her that does. So she stays stuck—stuck in the sticky, obstinate superglue of unwillingness—because she knows that she will have to heave a million times more to forget how much it hurts to not have a mother—to not have *her* mother—and to forget how unpredictable, unfair, and out-of-control life can be. As long as not getting fat is the most important thing in her life, she will not have to stand in front of the typhoon of grief that keeps threatening to come her way. And besides, her mother, Sandi is fairly certain, would have liked her to be thin. When you hang on to the disorder for dear life, you most often believe you have a good reason.

———————◆———————

Functioning Fine, Thanks

To get unstuck you absolutely must acknowledge and greet the part of you that does not want to get better, does not want to let go, is unwilling or not yet ready. Come up with a few guesses about why that might be and what it means to you to stay the way you are. You do not have to actually get better. You do not have to make any movement at all. Just study that list.

Ask the part of you that does not want suggestions to work, "Why not? Why do I not want this to work?" That's question one.

Ask the part of you that wants recovery to work, "What's in the way of my doing what I need to do? Where is my willingness?" And then go back to question one again.

When I ask Sandi why she did not seek help sooner, she says, "What kept me in the disorder for so long was that I was functioning just fine with it. That's how I did the amount of damage to my body and mind that I did. I was functioning well. At least on the outside."

"Functioning well" puts a fancy dress on the disorder. It lets you believe that you do not have to take a good look at the downside. It lets you believe that you are really OK in some way and that the work it takes to face things is not necessarily worthy of the effort; that your deeper demons can wait. And that might be true. But it's hard to know at just what point your body will take a hit that is bigger than you ever imagined. Or when the damage will truly be out of control. And it's hard to measure the effects on your soul and your spirit; hard to know what kind of life there could be, or would be, if you were not living in the world of the disorder and in the belief that you need it.

Clare, twenty-three, who is finishing college and feeling lost at sea, has a moment of deep truth. She tells me in one particularly painful session that she wants to be sick. Ever since she was a little girl, she has fantasized about being in the hospital. She made up a pretend illness, and there, in her head, she got tended to by all sorts of kind, loving, gentle people—doctors, nurses, visitors, not even anyone she knew or was related to—strangers who loved her and whose only concern was taking care of her, nurturing her, and worrying about her. She felt so loved and protected in this fantasy. Over the years the doctors had names, and one fell desperately in love with her and became her husband. He knew her true self and understood her when no one else could or would. He said all the things that she wished her father would say. He always gave her good advice and the benefit of the doubt. He was reassuring and concerned and never intrusive, critical, or mean.

Whenever she feels alone or afraid or angry, or has a fight with someone, or is reeling from the pain of having cut too deeply into her thigh, she puts herself in the hospital room in her mind, and all the lovely doctors—her angel husband especially—gather around her and take care of her. They check on her while she sleeps and soothe her when she feels any pain at all. They are serene and calm and totally focused on her.

Clare thinks that giving up the cutting means she will have to give up the love and care of her fantasy caregivers. Now, in recovery, Clare uses this fantasy whenever she wants to, but without having to actually hurt herself. She knows that whenever the fantasy comes to her it's a signal that she is hurting deeply and needs tenderness, understanding, and support.

Slowly the belief that being sick will get her the attention and love she craves shifts. She begins to find ways to fill up spiritually, to be and feel loved in real life, and to not need or want to be sick anymore—even the pretend sick. Wanting the sick was part of why Clare was not so open to willingness. She believed that the sick would actually be better for her than being well. She did not yet know—and how could she—that she could get what she needed in other ways—ways that honored the adult in her and would leave her feeling whole and confident—and that she could actually feel well and feel good about feeling well.

Hiding in the shadows of Clare's psyche was a lot of confusion about how getting better would affect her parents. The possibility that getting better would make her parents happy was in the way of her willingness; she was not interested in being that cooperative. She felt ashamed on one level about this, but liked the screw-you-ness about it on another. She worried, too, that she would lose a certain kind of connection, attention, support, or power.

Whatever is in the way of your willingness is personal, and most likely not something that is easy to spot with a glance or let go of with a shrug. It takes some contemplation, some good guesswork, a listing of possibilities, and some real, honest conversations with yourself (and/or someone you trust). You might have to dig around for a while, but you will find the gold eventually.

By definition and nature, eating and self-injury disorders like to tell their owners all sorts of things to block willingness, including that the disorder doesn't really exist all, that it's not all that painful really, that it's not necessary to work on recovery, and that it's too hard to work on it anyway. Deciding to get better is about fighting a problem that tries to tell you that it's not a problem, that it's actually the solution. And this gets in the way of being willing.

Another block to willingness is the fear of making mistakes. Some part of you might reason (perhaps not even consciously) that as long as you are in the muck of your problem, whatever mistakes you make are par for the course. And if you start to get better, you will then really be a screwup when you screw up. At least that's how it can look before you get willing. So much fear. So much fear of fear. But it doesn't usually go that way, really. In the world of willingness, mistakes and mess-ups are just part of a good day's work.

One wise old recovering addict once told me that she was too scared to make a decision because that meant that she would then have to back it up. It was no longer about her emotionally charged good intentions or pain-filled oaths after a bad bout over the toilet; it was about deciding in a moment of rare calm and sanity that she would make a plan and follow it, come what may. She would just have to risk losing everything she was, or thought she was. She would have to risk her controlled, up-throwing, double-lifed self for a new and unknown version. She would have to adopt the crazy notion that whatever lay ahead was better in some untasted, unimaginable kind of way than the private genie bottle of solace and self-righteousness and protection she was currently holed up in. She would have to risk being wrong and living through it.

If you can suspend your skepticism just long enough to do one thing on your list of coping alternatives; if you can write out five reasons why you don't want to get better but are going to eat breakfast anyway; if you can have some small morsel of faith that life is going to get better if you keep going, sometimes inch by tiny inch, toward the solution and through the fear into the unknown, you can open the door to willingness and stand back and let it in.

Sometimes the key to willingness is to act "as if"; to pretend that you are willing and do what comes next; to say, "If I were going to be willing, I would . . . ," and then do it. And then repeat. There is every reason to be confused in your heart and head when you're considering getting better and deciding to move forward. It's normal to have voices arguing in your head about what to do. But you can begin to detect the truth from the lies.

A good indication that you're lying to yourself, or your disorder is lying to you, or that your old unhealthy thought patterns are pressing on is if you are feeling worthless, depressed, hopeless, guilty, resentful, full of self-pity, or irrationally afraid—as opposed to sad, angry, concerned, or disappointed. Another good indication that you are being lied to is if you have the idea that being willing to recover will make you fat. And that you are the only one in the world who really knows this to be the truth, that the rest of us don't *really* get this, so it's up to you to secretly carry on. If you are telling yourself that you are a piece of dirt, don't deserve recovery, and can't do it, *and in fact, better not do it*, you are listening to the lies of the disorder again. If you have any doubts about what the messages are—and you can take pen to paper, listen to your head, and write like crazy till you see the lies. Most self-attacking, self-defeating, scare-tactic messages and thoughts are lies. The lies block the willingness.

If you have decided that you are willing, or willingness has started to grow in you, but you don't want to let on to whoever is trying to push you down the recovery road, you can keep it a secret until you have enough willingness and recovery that you don't care whether others are happy or satisfied. Or you don't mind. Because you are doing it for you—at last.

Even when the part of you that wants recovery or out of the pain and into life is bigger than the other part, and is even cruising sometimes, the other part will keep popping back up like one of those weasels in the hammer game at the amusement park. And that's the rest of the news about willingness. You cannot get it once and be done with it. Sorry. And you cannot take it for granted once you have it.

It's a gift, like the sun coming up every morning. Even if you are not there to witness its arrival, you're still glad and grateful to have it. You'll have to sludge and nudge yourself sometimes to keep it and not give it back—to hold on to it with the same obstinacy that prevented it from coming to you in the first place. The light of willingness on your face is what is ultimately going to carry you forward.

When willingness is evasive, or you are stuck in a seemingly permanent shoulder shrug, it helps to ask yourself what would make you willing. What would it take? Is there any motivation in the world to bring on willingness? There is always prayer, of course, and more on that soon. But here and now, if you don't know well enough yet what's in the way of willingness, ask yourself what it would take to get you or keep you willing. Think it, talk it, write it out, but don't let it slide away into protest and get lost in the shrug.

The definition of *willing* is "ready to do something voluntarily, without being forced." Sometimes willing is in small steps—little raindrops of agreement to hear something new, or something old again, and to allow it to sink in instead of drip off your thirsty skin. Sometimes it does just come to you, but usually you have to open the door just a crack.

I know plenty of people who needed to be protected until they were willing, and then protected again once they were willing, because willing does not always mean ready, and ready does not always mean willing. *Ready* means you are prepared for something that is going to happen. When you agree to open up your psyche to new ways of living, you have no idea what is actually going to happen, so you might not be prepared. That's why I sometimes recommend moving slowly, because willingness has to unroll in front of you like a red carpet so that readiness can walk on it, one tender step at a time. If you are pushed before you are ready, and without being willing, you can trip and fall.

Sometimes you need a push. But from where I sit, it's better to pull. That way if you go down there is someone ahead of you to break the fall.

Clare asks me one day, "What do I do when my stomach is literally knotted shut, the pain is just so bad? Or sometimes, it's a bottomless pit. What then?"

"Be brave," I tell her. "And be stubborn about being brave. Find support wherever you can to pull you in the right direction, one brave step at a time."

Please Don't Talk to Me About Feelings

I am quite used to the following answers in my office, given in any number of different tones from annoyed to afraid to totally flat: "I don't know." "I don't care." "What?" They are usually accompanied by, or replaced with, the following body signals: wincing, shrugging, eye rolling, head tilting, and staring out the window.

Not being one to push too hard to find a feeling, I usually back off. Besides, you can object all you want to feeling, but you feel anyway.

No matter how many trinkets you lift from the drugstore, or how many times you slice at your calves or throw up your dinner, you will not be able to stop the feelings. You can do this for days and months and years on end, but the feelings will still be there—old ones and new ones, good ones and bad ones. They will not go away until you turn around and say hello to them, agree to feel them, and learn how to bear them.

That goes for bodily sensations, too. Tense, tired, relaxed—it's sometimes hard to tease out the body sensations from the emotions. They are often related and intertwined. Being willing to just take note of yourself before you binge, skip a meal, or run too long or too fast on the treadmill is a sign of willingness. It is opening the door that necessary crack. And it gets easier as you go. Once you start down the path, the path gets easier; and that old truck you are pushing up the hill gets a little lighter.

It takes practice to recognize feelings. And I am not yet (stay tuned) suggesting that you feel things full-on, especially if you are not ready yet, just that you be willing to find out what you feel. You can start now if you like. Are you bored? Annoyed? Anxious? Interested? Calm? Do you think that if you let yourself know, the sky will fall? It won't. For one minute just sit still and put a name to how you feel in this moment. No criticisms, corrections, or consequences in this moment—just tell me how you feel. And if you don't know, guess. Out loud. Plow through the blanks and just guess if you can.

Good. Thanks.

Except for Me

Everyone I have ever worked with is an exception to the rule. I am also an exception, especially when I'm really angry. All of the good theories of all of the good therapies and 12-step programs apply to everyone except my clients. And me. And you. We are too sick, too far gone, too compulsive, alone, afraid, skeptical, intelligent, charming, angry, pathetic, savvy, stubborn, or right.

You have tried it all, read it all, and heard what everyone has to say, and it does not work. Or at least not well enough. Your parents are too far gone or too messed up, or your situation is too different from the "regular" cutters, who are really not so bad off. Or really you are not so bad off. Or really you are the only one who can't consider doing things differently because you really will get fat or because your stomach really cannot hold anything more than the black coffee that you allowed yourself this morning. Other people have better stomachs.

And you need to protect them (and you) from your fury. If you start to deal with your feelings, all hell will break loose. Feeling feelings might be good for everyone else, but you know better.

Staying the exception to all helping theories, great and small, is one more way not to make the decision to crack open the door to see if willingness will blow in. But here is the good news: If you open the door that crack, enough willingness can blow in to lift you up and carry you to the next right small thing.

If any part of you thinks that perhaps there might be a better way to live, and you are interested ever so slightly in letting willingness and readiness have their way, then *you must consider that you are not the exception to any rule.* This does, inherently, imply hope, often followed by its friend, fear. But if you've been making the rounds through treatment for years, there will come a time when you have heard something enough times (and some things we have to hear a lot of times before they finally slide down from the brain to the heart, and vice versa) that you realize you are not really exceptional in the sick sense of the word, and that you are standing at the intersection of readiness, willingness, and me-too-ness, and you can pick a path that is yours uniquely and start walking forward—fear or not.

I get a call from Dr. Now. (OK, I made up her name, but you will see the point soon, I hope.) She is my client Marcia's primary care doctor. She is alarmed because Marcia has been seeing me for sixteen months, and while she no longer wants to kill herself, and has pretty much stopped putting cigarettes out on the caps of her knees, she is still not eating very much. Dr. Now would like me to speak to Dr. Yesterday, the psychiatrist, about this. She would also like me to consult with Ms. Plan, the nutritionist, to figure out what exactly can be done to fix things.

Mrs. Iloveyouandlampayingforallthis (Marcia's mother) would like to know why Marcia is not taking a more active role in her own health and recovery, and what exactly has been accomplished with me (Mrs. Justkeeptalking) these last many months. They have all united and agree that Ms. Iamaworkinprogressbutlamgettingbetter (Marcia) should be moving along at a faster pace. They have all (except Mrs. Justkeeptalking) become impatient with Marcia's progress. They don't like it when she says she is still depressed sometimes, or when it takes a lot of effort for her to eat because she still does not really feel like she can put one morsel of nourishment into her starving body. When she says she is having trouble, they move in for the fix. Or they call me and tell me to hurry up.

Cooks in the Kitchen

If I had an outline for recovery that was a straight shot to freedom, I would hand it over in a flash. Less than a flash. But willingness and readiness are up to you and you alone. You can be helped to get ready and helped to find willingness and helped to figure out what's keeping you from both, but they cannot come from someone else.

I welcome being questioned about what will be helpful to your recovery. Questions about how the therapy is going and what kind of progress you are making are gateways to better work. I welcome them most when they come from you. When you are in therapy, your progress is a very serious and important subject. But it is also tender and tentative, and it moves at its own pace. And a little humor is OK now and again.

Knowing what path to choose is no simple matter, and it's not a once and done. Just like willingness, progress is fluid and alive and ever-shifting in meaning and definition. And among all the voices that want to fix you, help you, support you, and advise you, the most important one is your own real voice. Hearing this voice and learning about your options, what you want, and what's in the way of your going forward can take some time and some talking. Sometimes it's the willingness to say everything that's in your head and heart that brings the willingness to recover out into the light.

When you are not even sure if you want to recover, how on earth can I suggest that you drive your own recovery mobile? If you are not able to drive it, you are likely to be pushed along, so you might as well consider having a say and picking up some ideas about how to work well with the people from whom you are seeking aid, even if a huge—or even majority—part of you still does not yet want help at all.

Call Me George

Marcia makes fun of me for telling her too many times that we could be curious about how it is she arrived at this point in her life, and curious about where she might like to go from here. We can be curious about how she might feel if she goes to a treatment center, or how she might feel if she goes to a 12-step meeting. We can be curious about what would happen if she gave in to her desire to have sex with her best friend's boyfriend, and curious about her feelings for her biology professor. We can be curious about why her father loses it every time she comes home late, and curious as to why she keeps coming home late when she knows it will send him to the moon. And we can be curious about what will happen if she eats when she doesn't feel like it, or calls me instead of taking nineteen chocolate ex-laxes. We can be curious about why all these people feel so damned urgent about getting her better faster, and curious about why she herself is going along at the pace she is.

She says I should be called George—for monkeying around in her psyche like this.

The primary care doctor wants her to go back to an intensive outpatient program (IOP), and the psychiatrist thinks inpatient is worth a try. The nutritionist thinks it's best to just work harder at writing down her food and filling in her food/feeling worksheets. I think that it's really about what she thinks. And therein lies both the problem and the solution.

I have seen people go in and out of inpatient, IOP, group, rehab, therapy, and psych units over and over, around and in and out, and back and forth like they were square-dancing at town hall. There is a bottom line, and that is this: If you are going to risk your own life—either quickly or slowly, and whether you are in touch with the fact that you are harming yourself or not—you are not going to get to be in charge of where you land unless you sound somewhat cooperative. You are likely to be put somewhere; sometimes quickly, sometimes slowly, but you will be placed—willingness or not.

Sometimes that's what you might want. To be placed. But whether you are suffering alone, have people who are pushing you into recovery, or are making the choice yourself, willingness is still going to be circling above you until you let it land. And you won't get anywhere without it.

If you can reach into one of the hidden rooms in your psyche (where you have, unbeknownst even to you, a storage of courage, wisdom, and faith) and open the door, some of that elusive willing-ness—just enough to sound sane—will help you have a real say in how you can proceed with your treatment and your life, even when you are not sure what you want. You could really get something out of it. And because there is quite possibly a growing part of you that believes, or wants to believe that you *can*, in fact, be helped, that you do, in fact, *want* to be helped, it's OK to quiet the internal naysayer and crawl onward. This applies whether you are not in treatment, are in and out, or have been in treatment for a while.

As you go along, you might need to continually list and study all the treatment options, writing down the pros and cons of each. You might need to do this several times as you move through the maze of possibilities. You might have to repeatedly ask yourself the following questions:

What are my fears about treatment?
What are my hopes?
What is the worst part of being how I am now?
What is the best part?
To what lengths am I willing to go in order to feel better?
Am I willing to tell whoever is involved my true thoughts
     about what I think I need?
What do I most want help with, and why?

In recovery there are often lots of cooks in the kitchen. But you should be the head chef, even if all that means is asking for others' opinions so you can consider them; even if you want to be told what to do because you are afraid of making a decision or of knowing what you want; even if you don't think you care (which usually means you are angry, afraid, or confused); even if you still won't be sure what's the best thing to do. And you are, by default anyway, the director of your life. You can give the doctors, your parents, your therapists, whoever, whatever ideas you want. You can't con-trol what they say or think, and you are not responsible for how they treat you or how they proceed, but you can contribute to the problem or to the solution by how you express yourself.

If you tell the psychiatrist that you are more depressed than ever and you are not sleeping, and you tell the nutritionist that you are eating according to plan, and the primary care doc weighs you and you have lost four pounds (and you are happy and victorious about this) and she is upset, and you tell her it's because the psychiatrist isn't changing your meds and the therapist doesn't give you tools, and then you tell the nutritionist that the primary care doc thinks her food plan is bad, and you tell your mother that your team is not talking to each other, and then she gets more in your food than ever—you are helping to tie everyone up in knots.

If you are doing this, consciously or not (and I say this with love), it's time to be *curious* about what is really going on inside you. If there are too many cooks in the kitchen and you find yourself running around in circles, it might be that your willingness has escaped out the window, and you might be only vaguely aware of this fact. If you don't go chasing after it, you are going to be spinning in circles until it finds its way home.

Helping Your Helpers

There will sometimes be doctors, shrinks, therapists, coaches, nutritionists, and hypnotists who are not the right match for you and the disorder. It's difficult to figure out who is right, especially if you are particularly adept at blaming yourself and are not sure who can really be trusted to help you work out your own ideas and find your own real voice. When you have these doubts, it can seem like your willingness is going away. It's important to distinguish between losing your willingness and having legitimate concerns about your treatment choices, path of recovery, and treatment team. It is OK not to know; it is less OK not to find out.

Here is my number one guiding factor: Whomever you are working with must be able to hear your concerns, and they must be interested in understanding you and your concerns and helping you assess the situation. They should be willing to look for ways to work that are agreeable to you, and to help you discern the voices of resistance and disorder from the voice of reason. They must have a good ear that can hear the disorder as well as the healthy parts of you.

If they are not curious, accepting, understanding, interested in studying the problem and learning about what is most helpful to you, and interested in helping you learn about what is most helpful to you, consider a different professional. This does not mean that they should not work with you on a particular or specific method, or tailor things as they go. It does mean that they should not insist on something that is not helping you unless it is to keep you safe and alive.

You do not have to manage all the cooks in the kitchen. You do not have to know what you want or how to get it. It is part of your therapist's job to help you figure it out. But it does help if you are willing to talk, even if it's just chitchat for a while. You have to start somewhere.

And you have to be honest—as best you can be. If you get a bad response, say so. But at least give it a try. Most of the time when my clients don't talk to me, they are protecting themselves. They fear being judged, corrected, criticized, or told they are being disrespectful, not taking responsibility for their behavior, at fault, crazy, or stupid. Sometimes clients are silent because they are afraid to hurt or alienate the person they are angry with, even if that person is not in the room. Sometimes it's because they don't think talking will make a difference, or they think they will be disappointed or hurt yet again. And you know what? It happens sometimes, even in therapy. So it's a risk. But if you have to hold back too often or lie to a professional, either you are cheating yourself or you might not be in front of the right person. Either way, you won't get the benefit of real relief, which you definitely deserve.

When there are a lot of people involved in your treatment, you are going to get caught in the cross talk sometimes, and your helpers are going to say stupid things from time to time. It helps a lot if you can share your real feelings, ideas, doubts, and hopes with each member of your team. It is good to be able to generally trust your team, even if you don't always like what they say; to take or at least consider suggestions from people you have agreed to let into your world. Think about getting ready and being open to willingness and to turning your energy to the solution.

Even when willingness fills you, recovery is often a long and winding road. Sometimes it's not having less that brings willingness on, but having more—having good things in life that you are too sacred to risk losing or missing out on. There is no right formula for getting willing. A good chunk of the equation is, again, from your unconscious mind. They say in 12-step programs to pray for the willingness to be willing to be willing.

Having the disorder or being stuck does not necessarily mean that you are a rebel or a refuser or are choosing to have it. But it does mean that in order to want and get a better life, you will need to take a look inside your psyche to find out what's keeping you from going forward. Knowing won't automatically propel you into freedom, but it will help.

CHAPTER 7

Who Are Your Real Friends?

Piglet sidled up to Pooh from behind. "Pooh?" he whispered.

"Yes, Piglet?"

"Nothing," said Piglet, taking Pooh's hand.
"I just wanted to be sure of you."

—A. A. MILNE, *Winnie-the-Pooh*

BRAVE AND angry, Sarah talks a lot about friendship during our sessions. A few weeks ago, she told her college roommate all about her eating disorder. She poured her heart out in the darkness of their dorm room, with only the light from the full moon spilling in through the big windows that look out over the hills behind their small college campus.

She had wanted to talk about it for months. Not sure what the real goal was, Sarah just thought that maybe her honesty would add new depth to their friendship, gain her an understanding ear, and pull her toward the world of people who do not get on the scale sixteen times a day and create new ways to eat bagels without touching the crust. She wanted a solid friendship with someone who did not have her habits—someone who would not compare who had cut deeper, longer, and with the most interesting objects—a friendship that would not deteriorate into a competition about who was sicker or a contest about who was healthier. With her other friends, she played her usual role of listener and caregiver to the world. This time she wanted someone to listen to her problems. Though she certainly did not have to open up to her roommate, she wanted to see if a new kind of closeness was possible with someone she truly liked.

Sarah was trying out a human friendship because for a long time she has thought of the eating disorder as her best friend. Deep down she believes the disorder protects her, holds her, rescues her, and contains her. The ED voice talks so loudly, so convincingly, so lovingly, that she has come to trust its dual messages of love and hate. In her mind, the disorder is her most real friend, tried and true. It can be commanding when she needs to obey and gentle when she needs the comfort and understanding that she can find nowhere else.

Choosing Between Sharing Razors and Jelly on Your Toast

When we talk about it, Sarah and I are amazed at how the longing to be alone and the longing to build friendships can coexist. And we are troubled by how disloyal you can feel to your "friend," the eating disorder, if you step outside and take a chance with people. Servicing the disorder saps your ability to tend to real friendships, and while you know this, you often feel helpless to do much about it. You hazard the thought that maybe, at first, it does not have to be such a choice. Maybe you can take tentative steps into the real world without leaving the solace of the eating- or self-injury-disorder world behind. Small steps: just do the next right thing.

Sarah's roommate listened for a long time in the quiet of the night, and Sarah felt somewhat mesmerized at the telling of her own story. She was timid at first but got bolder as she went on, feeling a mix of pride and panic, hope and stupidity. It was all at once exhilarating and embarrassing. When she was done, her roommate said, "Wow, I had no idea," and "I'm glad you told me." Sarah went to sleep somewhat let down and confused.

Going to sleep was an attempt to tunnel to new and better feelings. She figured that maybe she would get the elusive feeling she was looking for in the morning. Besides, being able to sleep was a victory in itself. She remembered something I had said to her recently: Bad feelings are like vampires—they like to come out late at night and bite you.

At breakfast the next morning, Sarah stared down at what she considered her disgustingly fattening breakfast, a difficult nod to her new food plan. Her slice of toast, coffee, orange, and hard-boiled egg were taunting her. Then her roommate asked her if she wanted jelly on her toast! A mixture of anger, frustration, fear, and shame washed over Sarah. She had spent the night before explaining that food terrorized her, that she both craved and refused it, that every meal is a battle and every calorie a bullet. And her roommate wanted to know if she wanted jelly on her toast?

Sarah and I decide that her roomie just doesn't get it. Maybe she doesn't want to get it. Maybe it is too much for her.

What confuses Sarah is that it was such a different reaction from those of the girls she knows who are like her. They share their confidences and then offer to share their razors and bond in the secret society of rebellion, defiance, and slavery to the pursuit of thinness. These friendships seem fraught with jealousy and competition for attention to the point that Sarah has become somewhat suspect of other people's motives when they disclose their rituals. And she herself fights feelings of competitiveness and annoyance, even though they are natural, normal, and part of the struggle to find your way in recovery and in life.

It seems to Sarah that negotiating friendships while trying to recover—even while trying to get interested in recovery—is like traipsing through a field of wildflowers with land mines beneath it; while it's alluring and beautiful, you risk getting blown up at any moment.

Why bother? Because connections are so necessary, especially with those who understand. You need the companionship, the give-and-take, the feeling of not being totally alone in the universe, even if you normally live with the feeling of being in solitary confinement.

When she was hospitalized, Sarah got especially close to two other girls, Chloe and Kim. In group therapy they supported each other; at meals they sat together. They ran interference for each other if the nurse was getting too close when they wanted to be left alone.

Chloe was pretty set on ducking the system, hiding her food, and trying to dupe the social workers. She cut habitually and was always offering to show Sarah a few new tricks. She was happy to share the one razor blade she had managed to sneak in with her and kept tucked away in her socks. With Chloe, Sarah felt included, connected, and steeled to withstand the anti-ana world. Chloe got it. She got the frustration, the pain, the fear, the pressure. She understood being misunderstood and thinking everyone was thinking about you, judging you, and expecting you to drop your game and get back to a life. Chloe understood how terrifying it was for Sarah to walk into a Starbucks, a mall, anywhere sometimes. She understood curling up into a ball and hiding in the closet.

But Chloe had a strong competitive streak. When Sarah got attention from the staff for not finishing a meal, Chloe would up the ante and refuse to come to the next meal altogether. And when Sarah seemed to be doing better, Chloe backed away a bit. Sarah feared she could lose her friend due to her own progress. Things could get pretty confusing.

Kim, on the other hand, was always trying to snuggle up to the staff. She showed up on time to group, cleared her plate, and kept her journal. She was Miss Recovery. Annoyed with Kim for being such a kiss-up, Sarah paradoxically admired her progress and perseverance. And her relationship with Kim was even more complicated than that. Deep down Sarah related to Kim's genuine desire to recover, but Kim was much more out of control with food than Sarah was and considered herself the expert on all things purge. She had fessed up to being jealous of Sarah's ability to restrict for months on end, and her jealousy made Sarah uncomfortable. Yet somehow it was worth keeping Kim as a friend because her compassionate nature and connection with the staff gave Sarah hope.

Sarah stays in contact with both Chloe and Kim, but she feels that she can never be sure whether they are calling to see how she is doing or to see how they are doing in comparison to her. Since she has been doing better, she's not sure what to say to them.

It's hard for Sarah to figure out whom to trust among her ED friends; some of the people who seem sincere in their quest for recovery at times seem even more dedicated to fighting it. And some seem to understand her pain, but they are so caught up in their own struggle that they are not able to be there for her.

To keep up the friendships, Sarah feels she cannot land too heavily on wanting to get better because that puts her out of the loop. But she can't stay sick, either. That, too, seems to create distance.

Sarah often plays the role of listener in many of her friendships—the human valium for everyone in her life. She's the sponge for her friends' problems, giving them the emotional sustenance she wishes she could have—unconditional love, unending support, deep compassion, patience, praise, and a "fight on" message. She wants to be liked and pays for it with hours and hours of generous listening, leaving her without any assurance that *she* can get something from the relationship too.

So Sarah thinks she will try to confide in her roommate to establish a friendship outside of her ED circle. But her roommate's clueless question about the jelly only reinforces Sarah's belief that the only friendships she can have are grounded either in the race toward recovery or the shared culture of craving, starving, and self-attack—friendships in which she can at least be somewhat understood. Beyond that world is the habitat of civilians who will wound her with their clumsy, clueless real-world pursuits. In the former, she stays at risk of never having a life that feels whole and true. In the latter, she feels overwhelmed, lost, and silly.

We talk about how disappointing people can be at times, and about how hard it is to have to help your friends be better friends by letting them know what you need in a particular situation, especially when you're not sure yourself and part of you does not think you deserve friends to begin with.

We talk about how it's OK to get your needs met by different people at different times. Not everyone has to understand. You can forgive them their limitations—something you probably ought to do more of with yourself anyway. Self-forgiveness doesn't come easy to those of us rooted in stubborn self-hatred and perfectionism.

At her angriest, Sarah does not want to grace her roommate a drop. But one day her roommate asked if Sarah could let her know the right things to say when Sarah was having a bad day so that she could help. That stopped Sarah in her tracks. Hope lives, we think. Her roommate might not get it, but she is willing to be there for Sarah. And Sarah has just enough hope to be willing to tell her.

To do that, however, Sarah has to fight her fear of needing too much, which pushes people away from her. It has always seemed to her that the unspoken charge of friendship is to fix other people's lives or have them fix yours. This is such a strain that it adds weight to even the lightest social connections. In order to recover, Sarah will have to forge new ways of thinking about her friendships, forgoing the fantasy of "perfect friendship" for friendships with real people who sometimes say dumb things and frustrate and disappoint.

It's a question of balance. A friendship should be loving and gentle and sprinkled with laughter, goodness, and companionship; occasionally it mandates a good ear and support when you need to reach out. Sarah had to learn to make those distinctions, and it was a tough tightrope to walk.

So Who Needs Friends Anyway?

Self-attack requires enormous energy and intensity. Think how much effort it takes to push feelings away, slice up forearms, stick pencils down throats, play roulette with body weight, or run on the treadmill till your feet throb.

Is the idea of channeling your energy into forming a true friendship intimidating to you? Being close to others can be as frightening as being separate from them. Fear and loneliness are equal-opportunity destroyers. Being close brings with it fear of dependency, responsibility, vulnerability, betrayal, rejection, and judgment. Isolation can offer the relief of being sheltered in your own cocoon, but it does get awfully dark in there.

If isolation is the preprogrammed setting in your brain, building friendships can seem about as desirable as body fat. The yearning to be alone and the yearning to be connected are just different parts of the same you. They can coexist, but as long as you think you have to choose between them, you will be stuck. You do need real friends in order to want to get well and stay well. If waves of self-doubt, frustration, and annoyance with others lead you straight to the kitchen or bathroom, hold on to this thought: like recovery, good friendships take time. You can't be close to everyone, but if you let a few choice friendships take hold, at whatever level, they can catapult you over the edge of resistance and into recovery.

Since recovery requires talking about the food, the fat, and the feelings, building friendships that will endure means having a general sense about how much to talk. Some people I know are afraid of talking altogether. They are afraid that they will never be understood, or that no one keeps confidences anymore, or that whatever they say will be used against them or considered a commitment to action. They think words are like bricks, blocking them into a corner where they will be helpless against the advice-givers and naysayers that surround them. Some fear that the need to talk will take on a life of its own, just like food. They are afraid they will binge on the words, the emotions, the momentum.

Talking can be scary because it can trigger you without notice and bad feelings can rear up, sending you right back to eating yourself senseless or rededicating yourself to secretly getting your weight back down under your nutritionist's "into-the-hospital-you-go" line.

And then there is the fear that talking from the heart and soul is the last frontier, the final resort; so if talking does not help right away, you are doomed to a life of darkness and pain.

But . . . if you can help yourself and others talk well and safely, you get the double benefit of building friendships and moving forward in recovery. You can learn not to talk to the point of gorging on the conversation, and you can help yourself speak without commitment or confession. Words are weighty, it's true, and too many or not enough can take a toll on a friendship.

As part of our work together, Sarah and I like to keep a running list of our favorite words. Whenever we find one we like, we tell the other and add it to our list. We are especially fond of the word *serendipity*. We also like *flummox, discombobulate, apocalypse, ameliorate, sublime, sacrosanct, arcane, insidious, impervious, truculent, gourmand, elucidate,* and *insouciant*. (Feel free to add your own and send them to me; I am always happy to expand the list.)

Part of the joy of our word list is that it reminds us that besides all the terror that words can bring, they can also be vehicles for carrying us to better feelings. They remind you both that there is joy in the simple things and that there are things to talk about that do not revolve around body mass index, carbs, grief, crazy parents, or black moods. (Yes, it's true!) While wanting to live in your PJs all day in the privacy of your own hell is sometimes all well and good, you have to fess up to the idea that some part of you longs for lightheartedness, connection, and love. That part needs friends too.

Some of Sarah's caution about trusting women and forming friendships comes from her bumpy relationship with her mother. Sarah would like to have much more of her mother's time and attention, though not for her food stuff. She longs to spend some time with her mother, hanging out or just connecting. Sarah wants her mother to be more of a confidante to her, but things just don't seem to go that way (more on this in Chapters 8 and 9). She has the feeling that her mother does not want her around much. She assumes that other people also have this feeling of not wanting to be with her, and that only adds to the difficulty of reaching out, trusting, and staying connected. It's hard to know how to negotiate all the feelings that come up, but she and I agree that the benefits of true friendships outweigh the complications.

When it comes to friendships, you don't need perfection, you need safety. Sarah is especially sensitive about safety because her mother has a tendency to tell Sarah's personal stuff to just about anybody. Though Sarah and I are working on ways to help her mother not do this, she has a hard time getting it. So Sarah is always on guard, wondering if her secrets are being told to strangers and others are talking about her.

One time when Sarah was home for the weekend, she overheard her mother on the phone talking to the electrician. *The electrician!* She was telling him that Sarah's weight was stable again, but her moods seemed to be more erratic than ever, and she thought Sarah needed to talk more about her pain over being molested by her uncle some years ago.

We are trying to get her mother to understand, but it's slow going.

———————————◆———————————

In regard to friendships, Sarah and I talk about the importance of having fun and levity, of wanting to share life's ups and downs genuinely and with humor and compassion. We think that as much as you need attention, you don't actually want pity—occasional praise, perhaps, and someone in your corner. But no one person can fill up the canyon inside you. You have to be careful about imposing this on your friendships. And you have to know that some friendships come and go, while others endure.

It's best to take risks with those who are not exclusively pulling toward the ana/mia world, especially if you know that somewhere inside of you there is someone who wants to and is willing to grow. Though Sarah thinks that she might never be totally free of the eating disorder, she is learning to have a good life anyway. And somewhere in her depths, she is excited about that. Somehow willingness has taken hold and hope no longer hurts.

Making It Happen

We came up with some ideas about building friendships, connecting, and talking with some safety. Even if you're not ready to take on all the general guidelines that follow, it's good to keep them in mind:

- ◆ **Be open to the idea that talking and listening will help you get relief from emotional pain.** Good conversations are a major part of most friendships. Conversations do not always have to be heavy or deep, but words are a big part of how we connect, create relationships, and heal. They are a good route to relief—maybe the best route if you have the right ears in front of you.

◆ **Use words, even though you wish that those closest to you would just *know* when you want to talk.** Say, "I need someone to listen for a bit. Would you be willing? When would be a good time?" (True, you could get a no with a bad-feeling chaser, but it won't be any worse than having spent an hour talking only to get the sense that you exhausted and bothered your listener.) No one likes to ask for what she or he needs, but it's not so bad once you get used to it.

◆ **Say honestly that you do not want advice,** just some kind attentiveness—unless, of course, you do want advice. But be prepared not to like the advice or to feel judged, annoyed, criticized, or misunderstood—or to actually consider it.

◆ **Avoid burning out your friends.** No one can be expected to listen with undivided attention for fifty minutes straight on a regular basis except your therapist. So watch your time. I am not suggesting that you have to set an alarm or regulate minutes with good friends. But I am suggesting that you honor both your need to unload and your friend's capacity for listening. Overstaying your welcome with someone's good ears does not bode well for that person being available the next time you need to talk. Check in now and then. Say, "Can I keep talking, or do you need a break?"

◆ **If you are listening and you are getting frustrated about doing all the listening, say so.** Even if directness is not your strong point, see if you can muster up some words like "I want to keep talking with you, but I need to take a break. Can we pick it back up later?"

◆ **But do reciprocate; be good ears.** Find out how your listener is doing. It might trigger you, but if you picked her, she merits your interest, even if you have to fake it a bit. Ask questions.

If you feel stuck for things to talk about, you can always try questions like "What's going on in your life? How are things with you?" Or if you want to keep things lighter, ask about movies, music, even the weather. Remember to evaluate reciprocity in friendships over longer periods of time and multiple experiences. Sometimes we have to pay it forward a bit and sometimes we are more on the receiving end. An overall sense of balance and give-and-take is what makes a friendship withstand the momentary glitches and endure over time.

◆ **Hold off on advice unless asked for it.** Use eye contact and nonverbal cues like nodding in understanding. If you feel judgmental, make mental notes to think or write about it later but hold off on reacting in the moment. Stick with more supportive questions and responses like "How did that affect you?" or "That sounds hard."

◆ **Adopt your own "don't tell" policy.** If your friend expresses something in confidence, it should go no further than your ears. If you are a gossip, no one will trust you.

◆ **Ask for help if you get stuck talking about yourself.** You can say, "I feel like I need to talk, but I can't seem to say what's really bothering me." Sometimes your listener can help guide you along. You can make people guess, pull it out of you, and beg you to open up, but that gets annoying after a while and it can strain a friendship. Yes, I know, the part of you that hates yourself will be glad to watch this self-fulfilling prophecy unfold. But grace yourself here, too; it's hard to talk about your father's temper, your sister's success, your fear of driving, or your inability to keep down ice cream.

◆ **Share the good stuff, too.** You can do this without bragging if you keep it simple. Even if we or our friends feel jealous from time to time, we can still feel happy for each other's successes if they are shared humbly and without self-deprecation. We are not usually out to inspire jealousy unless we are very annoyed by someone or feel particularly insecure around that person. It's OK to say when you feel good.

◆ **Guard your own confidences.** Not everybody has to know everything. I know I've just been saying that you have to talk to build friendships and now I'm saying not to say too much—what I mean is you don't have to tell everything to everyone. You can be choosy. Opening up can be slow and savory. It does not have to be a binge. Let things unfold in new friendships and give yourself permission to go at your own pace.

◆ **Go at your own pace, but keep going.** Time will do its thing if you let it. Shared experiences and moments build momentum in new friendships and even help you reinvent some old ones. Most of us feel vulnerable when we talk about our stuff, but everyone's got stuff. No matter what it looks like from where you sit, everyone has something going on.

◆ **Choose different friends for different reasons.** You might have a bestie or you might not, but usually we have different kinds of friends. There are friends we can just hang with and friends we can really talk to. You can share different parts of yourself with different people. No one person has to be your person for everything.

◆ **Deepen the conversation.** If you like someone and want to grow the friendship, start by sharing something real, but not too heavy. If the person asks how you are, you can say something true for you like "Actually I'm a little sad today," or "I had a strange experience at work yesterday." If you sense the person is warm to what you said, you can say a little more. You can also ask a more leading question like "How is your job going?" or "What's it like to be in school full time?" You can also use compliments to get things going; you can say, "Great shoes! Where'd you get them?" or "I love your earrings." You don't have to be gushy or false, but a genuine compliment can get things off the ground. Creating a connection can take a little while, and not everyone responds positively, but when someone does it's well worth it.

◆ **Be honest.** This can be harder than you realize. You do not always want to be a downer, and too much complaining can tax a relationship, so monitor how much honesty is enough for the time being. You can say you are sad or tired or happy or grumpy. And you can be honest about not wanting to go out or needing to change your plans. You can say, "I'm really not feeling up to going out tonight" instead of "I have a big test tomorrow" when you don't actually have one. I'm not saying that there are not times you can be diplomatic, but usually a gentle truth is the best way to go.

◆ **Pay attention to what you are feeling.** We are so afraid of rejecting and being rejected that the dynamics of friendships can seem too painful and unfulfilling. Sometimes even a hint of not being understood or respected can send you reeling. If it does not feel right enough, table the conversation or try again a different time. Don't decide that either you or she is pathetic.

◆ **Time apart sometimes helps friendships breathe.** The Rule of Three says, "If things get sticky, let some time pass; wait three minutes, three hours, or three days." If you get mad at a friend and want to tell her off, ask yourself, "Does it have to be said? Does it have to be said now? Does it have to be said by me?" The answers are often no. That does not mean shutting down about issues you have with her; it just means not doing it on the fly and not doing it via impulsive texting or Facebook posting, for example.

◆ **It does not matter who is thinner.** OK, it feels like it does, and the pain is strong and hard, but you will never win this one. Never. And this pain and this pursuit is a central driving force in many of our lives. But there will always be someone fatter, and there will always be someone thinner, and you will always be on the losing end of this if you are focused on it. It will always be the eating or self-injury disorder ruining your ability to connect if you keep this issue front and center. I know that letting go of this seems impossible, but try to believe, just for a millisecond, that you can live with the unfairness of it all. If you can, you'll discover that connecting to people is where the real sweetness of life is. (And it won't make you fat.) Then you can start to develop interesting friendships that bring you real joy—impossible, strange, and new as that might seem.

◆ **Give, but give gently. Giving is different from people-pleasing. It is behavior with good boundaries and no expectations.** You can give time, love, support, understanding, kind words, and maybe a flower now and then. If you feel resentful, you are giving too much. Give for giving's sake; because it makes you a person who thinks about others; because it gets you out of your own head. Give because it feels good. Give because it shapes you.

◆ **Show up. Go out. Say yes.** If you are feeling brave, initiate. Go for coffee with your friend. Go to the football game. Go wherever and whenever you can. When you can't, you can't, but try. Give others the idea that you are interested in them if you want them to be interested in you. Even if you are having a hard time, act "as if." I know it's tough. But here again you might have to push the truck up the hill to get somewhere, to see what's at the top.

Yes, I know to whom I am speaking. If you stay alone in your head with all that pain, you are living under the false idea that there is no point in trying and that you are better off in your cocoon than out there in the world of difficult people. You are living in the myth that either you are awful or they are.

So I am talking straight to you—the you who stays home every night of the week because you'd rather eat (or not have to). If you push yourself to try life on the outside, you might find that your protective shell is not as necessary as you thought it was. Going out, talking—just being with others—can take the edge off some of your pain, distract you a bit from the world of food and/or weapons, and lay a foundation for getting a better life.

That might be hard to imagine from where you are now. It might also be hard to imagine where and how to meet new people. Many young women, especially those in their early twenties, find it difficult to start new friendships or rekindle old ones. It's not easy. There are opportunities, though. Tune in to those around you at work, in class, at the library, at the coffee shop. Keep an open mind and an open aura as best as you can.

One note about forming friendships: Use Facebook with caution. I know people who use Facebook as a shopping mall for bad feelings. They scope out the pictures to see who is skinny, who is fat, and who is hanging out with whom. That information is often used to ignite comparison, jealousy, self-pity, and self-hatred.

Facebook can be False Evidence Appearing Real (FEAR). We get all kinds of ideas about what a great life everyone else seems to be having, not to mention snippets of conversations, ignored contacts, and unfriending issues. You might never know that a friend looked at your page and got upset that you went out last night when you said you were too tired, took it personally, and now thinks that you are dishonest or you don't want her around. Facebook is a whole new arena for offenses and injuries, for finding emotional grenades that blow up on us and destroy our friendships. It can trigger us to grab for our weapons of self-destruction.

Skinnier Than You

Sarah sits hugging one of my green throw pillows tightly to her chest and tells me that two of her old friends from her residential program throw up together. She says they take turns over the toilet one after another until they can get no more up. Apparently they compete to see who can get to bile first. I thought I had heard it all by now, except that I haven't. I know all too well how far an eating disorder can go—clogged toilets, ripped esophagi, crashed cars, heart damage, stolen money, broken bones. Death. In the private underworld of secret control, power, and pain, there is often no telling when exactly you have slipped into unstoppable insanity.

When I ask Sarah what she makes of her friends' behavior, she tells me that she used to want to excel in tennis, but since she injured her knee she wants to excel in thinness. She also wants to excel in sickness. There are no official badges for meals missed, food avoided, bones showing, life events not attended, quantities consumed, or blood drawn, but there are rewards. There are secret and strong feelings of having one-upped your friend, of having gotten just that much more of an edge. Sarah understands her friends' competitiveness, though she thinks they've gone too far.

It's bad enough that Sarah's older sister is gorgeous and her closest friend from high school is on her way to Harvard. To top it all off, she cannot get a jump on her two old friends from residential. She tells me that she used to be able to hold her own in this sort of competition, but as she recovers, she's losing ground. She's afraid that she might get caught in the hell of being good at nothing—not even chucking up her insides.

What a bind she's in: The girls she knows who are making progress in recovery can seem haughty and confident and full of advice and encouragement. But if she's in the wrong mood, that can make her feel lonely and pathetic. Yet to join in by flashing her razor marks or showing bones seems pointless, too.

Jealousy consumes Sarah. She is jealous of the girls who are sicker than she is and jealous of the ones who are well. She's not sure against whom she is competing anymore, or for what purpose.

Sarah wants a friend, not a competitor. Her non-ED peers are competitive, too, but somehow the race to be the sickest of the sick is more important, and it seems easier than the race to be well and kick the disorder out.

To Sarah, deciding to want to get better means changing roles. It implies stepping out of the race and culture of being sick and finding something else to compete for.

And that's pretty scary. It's easier to compete when you at least know the sport, and that's partly why she's afraid to give up the ED. She can lay claim to hurting herself and getting the highest buzz—her body's ultimate praise—from going without food for many, many hours on end; in that sense she feels she's the best at something, even if it comes at a price. Getting so caught up in the culture of the ED world can make you forget that you can actually achieve and compete in real ways.

Consider this: Outside the bubble of pain, hunger, and pierced skin, there can be an evolving self who paints or writes or sings in thousands of ordinary small moments. Success can show up in your journal or your heart or in being kind to animals. It can show up through learning to say no or thank you or smiling at yourself in the mirror. The recognition you crave starts when you agree to recognize, befriend, and credit yourself.

Sarah sees everything as black or white—you are either good at everything or good at nothing. You are either perfect or awful. You either have nothing or you have too much. You are either better than everyone or worse. You are either starving or you are bingeing.

We talk more and more about what Sarah believes is worthwhile to accomplish in life. She wants to write poetry, work with children, and celebrate her own accomplishments along with those of her friends—not instead of or in spite of her friends. Those seem like tall orders, but they are worthy goals nonetheless.

At times she still feels that there is only so much happiness and success to go around; that others getting what they want means there won't be anything left for her. But she is beginning to rethink these ideas and let in new hope. Maybe she can really do it. Maybe she can leave the narrow world of obsession, emotional pain, and self-harm.

Sarah knows that new, healthy friendships can be the bridge to getting out of that place, but that negotiating the space between avoiding triggers (and avoiding life) and taking care of friendships can be daunting. She tells me often that she is afraid of what she will say, wear, or eat when she's with friends.

I have witnessed many a friendship succumb to the rules of an eating disorder—the fear of having to make conversation, face a buffet table, put on a dress, or stand near others who are skinnier than you. I have watched as connections faded, excuses spawned, and self-righteous regret took hold. It's normal to want to escape the bad feelings of awkwardness, jealousy, and competition even though they are natural, human sensations. As much as they can be hard to bear, giving yourself permission to feel them and not going after yourself just for having them is a good start.

At its best, jealousy is an informant sent to us from our unconscious to give us hints about what we value and why. At its worst, it keeps us focused on what we don't have, which keeps us stuck in the problem rather than propelling us toward the solution.

My friend Maggie once told me that she remembered coming home from school one day with a math test she had failed. She got the lowest grade in the class and thought she deserved to die—not that she had better study harder next time; not that maybe she needed a math tutor; not "who needs math anyway"; not disappointed; not angry that the math teacher was useless; but death—she deserved death—for failing a math test.

The secret life of wanting to die—of thinking you deserve to die for not coming out on top all the time—is common for people with eating disorders and those who go after themselves with sharp objects. It translates into thinking you cannot be around people because you believe that everyone in the room knows how miserable you are and that all eyes can see through you at all times. They can't understand you, but they know you are a mess.

Sometimes when I am with Sarah, I find that I am starving. I feel so hungry I think I could eat the pillows on my couch. This hunger mostly comes on when Sarah is sitting quietly and saying nothing. I sit quietly, too. But I know that if I am this hungry, it probably has something to do with Sarah. I was not so hungry before Sarah came in and was so quiet. And then in the quiet it comes to me that in our silence is the loudness of longing.

One day when the silence goes on for a while, I look at her and ask if I'm going to have to work for it today, to which she replies that there is no point in talking about anything anymore; it's all meaningless.

After a bit she's ready to add, "I can't find the right words. It's so real in my head, but it's stupid. I'm stuck thinking about my own body while other people are truly suffering—and that's what makes me really stupid. My food plan, constipation, waiting too long at the doctor, my father calling my mother a lazy sloth—my head is like a freight train full of randomly connected cars. What good is talking about it going to do?"

But I know, and Sarah is beginning to know, that all her feelings and words are welcome. And that sometimes the talking is how we clear away the fog that is blocking our view of better. And that even her feelings of futility and frustration, when said out loud, can begin to dissolve into something different, something better.

I think that I feel hungry when we are in sessions together because Sarah is so afraid of her multiple hungers—her hunger to have meaningful, close, safe, reliable friendships; to work through her feelings about her parents; to be successful in her own mind; to be comfortable, confident, and relaxed in her own skin; to be liked and loved; to be whoever she is—to just be. I will feel all her hunger for her until she is ready to feel it herself.

My relationship with Sarah is a safe testing ground for all the dynamics and feelings that come up in friendships. She and I both value the relationship we have with each other, and we see it as a springboard to her opening herself up to new people and new ideas.

Moving forward in our work together, we continue to expand on how to nourish and protect friendships, and how to nourish and protect ourselves within those friendships, because the grooves of good friendships carry us along in the worst and best of times throughout our lives.

Just past the silence, the doubt, the frustration, if we keep going, there is something real. There is understanding, grace, and connection. And through it all we decide that friendships are worth the struggle. Just like recovery.

CHAPTER 8

Parenting Your Parents

"It's not always easy being her daughter."

"I think," she said, "sometimes it's hard no matter whose daughter you are."

—SARAH DESSEN, *Along for the Ride*

THIS IS not a "blame your parents" chapter. This is not a "blame yourself" chapter. This is a "your parents are part of the picture and it helps to talk about it" chapter.

———◆———

My friend Rita has always had a hard time with her father-in-law. He is often harsh, judgmental, and cynical. He raised his kids, including her husband, with a heavy hand and a stern demeanor. He was slow with affection and fast with the belt.

The other day she called to tell me the following story: "You won't believe it. We just finished Thanksgiving dinner and everyone is pretty much up from the table except the two of us. He turns to me and says, 'Did ever tell you about the time my father locked me up with the rats?,' and I am thinking, 'Huh? I have known this man for twenty-three years, and he has never said anything personal to me. And now, suddenly, he wants to share?' Please.

"And then he says, 'Do you remember Uncle Arnie? Well, one day he and my father got into a big fight down at the store, just as I walked in to give my father a message from my ma. No cell phones then. It was up to me to run down the hill to the store whenever my ma needed something. So I walked in and said, 'Pop.' That's all, just 'Pop.' Maybe, 'Hey, Pop.' And that was it. He was so annoyed at me for interrupting him that he dragged me down to the cellar, locked the door, and turned out the light. I sat there for twenty-six hours in the dark, from three o'clock on Thursday afternoon till five on Friday afternoon, when they finally realized I was missing. I was so bitten up by the rats by then, I had pus coming out of every limb.'

"And then he shakes his head. 'I think I was about seven or eight at the time.' Head shake. Honestly, I never in a million years thought I could feel compassion for the guy. But all of a sudden, I understood. I understood that he has a story, too. I'm not excusing him for the way he treats people, but the guy's got a story."

◆

They, Too, Have a Story

All parents have stories. When you become a parent, you will have a story. A hint of the pain that shaped her father-in-law's life experience gave Rita an insight into why he is such a nasty parent. Not all difficult or abusive parents had difficult or abusive parents. And not all children of difficult or abusive parents become difficult or abusive parents. But everyone has a story. And we are all shaped and influenced somehow—however uniquely—by our parents and our relationships with them.

No one really knows why people develop eating or self-injury disorders. We have a lot of good guesses but no real facts. We know that genetics and biology play a role. We know that birth order, culture, community, and peers are all factors. And we know that environment, relationships, and family figure in as well. But we don't know what the formula is—to what extent our interactions with our parents have shaped our character and behavior, and to what extent it's biology, genetics, or blind luck.

Parents loom large in our psyches and our lives. They are woven into our deepest, most intimate pains and needs as well as our hopes, aspirations, and goals.

To ignore the relationships you have with your parents in your quest for wellness would be like ignoring your arms when you are trying to swim. You are intertwined with them in ways that are deep and wide.

It might not be necessary to work things out with your parents in real time in order to recover, though if you are living at home they are a big piece of the picture. If you are out of the house, or if your parents are not in your life, you can just reflect on what I say in this chapter. But at some point in your journey toward wellness you will most likely have to learn a bit about your parents and focus on your experience of being their child.

The desire to be understood by our parents is one of our greatest longings. If your parents are in your life—no matter how old or young you or they are—you might have to help them understand you, your needs, and your feelings. It shouldn't be necessary, but you might have to lead the way.

It might be that your distress is the red flag of your family. Some theorists even believe that if one person in the family has a serious problem, it is really the symptom of the whole family; it is the family that needs help, not just the one who has the problem.

You should not have to be the bridge to everyone getting help, and you should not have to parent your parents. You should not have to teach them how to speak to you or consult with you or treat you with respect. You should not have to inform them that they should model respect, treat each other with respect, and treat you with respect as well. You should not have to tell them that they have some part in the problem and that everyone will benefit if they take part in the solution. You should not have to tell them that when they argue with your feelings, they are hurting you; that when they call you names, they are taking your insides out; that when they make it impossible for you to say what you need to say in words, it makes you want to slice your arms up.

You should not have to tell them that when they yell so much it makes your stomach curl inward, or that a lifetime of hearing them complain about their own weight has had an effect on you. You should not have to tell them that when they comment about your food and your body—even if they mean well—it makes you feel like pounding yourself on the head. They should not hit you, belittle you, talk to you about their sex lives, or borrow your jeans and tell you that they are too big on them. You should not have to tell them that while all families need help sometimes, if they cannot get along with each other *they* should get help and leave you out of it.

You should not have to tell them any of this because you are the kid. No matter how old you are, you are still their kid. Most likely you don't have the words to tell them these things, and besides, they should know.

But people are not always who they should be or who we wish they could be. You can, if you would like a better life, help them be better parents even if you believe they don't deserve it; even if they are drunk or demanding or difficult or demeaning; even if they are wise and wonderful and just sometimes woefully off base.

Most people, at every age, crave a connection with their parents. We are shaped not only by our interactions with them but by our need to interact with them. We might never outgrow our craving for parental approval, harmony, understanding, love, and acceptance, but we can eventually transform it into something livable. Why does the longing for parental love often lead to frustration and disappointment, and away from productive communication? How come things get so tangled? Why do arguments with parents sometimes make people feel like they just want to give up and die—or at least resort to some extreme form of communication? And what does any of this have to do with wanting to recover?

I met sixteen-year-old Shelly after she carved the word HELP into her thigh. She tells me that her mother exercises in her underwear in the living room. Shelly and her two brothers find this positively repulsive, and a bit of a head tilter. When she tells me about it, I can actually see Shelly and her two brothers standing on the steps that drop down into the living room, their heads angling on their necks like cocker spaniels, watching their mother do deep knee bends in her bra and panties in full view of the big bay window and three stupefied offspring.

Shelly is actually a rather quiet person. Her mom, the exercise nut, is very clear about what she expects from Shelly. There are a lot of rules in the house. Everyone must eat dinner together every night, no exceptions. Shelly's dad is pretty overweight. He chews with his mouth open, and she cannot eat when she is near him. This is a big problem since family dinners are mandatory. Shelly has gotten quite adept at hiding her food in her underwear while sitting at the dinner table.

Shelly is hopeful that she will not have to deal with her own body looking too much like her mother's, or with having eating habits like her father. And as a bonus, she champions the art of hunger endurance—she excels at it, in fact.

She tells me that she is ashamed of her parents and that she is ashamed of her shame. Such a storm inside her!

Surviving the Storms

There are storms of many colors. Ask Amanda. Amanda's dad is a very smart man who teaches high school English. The kids at school think he is pretty interesting. He is cool in front of the class, likes to tell jokes, and imitates famous people. He and Amanda have a monthly "date night." They go out to Friendly's for ice cream sundaes and talk about life. Sometimes her dad talks to her about her mom. At first these confidences made Amanda feel important and special, but now they make her feel awkward and uncomfortable.

Amanda generally likes to be with her father. He is the one who takes her shopping and buys her clothes since Amanda's mom hates to shop. Her parents get along OK most of the time. The problem is that whenever they fight, it's pretty ugly because Amanda's father is prone to throwing huge fits of rage. Usually his anger is triggered when Amanda's mother has lost something important like her driver's license or bank card—which her mother does often—or when the house is overly messy or the laundry has not been done.

When her father loses it, he loses it big. The way Amanda describes it to me is this: "First, he starts to breathe heavily. Then he clenches his fists and his face starts to turn red. His eyes get really wide and his eyebrows rise high up into his forehead, as though they would like to leave his face, but can't. And then he starts to bellow really loudly. He goes on for about ten to twenty minutes, calling my mother names, saying what an idiot she is. He hits the wall with his fists and kicks at the wall over and over again."

He has never hit Amanda or her sister or her mother, but Amanda is terrified anyway. No one is allowed to leave the room when her father rages. He says everyone must listen and hear him out. Everyone is afraid to move. After he is done, he usually walks out of the house for a while. When he comes back, he does one of two things: he pretends it never happened and just starts talking normally about anything, like the weather or the football game at the high school; or he comes in and puts his arms around her mom and says how sorry he is, and promises that he is going to get better. He calls her "love" and "darling" and "beautiful," and her mother nods and says it's OK.

Amanda's parents are the ones who suggested she see me, because they are worried that she is not eating properly and is too interested in losing weight. They don't think she is anorexic, but still . . .

It took about four months of weekly sessions with me before Amanda told me about her father's temper. She feels extremely disloyal talking about him, and she wants me to like him. Most important, she does not want me to tell him what she has told me—which of course I would never do.

I want to help Amanda survive the storms without starving to death. All this storming in Amanda's house has affected her, and talking is one of the best ways I know to survive storms. I want her to talk about what it's like to be in her body and in her house; what it's like to love and hate a raging father and a strict but well-intentioned mother; and what it's like to need them both so badly.

But we mustn't hurry. We must go step-by-step—no sense getting blown away by talking too much too quickly. Amanda notices that when her father starts up she does try to sneak away, but if he sees her he tells her not to move. She had not realized this before. She had not remembered trying to leave. She now knows that she feels trapped at these times, and frozen with fear. In those moments she feels out of control and wants to die. And now, even on their dates, she just feels weird because she can't understand how this dad whom she mostly loves can get so crazy and not realize the effect he is having on everyone in the house.

Amanda also starts to feel that she does not like calling her outings with her father dates. She is sixteen, and dates are for guys, not her father. Even though the name is innocent enough, it makes her feel weird.

We are trying to figure out the best way to tell him this. Eventually we come up with some ways she can stay connected to her father without getting weirded out. Moreover, she has found some ways to learn about him that will help her weather his storms. She is going to observe him, thinking of him as someone to analyze. When he is calm, she will ask him questions about his childhood, his favorite color, why he chose to be a teacher, what it was like growing up in his childhood home. She will ask him, when she feels safe, what he would wish for if he could have three wishes, and what his dream vacation would be. She will never push him for an answer, and she will not ask anything about his relationship with her mom.

If her parents' relationship ever comes up, she will tell him that if it's OK with him, she doesn't want to talk about her mom to her dad, and vice versa. Even if her dad wants to talk about her mom, she will just ask him again if he would please not ask her to do that. She will ask it as casually as possible, saying it the same way she would say, "Pass the butter" or "By the way, I brought in the mail."

When her father goes into one of his fits, if she can't get away she'll think of herself as a reporter. She will notice, as if she were covering the scene for the nightly news, what sensations she is feeling and what thoughts and ideas cross her mind. She will also observe her father, perhaps as if he were a science experiment and she is collecting data.

Doing this, Amanda can both notice and allow her feelings and mentally remove herself, just a bit, from the moment. She can't veg out altogether, since he is so loud, so the reporter idea works for her.

Observing as though she were an outsider might yield valuable results. Besides giving her a way to step out of the storm mentally, even if she cannot step out physically, she might get to understand more about her father and herself. Sometimes understanding someone else's pain and/or motives can help lessen your own fear or hate. It can help guide you as to what you can say or do to protect yourself and the relationship. Amanda can take note of when her father is loving and appealing and when he is threatening and distant. She can do this when she is out with him, and she can do this when he is off on one of his rages.

Is it Amanda's job to help her father stop raging? Nope. But can she help herself by taking care of her relationship with him? Yup. Tall order, but it can be done. Amanda can acknowledge and allow all her feelings as well as the effect her father has on her. She can begin to learn new ways to think about him and to feel and be safe without having to stop eating and shrink away.

Then there's Amanda's mom, who is pretty strict about food. They eat meat only once a week and are heavy on the health foods—lots of hummus and whole wheat. Amanda's mom is freaky about anyone having too much sugar, and she doesn't approve of too many snacks.

She is also picky about how Amanda dresses, and she never gives an inch. Part of Amanda wants to please her mom, and part of her wants to punish her. Either way, she isn't eating much. When her father goes on his rages, she finds it hard to eat. Her stomach is really, really tight on those days. She notices that her not eating drives her mother crazy and gets her to pay attention to something other than Amanda's clothes.

Somewhere in Amanda's psyche an idea took hold. She thinks that between her mother's strictness and her father's yelling she is finding it more and more difficult to eat as time goes by. Only lately, she is glad of it.

New Words and New Ways

We've been working together for two years now, and Amanda has started to learn and use new words. She's picked up some of my language; she speaks Melissa. We laugh when she tells me that she finds herself thinking and even saying some of my old favorites. It's the language of curiosity, not criticism; of acceptance, not agitation;

of self-reflection instead of self-attack; of safety, not fear; and of respect for her own ideas, not what she thinks she is supposed to say. And especially it's the language of self and not shame.

After two years of hearing me say, "Let's shine the light on it a bit and see why it feels so intense." Or "Should we unpack that more?" and "Tell me your ideas about this," Amanda has started to speak nicely to herself and changed slightly the way she speaks to others. My "What if you had a different idea?" and "Was there something about our conversation that hit the wrong note?" and "Let's study it a bit" have seeped into her brain. And perhaps my own confessions of imperfection ("Is it OK if I don't get it right all the time?" "I must've missed it, can you tell me again?" and "Yes, I said the wrong thing.") have helped her feel that neither she nor her parents can or need to be flawless all the time. And that's fine. That's human. She catches on to the idea that mistakes and angers can be talked about safely and with interest—lightly even, and with love. And that feelings, while powerful, allowable, and meaningful, are not always facts.

"Stay out of my food!" is not going to go as far in the long run as "Mom, can I tell you how it affects me when you get into my food?" or "Dad, would you be open to hearing how I feel when you comment on how I look?" And what should be her tone? Same as "Please pass the butter. Thanks."

Words and tone both send messages. It is so much better to be *asked* if you would like a suggestion than to have one shoved down your throat. It is so much better to use words than to use a pocket-knife. It is better to allow yourself mistakes—even the spectacular ones—than to pummel yourself into the ground for them. And we all make those mistakes, don't we?

What you want from your parents can seem impossible, unattainable, or downright silly sometimes, but you are allowed to want what you want. (You might not get it always, but you are allowed to want it.) I know that you should not have to do this, but sometimes you have to lead the way in order to get what you want; sometimes you have to teach them; sometimes you have to show them the way. And this can take time. It should take time, actually—lots of time and patience and a dozen mess-ups and flops. But some successes will be mixed in, and the few rays of light make it worth your effort.

That's assuming that you want things to get better. I know plenty of people who are content, on some level, with torturing their parents. If that's where you are, then that's where you are. And if you will get harmed or hurt, then you might not be able to give these strategies much of a try. You cannot control the outcome of your effort, but making the effort can help things along to a better place. So if you can, despite your own frustrations and pain, put some new words out, perhaps you can get some new results. Here's how:

- ◆ **Show gratitude.** You can never go wrong expressing sincere gratitude. Try some well-placed thank-you statements such as "Thank you for washing my jeans" or "I know you had a long day at work; thanks for picking me up so late."
- ◆ **Give information about yourself.** In moments of calm, you can offer, "I really like it when you ask me instead of telling me" or "Is it OK to ask you to knock before you come into my room? I know it's your house, but I really like it when you knock." Try "It means a lot to me when I can just tell you how I feel" or "I get too frustrated when we shop together. It would help me if I could go with a friend." Say it all in that "Please pass the butter" tone.
- ◆ **Notice and check.** "It seems that when I tell you I am having a bad day you get upset, right?" or "I know you mind it when I want to stay home. What if I really feel bad when I go?"
- ◆ **Consult.** Get their opinion—but only when you really want it. And be prepared to hear (their idea of) the truth. Don't invite trouble. Asking, "Does this make my tush look fat?" is most likely not going to yield you anything good. You probably

won't believe them if they say no, and if they say yes you will want to shrink into a genie bottle. So try, "Do you think green or blue looks better on me?" or "What do you think is the best way to write this essay?" or "Which of my friends should I trust the most?" It's best not to ask something like whether they think your friend Julie is a user if you don't really want their opinion on Julie.

◆ **Apologize.** Even if you don't get good results at first, and even if your parents never say they are sorry, they can learn from you. This is not about putting yourself down, fessing up to things you did not do, or expressing anger with sarcasm ("Soooo sorry I didn't wash the stupid dishes"). I'm talking real apologies when you really mess up, such as "I'm sorry that I didn't call when I said I would." And though it may be hard, you can even say, "I'm sorry I lost it and called you an idiot." No need to go into fancy explanations of your character or your reasons or why they deserved it. Just admit you messed up and apologize. Keep it direct and simple.

◆ **Respect.** You might not have it for them. You might not think they deserve it. But they do. And you do. How you treat them shapes *you*. Even anger and the worst pain can be dealt with respectfully. In truth, this is hard stuff for everyone. When you fight, emotions take over. Your brain goes into flood mode, with neurons firing up, heart racing, and all those bad feelings rushing at you at a hundred miles an hour. You can still be respectful. It takes practice, but you can do it. It is not easy in the heat of the moment or in a sea of bad feelings to use new words, but you can create the possibility of it in your mind and decide to practice when the opportunity arises. You can practice, too, in calmer moments when your mind is not on rev. Even in the heat of an argument there should be no name-calling, no cursing, and no trying to embarrass anyone. Save it for your letters, for your shrink, for your best friend.

Don't hurl the worst of it at them. You can say how angry you are without being disrespectful. I give you full permission to *feel* like a raving lunatic and to *want* to punish them, hurt them, inflict pain and suffering on them, and let them know what they've done or how awful they are. Give yourself permission to have all your feelings. But whenever possible save the full force of the storm for a calmer moment and/or different ears—ears that will coach you through it and not throw you down. Sometimes when you are in the thick of it just deciding to pause and be quiet can cool things down. You can also drop a bomb diffuser in by saying something loving like "You know, I don't like it when we go at it like this. I respect you and I really want to work it out." Most people react defensively and protectively when rage or criticism comes flying at them, so if you can keep your words in respectful boundaries, everyone will fare better.

You and your parents might have different ideas about what those boundaries are. Some parents can tolerate more unhappiness and frustration and expression of emotion coming from their kid than others. Whatever their boundaries are, if you can respect them (even if you disagree) you will get better results. Even as you deal with the push and pull over how much closeness you have, how much you rely on them, and how much you value what they think, it's always somewhat easier on everyone if you muster up some respect.

◆ **See what's good.** Find what is positive, alive, interesting, inspiring, and supportive, and acknowledge that, too. Even parents who are caught in their own addictions or problems love their children and wish to protect them. They might hurt their children because they do not have the knowledge, experience, or ability to be good parents. As far as you are concerned, you're better off fostering good, healthy connections with them rather than viewing them as totally flawed, disappointing human beings. Remember that culture is a potent force in shaping families today. Like you, your folks live in a confusing world.

If you can find and highlight all the ways that your parents support you—the times when they are loving and kind, generous and thoughtful, protective and helpful—and tell this story as well, you will find relief there, too. Even Kate, who calls her alcoholic mom Satan, visibly relaxes when I suggest that while we are acknowledging her struggle with her mom we should also acknowledge her mom's good qualities. Like most of the young women I work with, Kate feels both guilty and gratified when trashing her mom but still yearns for the connection to be fixed and the mothering to be restored (or the relationship to be healed and healthy).

There is one more very compelling reason to find and focus on the things our parents do well and their positive traits: We inherit much of who they are, both through DNA and osmosis. We are like them in many ways, yet often we don't even recognize that until later in life, or after much therapy. We *suspect* we are like them. Sometimes we fear it. Sometimes we rebel against it. Sometimes we appreciate it. The process of accepting, tolerating, appreciating, and forgiving our parents for who they are is a lifelong one. But it's important because it parallels our own journey to know ourselves and give ourselves some slack.

The truth, then? It is not about changing your parents; it's about forging new pathways. Being the leader in good communication is rarely wrong. There is a wide range of emotional responses you can get from your parents when you use new words. There are no guarantees that new words will yield new feelings or different results, but it's worth a try. New words will certainly yield you dignity. And they will yield you the knowledge that you are trying and can, in fact, do something different. They show that you have options, choices, and some tricks up your sleeve.

You can be angry, hurt, and right, and still use new words—better words. You can feel hatred, frustration, anger, and fear; let them breathe; and then come back around to the other side of the street where support and love still live in some form. Good intentions can and do count in your parents' favor, and effort matters, too. You and your parents know that your own biology and being young come with age-appropriate wacky moods. Sometimes this is just the stuff of growing up, even if you are well into your twenties.

Sometimes parents remain stuck and stubborn in spite of new words and a calmer tone. They are not likely to readily drop their defenses, own their own mistakes, respond compassionately and appropriately but not provocatively, and swaddle you with understanding; new words often need a lot of repetition over time. But they might. They might yield a little. Even if part of you wants to continue the battle, if you are willing to give some new words a chance to take effect, you might get a better kind of attention than you ever dreamed possible.

CHAPTER 9

A Separate Peace

*I suspect the most we can hope for, and it's no small
hope, is that we never give up, that we never stop giving
ourselves permission to try to love and receive love.*

—ELIZABETH STROUT, *Abide with Me*

WHENEVER THE subject of parents comes up in my office, I know
that it's time to be extra softly vigilant about protecting everyone's
feelings. So many different ones come rushing to the surface. Guilt
about talking about them, relief at being able to discuss the problem, pain, anger, and shame. Fear of hurting them, betraying them,
losing them, and not ever getting what we need from them. And
longing. Longing to work it through. And desire. Desire to not just
be able to act or have them act, different, but to feel different and
different about them. To shift away from experiencing them only in
their shortcomings, difficulties, or addictions. And you can. It takes
some patience and some willingness to sort it through, but there
is light on the other side of your anger, your hurt, and their stuff.

Who Are These People?

"And why are they so important to me? Damn. Why do I both crave
their attention and hate them at the same time? How do I stay connected in a healthy way?"

I hear these questions all the time, and they are hard to answer. I think the sprint toward independence starts when you leave the womb. Really. It's one long goodbye. And it's a goodbye you both want and don't want at the same time. But it's also one long hello—a continuous negotiating of your physical and emotional dependency, your separateness, and your sameness. A hello to your real self and a hello to a relationship with your parents and a way of experiencing them that is healthy, nourishing, or at least workable.

Certainly if you come from a stormy house, or even one with gentle breezes of conflict (most of us do!), you can go round and round with how to do this and with wanting to be close to your parents and wanting some distance from them.

Some of us have parents who don't pay all that much attention to us. They are busy with their own business, and we are just mouths they have to feed—or at least it feels that way. Others grow up at the epicenter of the house—as either the joy of their parents' hearts or the pain. And certainly if your parents are very ill or actively in an addiction, the process of getting to a better place with them and with yourself vis-à-vis (or in relationship to) them, has many more folds to it. Much is expected, much is hoped for—and much is the burden. It can be difficult either way. That's why it helps to understand more about who our parents are and what they are and are not capable of. And to understand more about how and why we see them the way we do, because that can change, and that change can help—a lot. Parents can be great at certain things while falling flat on others. This can feel jolting to us and frightening at times. One young woman I knew was so confused about her parents and how to get some attention and understanding from her mom that she incited riots.

Knowing exactly how to provoke your parents is a wonderful way to get things all revved up. It's a gift, really (though there might be a better way). It is most definitely a way to get love and hate going all at the same time.

Kelly, seventeen, who is just barely maintaining her body weight agreement with her nutritionist, routinely likes to annoy her parents—just to, well, annoy her parents. She tells me that she often shouts obscenities at her mom. Without fail, this always wins her a slap in the face. She then recedes into muttering under her breath, and it escalates from there. It usually ends with Kelly walking out the door.

I ask Kelly why she starts this routine. "I don't know," she replies. "It's just what we do." But then she adds, "She gets me so angry with all her yelling that I just have to yell back. I just have to take her down, even if it gets me slapped. Hey, at least she knows I'm in the room and not just the person who is supposed to walk the dog."

"Hmm," I reply, which is therapist talk for "Tell me more." So Kelly tells me that she doesn't really mind the actual hit itself, and she really likes getting a rise out of her mother and watching her get out of control. In fact she does other things to provoke her, like sneering at her, hiding her car keys, and refusing to eat dinner. Kelly wants her mother to lose it; then Kelly can be sure who the crazy one is—and it's not Kelly.

I think that we have some road ahead of us. Best to settle in. This might be what Kelly really needs—someone to settle in with her—no cures, no mandates, no weight checks. Just some settling in.

Many sessions go by; the weeks roll on. We sit together and talk. We think about slapping, love, attention, and being hungry. We think about fat, fear, never getting enough of anything, and having to do too much for yourself. We talk about how being too important can feel like a burden and not feeling important enough can feel like rejection.

Eventually we figure out that provoking her mother is Kelly's way of letting her know how angry she is and how unsettled she feels. It's a terrific way to let off steam, but while it's mildly scratching the itch for attention, it is not leaving Kelly with much dignity or true relief. Kelly is holding a huge grudge against her mom for many things, but mostly because her mom couldn't keep Kelly's dad from moving out (at least this is what it looks like from Kelly's angle).

It's not only that Kelly wants her mom's attention, or even that she wants her mom to get crazy; Kelly wants to communicate how crazy and angry and messed-up she feels. Kelly is getting her mom to experience all the feelings that Kelly herself is feeling. She wants her mom to suffer because she is so frustrated and angry with her.

Think about it for a sec. If you don't have the words, or you think your words will fall on deaf ears, what can you do? You let your subconscious self take over. You do things to get your message across without even thinking about it.

Kelly and I decide to study her actions a bit more objectively and consider what they really mean. We consider how to have a better relationship with someone you also want to make suffer. We muse over the fact that parents are not just part of the problem; they are part of the solution. And we marvel at how complicated and confusing it all is.

Over time we figure out that even small changes can help (like no more name-calling or a few well-placed apologies—even a "thank you" here and there). Kelly does not want to lead the way with her mom, but she is doing it. I don't mind her swearing or her in-your-face attitude in our sessions together, but they're not leading to a better place outside my office. Sooner or later she'll start letting up a bit and mellowing out some. And as we talk, life becomes a little less hostile. The words are feeding us, and we are not starving anymore.

Moving Out

One of the most difficult challenges for young women who are thinking about recovery is how to make progress when you are living under the same roof with your family and swirling around in the same old family dynamics, even if those dynamics are not necessarily difficult ones. Even good situations can keep you stuck sometimes, especially good situations in which you are comfortable in basic and predictable ways. It's hard to leave when things are bad, but it's often harder when things are good. This can be a real snafu because many young women live at home well into their twenties or even longer.

Since at least some eating- or self-injury-disorder stuff has to do with parents, can you get better if things are not resolved and you are still living in the turmoil? The answer is yes, you can. If you are ready to get better, you can get better no matter where you live or with whom. And if you are not ready, no matter what kind of geographic change you make you will still be where you are.

But for many people, recovering is a lot easier out of the house, just like it's easier to put on skis when you're not sliding down the hill and it's easier to see the landscape from a distance.

It is true that the support of living at home is a great relief in many ways. Even if you are old enough to live on your own, the financial and security benefits of living at home can outweigh moving out. But relationships with parents get better when you are not constantly up against house rules, daily expectations, disappointments, annoyances, and arguments, and when you are not bumping into each other's characters all the time. If even only part of your self-attack and your self-attacking voice is triggered by your parents, it's better to have some space.

I've known kids who moved out, either to college or just to be on their own, and blew it fast and big. The separation was just too much.

The comforts of home—even the battles and the frustrations—were better than being away. The craving for closeness can outweigh the need for independence even when things are rocky. And it can take a while to forge a new closeness from independence.

Therapists watch for repetitions—behaviors that repeat and patterns and situations that happen again and again in one way or another. Most repetitions are not done on purpose. Some therapists believe that you keep coming back around to things to try to work them out better. We repeat negative experiences unconsciously, setting ourselves up for them, partly because it's what we have learned to do to protect ourselves and survive, and partly in the hope that things will work out differently if we just keep at it. And sometimes going back to the same old feelings is comforting and familiar, even though the coping mechanisms that helped us survive childhood can hinder us going forward.

When you are trying to get well but are suffering from hurt and pain and general self-loathing, it's helpful to look for patterns in your life and in your relationships. And ultimately it's easier to discover your patterns when you are not living at home. Your recovery needs to be on your terms, because you are interested and ready to go there. It is best not to be interrupted too often by parents who are desperate, frustrated, or even loving; they will figure into the mix one way or another and you can end up in knots.

When I was little I used to worry about my parents dying. I always hoped that when they did, it would be at a time when I was angry with them. To my young mind, if they died when I hated them, it would hurt less. I'd be glad they were gone. It would make losing them easier.

It's not that you *want* to feel bad feelings toward your parents—and you certainly don't want to get stuck in such feelings for too long—but on some level you *need* to feel those feelings. Painful as they can be, bad feelings can help you create your own future; one that is separate from your parents—and sustainable; one that will forge a path to richer, smoother relationships with them. Sometimes it is the bad feelings that help motivate you to work toward the better feelings; they don't always have to pull you down further into the darkness.

There are no easy answers to if or when you should move out. Nothing is really the norm anymore. Certainly if you are dangerously ill, too young, or unable to support yourself financially, moving out is not an option.

At home or not, though, parents live with you in certain ways all of your life. You need to know that you can be close and separate at the same time, and you should learn those boundaries for yourself by sensing when your parents' involvement feels comforting and when it feels intrusive.

One of the advantages of moving out is that you will not encounter being told what to do as much. Being told what to do often has an oppositional effect. Most people value a parent's opinion (on some level), or are at least affected by it. Being told to eat can make you *not* want to eat; being told to stop eating can make you *want* to eat. Even the most well-intentioned, protective parents, behaving in the most low-key way possible, can induce a kid into oppositional rage and defiance. You are less defiant when you are not living under the same roof. When pleasing or infuriating parents becomes a diminished part of the mix, it's just a drop easier to face personal truths, take responsibility for your actions, and take on recovery for its own sake—for your sake, for goodness sake.

So It Must Be Me

Jane always keeps her coat on in my office. The season doesn't matter—she has cover and she keeps her small body wrapped up. Maybe she's hiding her body from me; maybe she feels safer with extra layers between us. Therapy can feel a bit too raw on occasion.

Jane and I talk about her mom a lot, a subject she is both afraid of and attracted to. She is different from Lani, who loves to talk about her mom, letting me know in no uncertain terms that her mom is a big pain on a regular basis. Lani's fury is front and center. But Jane's is tucked away somewhere underneath her guilt and confusion. Both girls have similar problems with their mothers. Both mothers compare their daughters to other girls, often saying things like "Most girls your age have jobs by now" or "Kaye looks so good these days. I'll bet if you exercised like she does, you'd feel so much better." Neither mother seems to think she is being insulting, hurtful, or critical, or is conveying a message of despair or judgment. Neither mother seems to understand that her daughter turns these comparisons into self-attack.

Not every daughter hears these kinds of statements the way that Jane and Lani do, or has the same frustration. But many do. And they suffer for it. Both Jane's and Lani's mothers tend to give advice instead of asking their daughters if they would like suggestions, and both mothers start many sentences with phrases like "You could have . . ." or "Why didn't you . . ." or "You are so . . ."

Both Jane and Lani sometimes think their mothers are right; that objectively what their mothers are saying is true: If Jane believed in herself more, she could probably land a good job. If Lani helped out around the house without arguing so much, she could get along better with her brother.

But it's not that easy. Jane and Lani both understand, somewhere deep inside, that their mothers really do want good for them. They know that even in their overzealous attempts to push them forward into recovery and life, their mothers are not really trying to hurt them. Yet they do hurt them. Often. And it's hard to separate out the right from the not-so-right.

When Jane and Lani hear these comments from their mothers, they feel anger, frustration, and guilt. It becomes a lose-lose situation. They figure, "If I agree with Mom's statements in my own mind, it must mean that I *am* idiotic, lazy, stupid, or slow." For many daughters, this starts the snowball of self-attack. Every daughter believes what her mother tells her—even if she doesn't want to. Emotionally, we believe.

Then they figure, "If I disagree in my own mind with Mom's words, that means my *mother* is wrong, stupid, and doesn't understand me. And that is often worse. So *it must be me!*" They constructed the perfect, ironic concert of fury and guilt. "Who should I hate, my mother or myself? Who is the dumb one, me or my mother?" Neither is a good choice.

Jane wants to cut when she feels like this, and Lani wants to eat like there's no tomorrow.

It's not uncommon to want to punish the people who frustrate you. This includes yourself, and it definitely includes your parents. It's always easier to punish yourself than your parents, though many people get rather good at doing both.

Just because your mother is right does not mean you are a lazy, stupid piece of disappointing garbage, and just because she is wrong does not mean that she is garbage.

Both Jane and Lani try to work out these complicated feelings. Jane works on the idea that she is allowed to get angry with her mother and that it won't kill either of them. Lani tells me that her mother always encourages her, even when Lani herself knows that she is being ridiculous about something. Her mother, who is always trying to get Lani to try new things to help her recover from the eating disorder, often does not let Lani know when she is upset with her. She saves it up until she blows, and by then it's so hot that neither of them can get out of the fight unscathed.

Lani and I talk about how she sometimes does not feel like walking the dog, the one chore her mother asks of her. Lani "forgets," and her mother ends up doing it. Lani tells me this with a mix of guilt and joy. I smile and tell her that she can be a real pain in the tush sometimes. She laughs and says, "You got that right."

The truth is that we are all a pain in the tush sometimes, and it can be liberating.

My friend Wendy, who is forty-three, says that every time her mother comes for a visit she makes a comment about how much dust there is on the ceiling fans and how bad that is for the kids' allergies.

Most of the time now, when Wendy is in a good place within herself, she knows that her mother is just, well, her mother, and that she's simply chattering. Maybe she thinks she's being helpful or she just wants to chime in and feel more a part of things, but when Wendy is not in a good place within herself, it still makes her want to crawl into a hole—or push her mother into one. She feels deeply criticized, inadequate, and frustrated, just like she did when she was younger. All kinds of aggression instantly come oozing out from the small child who still lives inside my middle-aged friend. "Will I ever totally outgrow this?" she asks me each time her mother arrives. "Maybe," I tell her. "But what's the rush?"

Part Three

TOOLS FOR LIFE

CHAPTER 10

A Wise and Gentle Mind

It's funny: I always imagined when I was a kid that adults had some kind of inner toolbox full of shiny tools: the saw of discernment, the hammer of wisdom, the sandpaper of patience. But then when I grew up I found that life handed you these rusty bent old tools—friendships, prayer, conscience, honesty—and said "Do the best you can with these, they will have to do." And mostly, against all odds, they do.

—ANNE LAMOTT, *Traveling Mercies: Some Thoughts on Faith*

I HAVE always loved train stations. There is to me, something thrilling about standing on the platform waiting for the rush. I love the quiet before the train is near. I love the first rustle of wind that hints at its impending arrival. I love seeing its nose peek around the corner or appear as a tiny dot in the distance. I love the whoosh as a train rushes past or the slowing down as it pull in. I love knowing that I could get on . . . or not.

To me, thoughts are like trains. My mind is full of trains, there are thousands of them all the time pulling into and out of the station that is my mind. Some of the trains I hop on, not even aware that I have done so. Others I let rush past. And some linger in the station. Others still I ride because they are familiar, they are regulars in my station. And even though they take me to the same destination every time, often not a desirable one, I still hop on.

One of the biggest drawbacks of riding the same old trains is that when I am on one, I am not in the station anymore and I am missing out on other trains, ones that might possibly take me to a better place.

I know now that I do not have to ride every train, that it is OK to let them pull in and pull back out of the station that is my mind without me having to hop on. I don't have to act on my thoughts and feelings. Often, if I just leave them be, they pull in and out all on their own.

But when the trains are coming fast and furious and the power of the feelings is overwhelming, and there is no quiet in the station, I need help sorting out the trains I want to ride and the ones that I don't.

At the Intersection of Emotional Pain and Recovery

Somewhere deep in your heart is a place where recovering from the disorder and healing emotional pain meet. There is a pool of quiet wisdom that when tapped into can bring you forward in the most unexpected and amazing ways.

I know that the disorder is not only or all about what you do with your feelings. The reality of dealing with food (and your body) and/or self-injury is a right-sized problem in its own right. But when things are totally out of control in your life, your food, your weight, and your body seem like the only things you can get a handle on, even when you can't.

Your feelings are guideposts to living a good and whole life with meaning and a strong sense of self. They do not have to destroy you.

Whether you are still grappling with recovery in its early stages or are some distance from physical self-harm; whether you feel justified in your hurt, frustrated by it, or knocked out by it, the energy in your feelings can be a life force that fuels your creativity, your sense of self, and your journey. So this is where your disorder and your pain meet up, and it is where healing emotional pain and recovery join hands and walk forward side by side, together.

The tools that follow can help you tend to and get relief from emotional pain so that recovery can get and keep a foothold—so that you can quiet your mind and open your heart. So that you can get on the better trains. You can use these tools over and over and over again, for the whole of your life.

Meeting Yourself

Sometimes well after midnight, when I am overtired, I start to imagine all kinds of eerie, spooky, deathly, awful things. I think someone might be in the hallway. I think about ghastly events that I've seen on the news. I decide that I am (God forbid) right that minute dying from some deadly disease and will not make it to a ripe old age. I decide that my writing is and always will be garbage. I consider whether there really are aliens. I stare at the night sky trying to figure out who created God, and I ponder my husband's favorite question: Can God make a rock that God cannot lift?

My heart starts to pump more heavily, my breathing quickens, and my head feels like it's sinking in. In my worst moments I might get on the computer and write (and send!) someone a message that comes from this place of distortion and desperation. I do not make good decisions in the middle of the night when I am tired and impulsive. Late at night my inner irrational fear monster and his naysayer pals wake up, yawn, stretch, and spring into action in my mind. These things I know about myself.

I can guess about why this happens to me; it's good grist for the mill. But I try, whenever possible, to go to bed before overtiredness sets in. I also know that heights make me nervous and that I can be horribly argumentative, impatient, and fixated on ideas when I think I am right. I have trouble crying, even when I am desperately and wretchedly sad. I am also loving, generous, kind, and open-minded, and I can always see the good in everyone. I'm a great listener (a good thing, given my job), and I know how to say no and feel OK about it. Most of the time.

I am often urgent about getting things done and have to ask myself, "Does it have to be done? Does it have to be done now? And does it have to be done by me?" The answers are sometimes yes. And because I am well and far along in my recovery journey, I usually show up and honor my commitments. Other times my urgency and compulsive overdoing act up. Then I know the answers are no. When food calls to me on sporadic occasions, it often calls much louder late at night, so hanging around the kitchen at odd late hours is a bad idea. Because I know these things about myself, I am better situated to make wise decisions.

My point: In the long journey out of self-attack, it's good to meet yourself. Knowing yourself well will not cure you, but it will help—a lot. It will help you protect yourself, take care of yourself, and leave yourself alone. It will help you know when and where you should or should not be, what you need to work on and plan for, and when to maybe get some help.

Knowing yourself means knowing your character traits, limitations, and fears, and what you value, look forward to, and dream about. The 12-step folks call it "taking an inventory." The eating- and self-injury-disorder folks call it "knowing your disordered voice and separating it from your true self." Same goals: to learn what your deep beliefs are and what messages your brain tells you, and to respond in a way that brings freedom, relief, and serenity. Those pull you toward life.

Without judging yourself, make a list—as long as possible—of all your positive traits. Be honest, be willing, and be fair. And if you really and truly can't get started, ask someone you think would be willing to help you out. But do it.

Then make a list of your negative traits. It is very important to know that "negative" character traits or "flaws" are just survival instincts (*defenses* in therapy speak) that worked well for us in the past and helped us to survive when we were younger but now as we grow do not serve us the same way and can even get us into trouble.

Before you make this list, imagine yourself holding a giant baseball bat above your head. Now imagine yourself putting down the bat and sitting in a comfy chair and saying, "Well, OK, honest and easy there, Love, it's just a pen." Remind yourself that taking stock of negative traits does not mean beating yourself up about them. It just means taking note of them. Then make your list. (This listing process can take hours, days, or months—and for some, years—and the lists are alive; they can change and grow.)

Next make a list of all your fears. You don't have to do anything about them for now, but write them down. When you are ready to do something about them, you can make a list of reassurances and responses regarding your fears. You will most likely need help with the reassurances from someone you trust. But first, know—know what frightens you.

You can take this list of fears and write down where you think each fear came from and how it might have protected you in the past. Sometimes it's helpful to study if or how you perpetuate a fear (like staying up too late, in my case, perpetuates my fear of being harmed or useless), and what you can do about it. (My fears may have protected me at one time in my life by keeping me from situations that I was not prepared to handle. Now, however, they hold me back from accomplishing the things I want to accomplish in life, like writing this book.)

Now make a list of all the things you like. And make another of the things you would rather avoid—things that trigger you and things that excite you; things that you know to be true about you and your body. (Try for now to leave out all things fat. This is not an exercise in healing body-hate or listing all the ways your body is awful. It's a way to get know what your body needs. Like how much sleep or vitamin D you need.)

◆

I know, for example, that my body craves sugar; if I start with it, I end up in the gutter. I spent most of my life trying to prove this wrong, without success. So now I know, and I accept that this is true. I live accordingly. I do not eat processed sugar. I eat many other delicious foods, but sugar, for my body, is a trip to hell.

I know that when I am hungry, I feel it in my thighs. Then my head feels like butterflies have taken up residence, and I get jittery.

Hungry or not, I am most often—even in the middle of a New Jersey July—cold. I can show you the goose bumps on my arms to prove it. So I dress accordingly.

When I am tired, my eyes burn, my feet feel like they are made of cement, and I am grumpy as all get-out. Do not try to reason with me when I am tired.

When I get a certain feeling building up in me like a freight train coming, I know that I had best use my Phone-a-Friend before I take any kind of action. Someone else needs to hear my intentions before I get myself into trouble. I know it's best for me to consult with someone I trust before I say or do anything I might regret. And I usually know which ears to tell. I know who will just agree with me and who will give me advice; I know who will feel competitive and who will be honest, even if I won't like what they say.

◆

It's a great idea to write out on paper, or at least visualize in your head, a map of your body. Study where you feel what. Differentiate feelings from bodily sensations. It's true that you can be emotionally hungry, or tired from emotional pain. With a nod of honor to the mind/body connection, start to study the difference between what your body is experiencing and what you are feeling. Notice where in your body you feel anger, loneliness, regret, and shame, and where you feel tired, sore, bloated, or stressed.

Make a wish list, a dream list, an "if I had wings" list, a list of what gives you pleasure. This one might be the hardest of all, but do it anyway. Start with a good book, or a funny movie, or having your back rubbed. Borrow some from my list if you're stuck—long walks, planting a garden, hot showers, sunshine on your face—if they suit you.

There is no rush, and as I've said, this tool is alive and changeable. It will help you pause and take a deep breath and learn as much about yourself as you can.

Back Talk

You are a fat ugly pig. That you cannot find a part-time job is proof that you will go nowhere in life. You deserve to die, and your parents are a mess because of you. If you do not lose three pounds by Friday you have to run six extra miles. And if you eat today you will look even more like a horse. You cannot stand your ugly sister and her stupid boyfriend. You are a failure and a disgrace. Cut. Eat. Don't touch that sandwich.

Hello Voice. Monster. Destroyer. Commander in Chief. Some call it their disease; some call it ED; some call it cognition or negative thinking. There are a thousand names. But I believe that you have to learn to hear it, and you have to talk back. You can, if you are able, think of the voice's messages as the trains that you do not want to ride, and let them pull into and back out of the station without paying them much mind. But if they are stubborn and if you keep hopping on board, then you most likely have to talk back.

I first learned about the voice from Dr. Terry Sandbeck, who wrote *The Deadly Diet: Recovering from Anorexia and Bulimia.* Dr. Sandbeck's method is a direct, easy-to-follow path. The Alcoholics Anonymous Big Book Awakenings method used by many in 12-step recovery programs is also a solid path to freedom from the voice. Though it is beyond the scope of this chapter, you can access it through most 12-step rooms.

Here are just a few examples of some wrong trains, ED thoughts or lies that many ED and self-injury voices have in common that are not necessarily related to food and weight:

There is no point in trying. You are worthless. You never do anything right. You are so embarrassing. Nobody else has these problems. You are going to end up even more alone than you already are. Nobody really cares about you. You are a loser. You are not as good as other people. You are stupid. You are not capable of love. Everyone has to approve of me for me to be happy. If I don't make someone happy I am a failure. My parents' marriage problems are my fault. I cannot be happy unless I have all the relationships I want with the people I want them with. I'm always missing out. I should know better. Other people don't have problems like I do. They are happier. I can't change anything. If I am not hard on myself I will really never accomplish anything. Pleasure is wrong. If you enjoy things you will get punished for it. I have to do everything I think of doing. It is awful to be wrong. I need to be special in the eyes of others or I don't matter at all. What other people think of me is the most important thing. My value and self-worth are dependent on what others think about me. I have to always prove myself. I am not safe. Everything is all about me. I can't get anything or everything I really need. If I really mattered other people would behave better around me or toward me. My body is awful. If I stop worrying something bad will happen. I should be able to fix things.

The sneaky thing about these thoughts is that there is usually a small kernel of truth to them, so it gets pretty confusing. For example, your ED voice might be saying something like "If you relax you are wasting time." So this might be true, but the voice behind the voice is really the problem—what I like to call the sneaky chaser voice, because we often don't keep listening after the first part. And that voice says "Wasting time is terrible and therefore you are terrible." But really wasting time is not always so terrible, sometimes it is wonderful and necessary and revitalizing. And either way, even if you are wasting time that you shouldn't be wasting, you are still not terrible or worthless or a skank. You are just you, growing and going along in life and not being perfect because nobody is.

In the many years since I first learned about the voice, I've seen many different approaches to hearing and responding to it. No matter what road you travel down in recovery, listen to that voice and the lies it tells you, and tell it the truth. It's like a storm during the day—you might not always see the lightning, but you hear the thunder. The thunder is the bad feeling. The thunder is the razor in your thigh, the finger down your throat, the scale beneath your feet for the hundredth time this morning. It is your racing heart, your empty stomach, your dizzy head.

Imagine if this voice were outside you, following you around all the time, yapping insults nonstop all day and all night. This is what you are up against. Learn to talk back. Tell it to shut up. Learn to hear what it says with discernment, get to know the worst things it says to you, and write out responses so you can be ready when you hear it.

---◆---

To find out if the voice is at work, you can pretty much bet that if you are feeling awful—not just sad, but awful—including self-pity, self-hate, and hating others—the voice is coming at you. If your fingers are down your throat, you are not allowed to eat until 7 p.m., you have had three pints of ice cream, you are pin-pricking your upper arm, driving way too fast, taking too many pills, or shoving your dinner in the garbage, the voice is at work. If you cannot get out of bed, doubt you can ever go to class again, think everyone is talking about you—yes, the voice is at work. If you are deep in depression, guilt, resentment, or irrational fear, the voice is at work.

And you have to talk back.

---◆---

Of course the voice does not want you to talk back. It will tell you that I am lying to you about that. It wants to survive. It will tell you that it is protecting you. It will tell you that you are the exception to the rule.

Every single client I have ever worked with—eating disorder, self-injury disorder, or otherwise—has had the voice. Sometimes the voice likes you to think that it serves the purpose of protecting you by letting you attack yourself first, with the idea that you will then be numb to whatever anyone else has to say to you or about you—like an emotional vaccination. Or maybe the voice that speaks to you is just a skipping record of all the mean, critical insults that have ever been hurled at you. The voice wants you to be comfortable whacking yourself because it thinks it will keep you on your toes in some way, or drive you forward to better things—like a whip to a donkey.

Either way, healing does not happen via abuse—your own or anyone else's.

If you were walking down the street and happened upon a small girl lying in the gutter, curled up in a ball, crying, fists in mouth, shaking with fear, you would not (I am guessing here, but I think I can say) walk up to her and kick her hard in the head, and then again in the back, and once more in the stomach, spit on her, and walk away.

When you attack yourself with words or weapons, you are kicking the frightened child—the frightened child in you. What if, instead, you ran a gentle hand over her head and told her that you know she is scared—that it's a big, wide street, but if she wants to cross, scary as it is, you are there to help. There is no rush; no one has to be pushed, bullied, or hurt to get to the other side.

Hearing the voice, discovering its lies, and talking back is soothing and life-giving and empowering to both the child and the blooming adult that you are becoming.

Clappers in the Closet

My friend Ellen says that some days, when her mood has been in the gutter and all she can manage to do is get to work, do her job, and get back home again, she feels like she should get a standing ovation. She actually walks over to the coat closet in the entrance hall of her home and opens the door and—yes, she really does this—imagines that there is a large audience of people in the closet clapping for her. On really bad days, they are on their feet, whistling and cheering and smiling and hooting. Ellen says that if anyone really knew what an effort it took just to get through the day when she is depressed—if they really understood—they would get on their feet and clap away for her.

I know what she means. We all need a cheering squad. I think this need goes beyond appreciation and recognition. I think it even goes beyond encouragement. I think it is a need for acknowledgment in some deep and psychic way. The clappers are saying, "You go, girl!" "You did it!" "We get it!" "We get you!" "We know what it took!" "We know who you are, baby!"

There are days when you've just done the ordinary, but given your life it really should count as extraordinary. And it does. To me, it does. When you need a good, genuine, knowing nod, with a deep look into your tired eyes, consider that this is that nod. Just for reading this sentence you can take a deep bow and say to your audience, "Thank you. Yes indeed. Thank you very much!"

When someone hurts you or ignores you or excludes you, and you can find it in your head to listen to what the voice is saying and talk back; if you can sit with that bad feeling; or run or walk or cry or write it out; or make a list of the top five reasons why what they did had nothing to do with you; or figure out what mistake you might have made and then count it as one of the normal mistakes that humans are allowed to make each day, and then forgive yourself—if you do any one of these things you get to open the closet door and let the clappers do their thing for you.

You Need Credit and Encouragement

We all need credit, and sometimes there is no one there to give it to us. So we have to use the clappers. And if you feel too silly to imagine your own clappers, you can borrow mine anytime you need them. They are really Ellen's anyway, but I checked with her and she said we are all welcome to them and that they do a fantastic job. They consist of all sorts of kind people. There's no need to go into detail about what they look like or who they are; just know that they are there, and that they know, and that they are doing whatever kind of clapping you need at the moment.

There are too few genuine and reliable sources of good feelings and good feedback, and you tend to excuse or dismiss the good stuff when you hear it. It's often no match for all the negative words that are already paved in your brain.

It's easy to forget that the basics of getting through a day when in recovery or healing from emotional pain are like running the 100-yard dash with flip-flops on. You can do it, but when you break the ribbon at the end and there is no one at the finish line (and often there is not), you have to clap for yourself. You can let someone you trust know about your victories, but you have to credit yourself. Do this without shame, without fanfare, and without hesitation.

I am not suggesting you cultivate conceit, arrogance, or entitlement. I am a fan of humility, so I am humbly telling you that it's not only OK but necessary to keep track of your successes, small and large. Stock them on a shelf in your brain where you can easily pull them down and look at them regularly. Or better yet, write them down.

Until your pain subsides and you feel more confident about who you are, you can use the clappers. You might not always need them, or maybe just once in a while, but when you are in need of some acknowledgment and there is none to be found, and not much inside you yet, borrow the clappers.

Your Side of the Street

Many of us walk around thinking that we are not allowed to make mistakes. We have the distinct idea that mistakes are only for the stupid and the slow. Striving toward perfection is considered to be at the core of many anorexic psyches; many young women are obsessed with perfection. When it comes to recovery, if you hang on to your idea that perfection is achievable, you are hanging on to a greasy rope.

Perfectionism gets a lot of bad press—for good reason. The raw truth about perfectionism is that it's a decoy for actually owning your own stuff and taking responsibility for when you screw up. You need self-responsibility like you need water because you will screw up along the way and the best way to deal with it is to take responsibility for it without being too hard on yourself.

Karen, a young woman I work with, had a huge blowup with her friend Amy. Karen and Amy had a ritual: every time they said goodbye after being together, one would say, "Love ya, Babe," and the other would say, "Back at ya, kiss kiss."

Amy's boyfriend Ted hated this ritual with a passion and often said so. He had asked them not to do it in front of him. One Friday night, after a few beers and a lot of laughs, Karen initiated the ritual in front of Ted. Ted blew up, and one thing led to another, leaving Amy and Karen in tears. The next day Karen got a text from Amy saying that if Karen started it again in front of Ted, Amy would just walk away. She just wanted to let Karen know this.

Karen is brokenhearted. She thinks, *Not only is Amy choosing Ted, but she is telling me what to do, and in a text no less.* So Karen ignores Amy, and then they don't speak for weeks, and when they do, things are off-kilter.

Karen thinks that she did not do anything so wrong, and that Amy is an idiot to have sent that in a text. Amy and her boyfriend must hate her. She never wants to talk to either of them again. She feels hurt, angry, embarrassed, and alone. "Stupid, stupid me" is the mantra in her head, along with "You should've known better. You never do anything right. You're a loser. Why do you even bother with friends?" And also, "He's such a jerk. I can't stand him. And if this is what she wants, then she can forget about being with me, too." And off to the bathroom she goes with her favorite piece of cutting glass. A few slices to the upper thigh, some bright red blood, and a few new pinked-up welts, and all is calm again. Karen is once again amazed at how physical pain trumps emotional pain, and she can forget all about it. Almost.

But what if Karen could think, "You know, I did say I would not do that in front of Ted anymore. And I knew I should not have been drinking with the two of them, it usually ends up in a bad place. And even though I think Ted is ridiculous and there is no reason for this to bug him, I could've been more respectful. And I did tell Amy last month that I hate direct confrontations, and that if she ever had to tell me anything, she could just text it."

What if Karen could be curious about which one of her fears or character issues were coming into play here? Was it her fear that she did not really matter or count? Is that why she did the ritual in front of Ted and forgot not to after Amy had specifically asked her not to? Did she stop speaking to Amy for a while and ignore her because in her earlier experiences saying her feelings usually got her into more pain and trouble and ignoring whoever had hurt her was the safest way to go?

What if Karen calls Ted and says, "I am sorry"? And she calls Amy and says, "I am sorry"? And then she calls herself and says, "I am sorry. I am allowed to screw up, own my end of things, and say I am sorry. Even if I think Ted is a jerk"?

I want you to know that I am always right. Except when I am not. And so are you. Except when you are not. And it's OK. I am not suggesting that you should apologize for things you don't do, nor am I suggesting that you blame yourself. I am suggesting that you find the grown-up middle ground where you take an honest look to see if or what you might have done better and what your role in the problem might have been. Sometimes we are too self-protective and sometimes not enough. We have to be curious about the truth of it.

It is far from easy to own your part in things, and often it's hard to sort out what your part is anyway. We get into snafus all the time, and it can take a lot of time to learn about and understand our different motives and needs and why we do what we do. It helps to have some assistance. And not from someone who has too much of a personal interest in your being wrong—or right for that matter. I'm thinking sponsor, therapist, mentor, counselor, or coach type. Or at least someone who knows about her own side of the street, that mistakes are human and amends are healthy, and that not every "I'm sorry" is going to land on good ears, create a good feeling, or bring relief. Sometimes it's best not to say the sorry, but just to know it. But either way, when you are thinking of having a different life that does not involve living in your secret bathroom world, you do need to admit it when you screw up. It can actually be a relief if you do it seriously and gently at the same time.

It's the stuff recovery is made of. It's the stuff healing from emotional pain is made of. It's the stuff health, wellness, and progress are made of:

> **Part one**: Know your character and your "shortcomings" as
> well as you can.
> **Part two:** Look at your role in whatever problems you have.
> Remember, when doing this: put down the bat—it's just
> you and your humanness. Or you and your effort to
> understand your unconscious mind better. You can decide
> that someday you will tend to your character flaws but for
> the moment it's OK to just know about them so that when
> they creep up again up and knock on the door you won't be
> so spooked by them.

Karen shares with me a particular memory she has of her mother yelling at her. There were ants crawling all over the kitchen, and her mother went crazy shrieking at her and calling her names. Then her mother was silent—for days. Karen begins to cry as she tells me this story, and when I ask what the tears are for, she tells me that they are tears of shame. She cries and cries, and the shame just comes tumbling out. She feels shame for leaving food crumbs. She feels shame for her revenge fantasy—for wishing her mother dead. She feels shame for forgetting to clean up the spilled apple juice that brought all the ants marching.

Then, after more crying, Karen tells me that she is feeling something new. She is not sure exactly what it is, but it smells like relief. We talk a lot that day about hating people we love, about blaming ourselves, and about the quirky way the unconscious mind works. We talk about how Karen often forgets things, like Amy asking her not to use certain words, and how that might be because Karen got used to forgetting things so she could make her mother furious just to get back at her, and maybe to protect herself from having to take more responsibility for things she does not want to do. We talk about how forgetting things sometimes makes her seem cute or endearing to her friends. And sometimes when she forgets things her mother lets her off the hook instead of getting angry. It's not always one thing. But forgetting does have a big downside, and for Karen it's starting to outweigh the upside.

After the ant incident, Karen tried to read, blast music, cut deeply—anything to forget the pain and fear of those moments. We marvel at how sometimes your mind repeats things unconsciously, like forgetting, in order to protect and defend you from too much hurt. And how learning about that can go a long way in getting to know yourself.

Some time later, Karen tells me that she and her mother were talking and the ant incident came up. Her mom said, "I was having such a bad time that day. I was getting my period, and my boss had just called to tell me he was cutting my hours. I hope you didn't think it was all about you."

So while we are taking a look at our side of the street, it helps too, to keep in mind that we can't overdo it. Sometimes it really is somebody else's stuff. And our role is to sort out what is and what is not our part. Sometimes, as the saying goes "It's not my circus and those are not my monkeys."

Karen tells me that she wrote a description of the person she wants to be. It includes what she wants to look like, but mostly she wrote about who she wants to be. She has certain role models in her life whose characters she wants to emulate. Her grandmother is one. She was kind—not overly generous, but kind. Karen also admires a teacher she once had who had a good sense of justice and treated people fairly and always seemed to try to understand her students' issues. Though Karen knows that she can't control what people think of her, she wants the world to view her as calm and interesting. She wants to think of herself that way. She wants to remember things better since she is becoming less afraid of her own feelings and of making mistakes.

Karen fears that looking at her side of the street will be the beginning of the end for her; that once her flaws or mistakes are brought out into the light of day, she will slide even further into the abyss of self-hate; that her longstanding feeling of "being a loser, so why bother" will take over.

But she is forging ahead in her effort to look at both sides of the story. She now sees the ant incident differently. She apologized to her mother for leaving such a mess, *and* she acknowledged her mother's overreaction. She sees the situation as painful, but not as evidence that she or her mother is awful—just human. Somehow there is relief in this.

Together we are taking a leap of faith that being open to looking at your stuff is not, actually, the beginning of the end, but rather the end of the beginning.

◆

Mean

A few weeks ago I was in the grocery store and bumped into an acquaintance of mine. He had ridden his bike and had brought it into the store and parked it in a corner while he did his shopping.

After saying a quick hello to him, I went on to the cash register to pay.

I noticed that one of the store managers was approaching my acquaintance, the bike rider. The manager asked, in a most calm and sincere way, if anyone knew who the bike belonged to. My acquaintance, who was wearing gloves and a helmet at the time, said, "It's mine. What are you, stupid? Can't you see I'm wearing gloves and a helmet?" He glowered at the manager and in a loud, menacing tone again said, "It's mine. Are you stupid?"

The manager, a short fellow, mostly bald, and sporting a long beard, looked absolutely stunned. I had turned to watch the show, as had everyone else in that part of the store, and I was studying the manager's ears, which cradled not one, but two hearing aids.

The manager looked at my acquaintance for a second more and then said quite sincerely and earnestly, "Nice bike."

I have to admit that I was in tears over this. First, because I had always thought my acquaintance was a really gentle, loving sort, and I felt like I had just seen him naked—and it was ugly. While I welcome all thoughts and feelings in my office no matter how ugly they are, it was jarring to see *mean* in action toward a seemingly innocent recipient. Second, because the manager either did not hear my acquaintance's malice or chose to simply ignore it. The look on his face was like that of a little boy who had just climbed off a mall Santa's lap after telling him all the things he wanted for Christmas but knew he probably wouldn't get.

This is the definition of *meanness*: "the state of being inferior in quality, character, or value; commonness; the quality or state of being selfish or stingy."

I think my acquaintance knew that he should not have brought his bike into the store, and he was justifying it to himself and felt defensive about it. I think he was attacking himself for it, and when the manager approached him, he assumed he was going to get reprimanded so he went to his own default mode, his own defenses went up, and he reverted to meanness. He assumed an attack and he sprayed like a skunk. And it stunk.

A friend of mine told me that she had heard that her own therapist was known to be mean. In fact, she had experienced him as mean herself at times. Her father had been mean, and she was frightened of being hurt by this therapist. She was considering ending her work with him and asked me what I thought she should do. I suggested that she tell him what she heard and felt, and ask him what he thought. And you know what? He told her she was right; he was mean.

When he admitted it, she felt relieved. She said that whenever she told her father that he was mean, he denied it, and that made her feel even worse. This time she felt happy because the therapist did not deny her experience of him. She thought this was a good therapeutic move, worth the difficulty. And he was willing to hear about it and own it when she thought he was being mean.

And I thought about this: Even though it was therapeutic in some way, the guy was still mean a lot, and the ends don't justify the meanness. They don't. You do not have to stay on the receiving end of meanness, nor do you have to translate your own mean feelings into mean actions toward others.

Sometimes people with addictions or eating disorders or who self-injure are more sensitive to the vibes others send out, or to being told no, or to what other people are thinking (or what we think they are thinking or saying). Sometimes things can seem meaner than they really are. It's good to check it out when you can. And check out your perceptions.

I'm not saying that you don't have to be firm and clear or direct and serious at times, and set boundaries (you do!) in order to protect yourself, it's just that there is rarely ever a reason to be mean that washes. You can *feel* mean, sure; that's a human response to feeling hurt, misunderstood, disrespected, or rejected. We are all capable of feeling and being mean. Eating and self-injury disorders are, among the many other things that define and underlie them, mean. The actions that go with an eating or self-injury disorder are, in some ways, acts of being mean to yourself.

Many people employ meanness as a protest or a way to protect themselves or convey to someone else what it feels like to be who they are or to be on the receiving end of someone's mean spray.

But meanness shapes you, no matter which end you are on. Karen's father is mean. She is afraid of his meanness. It seems to come out of nowhere. Sometimes he calls her names or yells at her to get a job or clean up the house. He is short in stature, just over five feet tall, and slightly built, but he can be very loud and frightening. Though Karen does not consider herself to have an eating disorder, she often throws up after one of her father's outbursts. She has begun to wish that her father would walk into a pole. The vision of this makes her smile. She has also started to think about all the mean things she can say to her father. She is beginning to get pretty good at mean, at least in her own mind.

But Karen and I notice that even though it is downright fun, not to mention relieving, to indulge her revenge fantasies and her meanness, her personality has started to shift and remold. Her attitude is getting haughty, and she has begun to shrug her shoulders at the world. Let the glowering reign!

But not. Though Karen is allowing herself to have all of her feelings toward her father, she does not want to be poisoned by them or by him. Nor does she want to pass along the venom. It is not who she is. It is not who she wants to be. There are other ways to defend and protect herself. She can be like the nearly deaf grocery store manager and just not hear it, pretend to not hear it, or walk away. She can even say something nice and perhaps defuse the bomb with a compliment, a smile, a soft look, or a brief, kind word. She does not have to engage the enemy or pass along the pain by being mean to someone else. And she does not have to think that she somehow caused it or deserved it and then be mean to herself. She does not have to pick at her undeserving, innocent legs.

We don't know for certain what we have caused or what we deserve. But we have a role in all the goings-on in our lives. It's not always a conscious role, and certainly not always, or even often, one we signed up for, but if it happened to us, then we were part of it in some way, even if it means that we were just in the wrong place at the wrong time.

What if you have made some real mistakes? Behaved terribly? Taunted, teased, provoked, prevented progress? Be honest about your mistakes (no matter why you made them) and say you are sorry whenever possible, in whatever way is safe for everyone. You can sometimes say you are sorry in your mind if doing it in person is not totally clear for everyone involved. Sometimes saying you are sorry is more complicated than not, but it does help. You can say you are sorry to yourself, too. (More on this soon, when we get to forgiveness.)

Karen's father's voice still rings in her ears sometimes when she messes up. She thinks, "I'm such a loser" (she gets mean to herself). The simplicity of knowing that she made a mistake and can own it, apologize for it, learn from it, and leave it still gets lost in grooves of mean that Karen was used to. She is used to blaming and being mean—mostly to herself—but more and more she has begun to rethink mean and take a stand for herself. And it feels good. In fact, it seems that the best revenge might be *living well* after all.

Karen and I work on defining what *living well* means to her. For now it means smiling to herself, taking deep breaths, and doing a kindness here and there, not just to others but to herself as well. Sometimes that looks like leaving a short note of thanks to a friend. Sometimes it looks like buying herself a flower, taking a hot bath, or just letting herself have all her feelings. Sometimes she goes to FreeRice.com and sends food to the hungry or visits other online kindness sites to get inspired. She likes these ideas. They are like gentle breezes that we think are just strong enough to blow her forgetfulness, along with her father's meanness, out to sea.

Stopping the mean and orienting toward kindness is a tool because when you are hurt and hurting, and inflicting physical pain to trump the emotional pain as a way to get relief, you are acting in a mean way, even if it works. Practicing kindness helps shift this around so that you can bear the emotional pain without hurting yourself.

CHAPTER 11

Mind Trek

He does not need opium. He has the gift of reverie.

—ANAIS NIN

My Dearest Marcus,

I created you in my mind, but to me, you are real. You come to me when I am at my loneliest and you hold me in your arms so that when the pangs in my chest are too much to bear, when human ears fail me, when everyone seems too far away in the hurt of the moment, I can call on you. I can hear your voice in my head when I close my eyes. I can feel your arms around me and your kiss on my forehead. I can hear you telling me that I am safe. That I will be well again. That there is good in this world and there is good in me. That awed as I am with how much I am hurting right now, you are right here with me. You are my private friend, and constant comfort.

My mother hit me again tonight. Drunk as could be, she finally passed out, but not before she laid into me again. I feel like dirt. I am heading for the drawer to get my blade, but I feel you here. You are saying, "Easy does it, my love." You are telling me to put down the blade and to sit quietly and look into your eyes, which I know are a deep and enduring brown. You tell me to feel you with me, that you are real in my mind, that I do not have to hurt myself. That I am not dirt, not nothing. You will help me bear the sadness, the shame, the frustration. The rage rage rage.

You remind me that I can go anywhere in my mind. To an island in the Pacific where the water is warm and clear, where the sky is so blue that it almost hurts to look at it. You remind me that I can feel warm sun on my face and can curl up beside you in the shelter of your loving words. That my mother cannot make me small. That my value is God-given. And that I can soothe myself without self-pity or self-harm. That this too shall pass, and I can survive it.

You are the best of all possible voices and the truest of all true friends. And since you are created by me, for me, I need not share you or tell anyone about you. I need only to call you when I need to, and you are here.

Thank you,

Cassie

Besties in Your Head

Cassie was twenty-three when she wrote this letter. She tells me that she has had her fantasy friend for years and years but is embarrassed about it. She thinks she might be schizophrenic or have multiple personality disorder or be really crazy. She says that Marcus talks to her, reassures her, and comforts her, and he only says good things. She wants to know what I think.

And I think it's fine. More than fine. You need all the help you can get when you are hurting. And using fantasy is a big help. Fantasy is not a substitute for the work of emotional maturity or real relationships; it's not meant to encourage unrealistic expectations of real people and real relationships or to keep you immersed in the younger part of your psyche. But using fantasies can help you through emotional rough edges without hurting yourself as you transition into being able to face and feel the most difficult of hurts. Fantasy used this way can also help you tap into and develop a more loving internal voice, one that does not attack you or urge you to attack yourself, and one that can help you validate your own feelings, think things through more logically and calmly, and not act so quickly on painful urges and compulsions.

I ask Cassie if she actually hears Marcus's voice like she hears mine, or sees him like she sees me, to which she chuckles, "Of course not. I know he is my fantasy. But I do think he is real. He is real and fantasy at the same time." And then she adds, "I know if he shows up in my mind that I am in real pain or have a real need to talk. Sometimes he is just a signal to me that it's time to slow down, that I need some extra tenderness, love, and care, or that something is really bothering me and I need to tend to it instead of hurting myself or getting on the scale again and again. When I imagine him with me, I feel less alone in my aloneness."

I tell her that some research shows that many children have imaginary friends in childhood and some carry them into young adulthood and beyond. These children are believed to have superior creativity, better emotional resiliency, and better verbal skills. Some feel that these children are better able to look at more sides of a situation and tap into more rational thoughts and ideas. They are considered to be healthy and normal. I tell her that adult fiction writers often experience their characters as real; some even believe they arrive in their mind already formed, and all the writer does is channel them. I tell her that some therapies encourage the idea of imagining an internal "wise parent"; this kind of fantasy can be healing and soothing.

Cassie also has trouble falling asleep some nights. And though we've talked about ways to ease into sleep (redecorating a room in her mind is one of her favorites—working on it a bit each night as she drifts off), talking to your bestie works pretty well too. It's not that she doesn't know what's real; it's just a comforting way to talk the edge off in her mind.

So I think that besties in your head are a good idea. Have one, have a few. Give yourself permission to create, to dream, to conjure up a comforter.

Beth, who lost her mother when she was seven and only remembers her vaguely, has many precious photos of her mother. She tells me that when she feels lost, she feels her mother. She feels the softness of her voice, the smoothness of her hands, and the warmth of her face, close and gentle. Beth says she knows that perhaps she has given her mother many qualities that she might not have had, and that if her mother were alive she would most likely not be so perfect, present, private, and tender. But she needs this idea. She needs the fantasy to carry her through when the pain is swirling around her and welling up inside her; when she has no vice anymore because she is eating and digesting her food. She is no longer using her eating disorder to bring her distraction, relief, and comfort. As she progresses in her recovery and is feeding her body, the needs of her heart and soul are making their way into the light. Tending to them with fantasy and without hurting herself smoothes the way to real relief.

She says that in her mind her mother listens wholly to her and says only soothing, loving things—all the things opposite to the harsh voice that is the eating disorder. Her mother's voice is one of reason, calm, and understanding. Going to this gentle place with her gentle mother soothes her and even helps her be more reasonable when she wants to be. She needs every available coping method to help her bear bad feelings without going back into attack mode.

I tell her that I think this is lovely and right; we should all have such a mother.

Vermont

When Tess, who is now twenty-eight, was a kid, she created a fantasy about Vermont. That was where she was going to run away to. Whenever the pain or the fear or the fury got too big, she closed her eyes and went to Vermont. She knew that somewhere in the fantasy were real feelings of fear, self-pity, betrayal, and grief. She knew that she had to, at some point, deal with those head-on. But in the moment of crisis, and to stop hurting herself, she let her mind have Vermont. It helped her feel safe in moments of danger when she could not actually leave, and it helped soften the blow of hard feelings without breaking skin.

Tess has never actually been to Vermont except in her mind, but she truly loves the place. She did not just go there, she traveled there. The more pain she was in, the more details there were in the fantasy. It went something like this:

First, she always had a secret bag packed. It was a blue North Face backpack, with sturdy black straps and many panels and pockets. She always had money. Some money she kept in the pack itself, and some was buried outside next to a tree in her front yard in a metal box, in case of dire emergency and the need for a quick exit.

In one scenario, she had just enough time to grab her pack and sneak out the back door. Sometimes she went back to dig up her money and sometimes she had to leave without it and run, depending on how hurt she was at the time. If she was in lots of pain—let's say she had just been yelled at, called names, humiliated, or hit—she got out fast. If it was just a mild form of general pain, she stopped for the money tin.

She took the train first to New York City. She always figured she could get really lost there, and in case someone was trying to follow her she would disappear in the Big Apple. From there she went north. In her mind Vermont was always green, always warm, and always full of soft, kind people. They were never nosy, always goodhearted, and only interested in helping her.

Upon arriving at the train station in what she imagined to be a small college town, she disembarked, after having watched miles of New England countryside slide by outside the train window, and walked in a daze around the town.

Depending on how much pain Tess was in, she sometimes saw all the people on the way as she meandered around the streets. She looked in the shop windows, noticed the narrow river running through town (her fantasies always had to have water nearby), or watched the light traffic on the small streets. She imagined a country store with a door that had a little bell that jingled when you opened it and banged closed behind you when you walked in. The store smelled like cinnamon and strawberries and old pine. The shelves were full of home-baked oatmeal-raisin cookies and honey jars and rows of apple butter and preserves. Of course there was a kindly, stout, red-haired woman with a fringe of grey smiling from behind the counter as she looked up from her quilting.

This woman would perhaps be the one to offer Tess a room, and then a job at the store, and then, later, hold Tess as she cried. She would never ask a thing of her or about her, but simply would hold her when she needed it and bring her warm, soft food (oatmeal, pancakes, rice pudding) on an old wooden tray and tell her, "You stay as long as you like, Darlin'. You're safe here."

Some people have a room of their own in their mind—Tess had a whole state. Sometimes she walked past the store and went straight on to an apartment complex. She would be given an apartment, and since she had stashed a lot of money in her pack and she was now hundreds of blessed miles from all that pain and those who had caused it, she had nothing but time. She spent this time decorating the apartment down to the faucet fixtures. (They were silver and shaped like swans' necks, with white porcelain handles.)

When Tess was younger, the apartment was sparse—a one bedroom, one bath with a little couch (floral pattern, reds and yellows) and a futon in the bedroom. It of course had a window overlooking a stream running through woods. There were neighbors; she did not want to be completely alone.

And then of course she met the boy of her dreams. He was looking for her, as it turned out. And he was the most adorable, hottest, sweetest, smartest, funniest, sexiest, kindest boy you could ever imagine. He was hurt, too. He, too, had run away from home to get away from his parents, who were (depending on the day) divorced, dead, abusive, mentally ill, or in prison. The instant Tess and the boy laid eyes on each other, they knew. They knew they were two lost, hurt souls who were meant to find each other and hold each other through long, dark, scary nights and promise each other that they would protect each other always and no one would hurt them ever again.

Tess used this fantasy for years. She doesn't use it much anymore because she has found many other ways to be and feel safe and take care of herself when she is scared, angry, and hurt. But she likes to know it's still there if she wants it. She knows that her escape fantasy has its limitations and that her maturing, emerging, and emotionally resilient self needs to work out real-time self-care and adult coping skills. But it helps get her over the impulse to act harmfully until she can weather her feelings better.

When she gives me permission to use her fantasy in my book, she says to tell you that you can borrow it anytime you need it and that she hopes it will help you, too, along the way toward getting to a better place for real recovery, not only in your mind.

CHAPTER 12

Tell Your Story

*All sorrows can be borne if we put them in
a story or tell a story about them.*

—ISAK DINESEN

MANY YEARS ago I experienced a loss that felt quite profound to me. It shook my self-confidence, my faith, and my emotional stability. My friends reminded me of all the blessings in my life; they sang my praises and reviewed my accomplishments. But all I could think about was what I had lost—what I did not have. In the midst of being upset, I made a list of things that I did have. Like feet. And lungs. And fingernails. And eyelids. (It is a very good thing to have eyelids. It would be awful not to have them. Think about it, but only for a second.) And water. And air. And grass. And sunshine.

It helped a bit. But I was still in a lot of pain. My colleague Roseanna says, "Emotional time is timeless," and the pain was going on and on and on. And because some of the loss involved another person's actions, often anger reared its head. I wanted that person to hurt the way I was hurting. Part of me wanted revenge. But I knew that one of the most important things to do when things are this bad is talk.

Talk

Talk. Talk. Talk. Tell your story. Tell it to someone or ten someones who will listen without correcting, criticizing, complaining, or creating a bigger mess for you. And perhaps can, if and when you are ready, and would like, give you some feedback and support.

The right someone can be hard to find, but look. Look and talk. (If you're stuck on who to talk to, make a list of possibilities. Consider a trusted relative, clergy member, teacher, coach, school social worker, therapist, friend, parent of a friend, 12-step group member, or teen librarian. Just like with friendship, you don't have to tell it all to one person, and you can go slow and test the waters.)

You can tell your story with integrity. Tell it without publically slandering the offenders (even if you feel like it). Tell it privately, in confidence to trustworthy ears. Say everything to someone who will hear everything and hold it all privately and respectfully for you. Telling your story does not mean you name or name-call the characters—though to those private ears you can. It means that you start to unravel the knot that is the pain that is the story. And you begin to find a way to live with and through it that is healing and healthy, even if the pain lingers.

What I experienced was a trauma of sorts. It was a shock to my system and a blow to my heart. It might be a raindrop compared to your ocean, but to each of us our pain is our pain. Comparing pain, while helpful at times, is not the point. (Yes, more than one billion people do not have fresh drinking water. It's good to have perspective. But emotional pain is still a thief and you are still suffering.)

When you experience a trauma, tell your story. Don't act until you have thoroughly and deeply discussed your potential action with another human being who is compassionate, rational, and honest enough to tell you if you are operating under the influence of your wounded soul and brain.

I have had to tell my story to a lot of people. I am telling it still. I am telling it to you. And each day I get a little better. I see now— ouch—how I might have contributed to the problem. I see how I might have been vulnerable to such a situation. I see, too, how I might have hurt the person who hurt me. I see now how I need to forgive myself as well as the person who hurt me. But I see. And I would not have seen if I had not kept talking. I would not have been able to release all the revved up feelings and quiet my mind without the talking. I would not have been able to put the brakes on making more bad decisions without the talking. The talking was how I cleared away the vines that were blocking the path to my rational and healthy self.

Some pain takes a billion words. It just does. But it has to come out of you or you will continue to starve or stuff your body or puncture your shoulders or walk around in the dark, grey haze of seemingly endless rage, self-pity, and hopelessness.

Telling your story, or stories, is like walking through the door to life. I have sat through endless hours of silence in my office until the suffering, silent, scared young woman in front of me can find the words, or until I can help her find the words. I have waited until courage and pain overtook fear and refusal, until the pain of not talking was worse than the pain of talking. And I can tell you that it pays off. The right words pay off.

You will find relief through actions other than talking, too, but some things—most things—are best left for after the urgency is gone and plenty of talking has been done.

I'm leaving out the ugly details, but I'm telling you about my painful experience because I want you to know a few things:

- Many people have some sort of deep pain or wound. It might not be apparent when looking at them, but you can be sure that you are not the only one. Knowing this helps because when you are suffering you often think that no one in the world knows what it feels like to suffer, and that not only are you suffering, but you are suffering alone.

◆ You cannot tell what people have been through by looking at them. In 12-step meeting rooms, there is a lot of discussion about comparing your insides to other people's outsides. When you do this, you usually end up feeling pretty awful. It's hard to know how people really feel unless you ask them directly and they trust you enough to say the truth.

◆ Though difficult, talking and telling your story has a big payoff in terms of healing. It is true that with some trauma, thinking about it and talking about it can be like reliving it, and all the feelings can come rushing back. This kind of trauma needs even more tender care, and you should not force yourself to talk about something that you are not ready to talk about, but usually talking about your trauma or problems opens the door to relief and healing.

◆ Don't downplay the importance of your story. If something is bothering you, tugging at you, or nudging you somewhere, then it's a story worth telling. Yes, there is a scale of trauma, and some things are far heavier than others. And yes, part of recovery is learning when and how to let some things go, but if it's bugging you, talk. Don't duck out by downplaying.

◆ The day-to-day bumps and ups and downs in relationships and life need attention too. Talking is not just about big trauma. The things you think are little are worthy of attention too. In fact, sometimes, taking care of the daily nicks makes all the difference with the bigger things.

◆ "Feelings are always real, but they are not always based on reality," an old addict friend of mine likes to keep reminding me. This is one more way talking helps us. Sometimes what we feel is based on what we think, and what we think is based on what we think we saw, know, heard, or believe to be true.

And sometimes, we don't get it straight. An objective ear can help us consider and discern the facts, and consider new and viable perspectives that can calm our emotional brain down, help our more rational brain step up, and bring in much-needed relief. There are times, after all, when we are being overly dramatic, and it helps to find that out too.

- Choosing recovery, getting better, and deciding to take a step toward a better life require honoring your own traumas and moving forward anyway. You don't have to let them go—some griefs and sadnesses stay with us always—but you can carry them differently in order to live a better life. Talking helps you to shift the burden.

Though you should not be pushed to talk before you are reasonably ready, give it a go when you can. You can start out very slowly. You do not have to tell your story to anyone you do not feel safe with or want to tell it to, or who might join in the riot and rev you up more, but look for some good ears and put your toe in the water.

Revenge Alternatives

I wanted the person who hurt me to feel bad for what she did because of the pain I was in. The ability to consider forgiveness rather than revenge came from a lot of talking. It is a great relief to have your pain understood by the one who caused it, but it is not always possible. It is possible to talk to and tell your story to other ears that will understand and to know about all the parts of you that want peace as well as the parts of you that want war—war and revenge.

Revenge is something that many folks think about but won't in a million years admit to considering. There is so much shame in that wanting—so much that you take out all the frustration on yourself.

Marla's parents give her most everything she needs and much of what she wants. They are at times very loving and understanding, and at other times very frustrating and demanding. Marla likes to steal candy from the grocery store. She loves to tell her father that she will be home at eight and then show up at ten. She loves to pretend not to hear him when he calls her and to fake sleep. She loves to get barely passing grades because it drives him nuts. She feels the most delicious guilty pleasure when he simmers over her report card or gets annoyed when he has to take the dog out himself. Serves him right. Good. Ha.

Except that she feels bad about it, too. She is not quite sure how to stop. She wants him to suffer the way she does, even though she is not exactly sure what his role is in the whole mess of her life. Maybe it's that he works a lot. Maybe it's that he seems to like her sister better. Maybe it's just because he is a jerk sometimes. Maybe it's all the yelling, or that he pretends to know how she is feeling when he never bothers to check with her first. He just thinks he knows.

Marla's unconscious has come up with many ways to get revenge on her father without actually formally plotting against him. Her best revenge is his continued frustration with her inability to eat much.

One day Marla admits wanting her father to pay for all the trouble he has caused her. We don't actually know why Marla has an eating disorder or whose fault it is, if anyone's. But we know she is pissed as all get-out at her dad, at least for all his yelling. I ask her if she thinks there might be a better way to get revenge than refusing to put food in her body.

A few months later Marla asks what I had in mind. We mull over the idea that ideally her real relief might come from not even wanting revenge anymore. From thinking about things in new ways and clearing the way for new insights, better feelings, and to her own inner peace. But since she's not there yet, I tell her I was thinking that there are other ways to get revenge without involving her body or taking herself down, too. She says maybe she could tend to her bingeing in earnest and not tell him. He would hate that. Or maybe she could get better and not let him know how well she was doing. Or maybe she would pursue her music career and write a song about how horrible he is. Or take up a percussion instrument and practice all night long. Or write a book about her life and how she got better even though he wanted her to because she will not sacrifice her life for the sake of making him sorry.

The possibilities are endless, and I have to admit that I like the idea of writing a book. It worked for me.

Write On

I have filled journal after journal telling my private stories, working through my private pain, and recording my changing heart and mind and my many joys and blessings. I have documented my recovery, my faults, my fears, my victories, and my gratitudes. I was not seeking perfection, only pensiveness, and sometimes not even that—just release.

I also wrote about 1,600 (OK, it felt like that many) letters to the person who was part of all that loss that hurt me so much, telling her all about how she wronged me and how I am not nothing. I outlined her wrongdoings and my nobility. I reminded her that God knows all about her shenanigans and that what comes around goes around. I made my case many times for how she should do the right thing. I told her every sordid detail about what she did that hurt me so much. I outlined each and every one of my feelings. I told her time and time again how much pain she caused me.

I also wrote her letters that were more reasonable. I explained what I thought would fix matters, what I hoped to accomplish, and why I thought it would be in everyone's best interests to make amends.

And I have, in moments of self-reflection and gut-wrenching honesty, written her letters apologizing for the things I did wrong that might have contributed to the problem. I have, gulp, admitted some of my mistakes and asked her for forgiveness.

In yet another effort to find relief, I even wrote myself a letter from her. In this letter she admitted to all the lousy things she did to me and she begged for my forgiveness. I even went as far as to offer up some explanations of her misguided, emotionally traumatizing actions toward me. This actually helped a lot because I was able to quite seriously admit that maybe she, too, had fears and circumstances and human shortcomings that contributed to the problems she also had in her life, and that maybe, hmmm, maybe, it was not all or only about me—which was both relieving and unsettling at the same time.

The only thing I have not done with these letters is send them.

I have not sent them because whenever I ask my friend Ellen about sending them, she tells me that they are great literary pieces, and most definitely important to have written, but there is no point in sending them. That is the beauty of letters. You can use them all the time, anytime, but you don't have to send them—not unless and until you have let a sane and supportive person read what you want to send and review with you the purpose of sending it, the desired outcome, and the potential consequences.

There is often a time and a place for dealing directly with those who have harmed you and those to whom you may owe amends. There are many instances in our relationships in which we must deal directly with the other person. But we write for relief, release, and to clarify and claim our feelings and our ideas. We write to learn more about what we need, what we wish for, and what we want to have understood. We write to clear out the clutter from our minds and make space for new ideas and for peace. Sometimes writing clears the path for direct interaction.

When I sat down to write those letters, I full-on told myself that I would send them, that they would be read—darn straight they would. I gave myself complete permission to write it all. Say it all, baby. Let 'em have it. And each time when I finished, I took a deep breath and said a prayer. I printed them and put them in my box— *my box*—my private box where I keep the letters I have written so that when I need to make sure I have recorded all the things I want recorded, said all things I want said, and made all makeable points, I can go and reread them.

Sometimes when my pain rears up, I reread my letters. In them I see my frustration, but I also see the very subtle stirrings of forgiveness, self-examination, and acceptance. And I see my progress, and that is huge.

There is no tool of relief as powerful as the pen—or the keyboard, if you wish. Writing can be even more powerful than talking. But I cannot advise you strongly enough, with my whole heart, not to work out your feelings in an e-mail or a text message or on Facebook or Twitter. The temptation to sound off and press "send" is far too great to overcome, especially when you are sitting in a pool of stirred-up emotion. Don't even log on. You can always send it some other time.

Some of my clients moan and groan when I suggest writing. It is not the balm on a chapped soul to everyone as it is to me. Not everyone wants to keep a journal. It seems hard in the heat of the moment to put down your razor blade or walk out of the kitchen and sit down and write.

You can tell me that you don't know where to start, or that it will sound stupid, or that you just don't think it will work. You can even procrastinate by going out shopping for the perfect journal. And the smoothest pen. Or the prettiest mouse pad. But if you can just *try* to channel your urgency, anger, fear, or frustration onto paper, you will find relief. If you are willing to write down your stories, ideas, and thoughts, good and bad, in whatever form, you will move along in new ways. Set yourself up to start writing. And then just go. Start writing and you will see.

If letters and journals aren't for you, try *listing*. When Marla and I first started working together, she abhorred the idea of keeping a journal. She did not think her mind could settle down enough to write. She even felt annoyed at the suggestion. But since it's never any one tool alone that works, Marla agreed to try listing.

Listing is a good way for nonwriters to start writing. It's a good distraction from the noise in your head, a way to exhale your to-do list or your rage or your hurt in order to sleep or eat or read. Listing is a safe activity if you are bored, angry, or lonely. You can never run out of things to list. Here is a list of some lists:

Your favorites (music, colors, food, people, etc.)
Things that start with *B*
Things that are red
Places you want to go
Things you would never do
Things you would change if you could
Things you are grateful for
Things you wish your parents would understand
Things that bug you
Reasons to recover
Reasons not to
Worst feelings
Best feelings
People that you are mad at
People that you are afraid of
Things that are good about you
Things that soothe

OK, I know, I digress. Your lists do not have to be therapy-minded or discovery-oriented. They can just be. Marla and I once did an

A to Z list of every coping idea or tool we could think of for each letter of the alphabet. She does not mind my sharing it with you:

Attitude. Acceptance. Agree to protect yourself. Ask for help. Align yourself with someone strong or loving. Allow new ideas and better feelings. Believe in yourself and your helpers. Be brave. Breathe. Bask in sunlight. Bathe. Brush your hair. Commitment. Consciousness. Create. Curiosity. Consult. Console someone else. Cry. Call. Calm. Catch up with an old friend. Center. Change of scenery. Compliment. Depend on positive resources. Distance from naysayers. Dance. Dress up. Dream. Distract yourself. Exercise. Easy does it. Feed your soul. Feed your body. Find something new to do. Focus on the next step. Friends. Family. Fantasy. Feel. Fight the negative voice. Grace. God. Go out. Hope. Hear. Hold a baby. Investigate. Identify. Initiate. Inhale fresh air. Just be. Keep at it. Kindness. Label emotions. Laugh. Look around. Look at something beautiful. List victories. List gratitudes. List anything. Letters. Love. Lie down. Lean on someone. Let someone lean on you. Love yourself anyway. Move your body. Meet a friend. Notice. Observe. Organize a drawer. Open a window. Pause. Perspective. Plan. Practice gratitude. Peace. Play. Ponder. Pets. Pray. Quiet time. Rest. Rub a back. Reassure. Rate your feeling intensity. Reach out for support. Read. Resist negative self-talk. Repeat recovery mantras. Risk. Study human behavior. Stop for a moment. Sing. Sit still. Stare at the sky. Smile. Say something kind. Stay safe. Talk. Touch something soft. This too shall pass. Teach. Tell someone something nice. Trust God. Trust yourself. Try something new. Tenderness. Tell the truth. Understand that feelings pass. Use your support team. Use this list. Validate your feelings. Visualize a resilient you. Visit someone sick or elderly. Voice your opinion. Write. Write. Write. You are worth it. Yell into a pillow. Your own pace. Your own path. Yes you can.

We could not think of any for X or Z. But you are most welcome to let me know if you've got one. Feel free to add to the list.

Color Your World

Or draw it. If writing isn't your thing, then draw. Make stick figures or round figures or give everyone in your world a symbol and draw them. Color, shade, or just leave it be.

Sometimes things come out better in pictures, especially when we can't find the words. Sometimes you can lose yourself without losing yourself—and find yourself too—by coloring and drawing and creating art. (And I mean art gently, without perfectionism and criticism, just you and something to draw with and on that is not your body.) Buy mandalas; color them in. Make a scrapbook; fill it with pictures you find, quotes you love, feathers, leaves, dried flowers. Buy a sketch book, construction paper, markers, colored pencils, charcoal, and let yourself roam over the pages with no judgment, no mandate, no agenda at all except to accept what you are feeling.

You can sing, make music, make jewelry, sculpture, act it out. You can take pictures, arrange or plant healing flowers, decorate a room.

Move It

You can also move your body. This does not mean (and you know what I mean) that you move your body according to all the rules that your eating disorder is demanding you follow. Moving your body for relief from feelings—good ones or bad ones—intense feelings of any kind, means giving yourself permission to move freely without having to keep going for hours, without deciding that whatever you are doing isn't long enough, good enough, fast enough, far enough. Enough.

Movement means you walk or swim or dance *when and if your eating disorder voice is not running the show.* If you can't tell the difference yet, or if exercise is a weapon, or if movement is too triggering, then it may take some time to learn how to use it safely. And you can. You can learn to move *reasonably* even if you are not able to move reasonably at the moment. And you can learn to not hate it, if you hate it. You can learn to *give* this to yourself, not *do* it to yourself. It may take some time, but you can learn.

Movement when done with the gentle fluid idea that you are releasing pent-up body rev and giving yourself some much needed space and attention feels great. Be open to believing that you are moving gently in order to lose weight in your mind, not in your stomach.

Start by having the idea that it's possible. When we begin to teach our minds to turn to expression instead of compression, when we begin to believe that we can shape ourselves, know ourselves, and heal by putting the pain onto paper, or molding it with clay or craft or creative arts, we are voting with our hearts *and* our hands and championing our right to feel and heal freely.

CHAPTER 13

The Heart of Our Matter

What I need is the dandelion in the spring. The bright yellow that means rebirth instead of destruction. The promise that life can go on no matter how bad our losses. That it can be good again.

—SUZANNE COLLINS, *Mockingjay*

MARLA LOOKS up at me with her bright brown eyes and says, "I wish I could just come hang out with you on your front steps whenever I feel like it." "Me too," I say, "I wish it, too." Then we do the therapy thing and get curious and talk about why she is thinking about this just now—about my house, my front steps, what they might be like, and what it might be like to just hang out there with me—and of course about how that would be different from hanging out in my office, me in my big ol' suede chair and she on my saggy beige leather couch.

We figure out that all this recovery talk is such hard work sometimes, and that's on top of all the rigorous endurance of hurting and feeling so low and so nothing and so revved and crazy . . . and that's on top of all the darn thinking that goes on in a crazy brain. Then there is just showing up for the day; that alone is too much trouble sometimes, and it's nice just to chill.

Can a crazy brain do that? Just chill? Maybe. Maybe on my front steps, away from the office and away from those four white walls, where you can really see the bright blue sky, feel the wind on your neck, and just not work. Not work. No more unpacking the pain, analyzing the problems, figuring out the feelings, putting urges into words, talking about parents who just don't get it, or answering back all the fears. How 'bout just some hanging?

Marla needs a break from trying to figure out who she is and what she wants to do with her life. She needs a break from the voice, a break from the work of recovery, a break from her thoughts. As we unwrap those thoughts, we discover that for Marla, to chill also means to be taken care of a bit—to just be, but not necessarily be alone.

Marla tells me that she wants to be held. She wants to stop thinking about all the things we have to think about and just be held, and for one perfect moment feel that she is not alone. This is a cry for arms—for arms around her, physically and psychically. It's part of wanting a vacation from all her stuff, some human shelter and some peace, for a few minutes at least. Marla tells me that sometimes she likes to chill alone, but sometimes she is tired of holding her own hand and wants a vacation from that, too.

Vacation Days

You need vacations, and you can take them. I am not talking about diving back into your drug of choice and taking a vacay from what you know is progress, sobriety, and commitment; or taking a break from your food plan and skipping a few meals or diving into the food head first. I am talking about a pause—for a minute, an hour, a day, if possible (on occasion)—and resting.

Easier said than done, I know. But you can. You can tell your mind that it's time for a break—no thinking, no hammering, no banging out recovery all day, and no diving into the war zone, either. It's about giving yourself permission to escape for a few minutes or hours at a time, from both the problem and the solution, and doing something else.

There are many exercises, ideas, writing assignments, and charts available to help you get out from under your own mind, live well, stop hurting yourself, and deal with and heal all the bad feelings. There are tons of ways to quiet your mind. But when even those things start to feel like too much work, you can get caught in the "I don't want to" cycle, and that leads to the "I just can't" cycle, which leads to the "Forget this altogether" cycle, otherwise and tenderly known as a case of the "screw-its."

You can take a break from everything, with my full blessing, encouragement, and permission, without it being a case of the "screw-its." And you can come back when you are ready. You can come and go without any formal tools, trickery, or fanfare. You can just put a sign on your pain, your work, and your thinking that says "Back in five." Nothing fancy, just a breather.

Marla and I decide that we can take breathers from our sessions sometimes, too, and just hang out together in the office and dream about my front steps. It does not have to be all work.

Do Your Work

Now that I have just finished telling you that you can take a break from your pain, your work, and your thinking, I am going to tell you to do your work each day. Whatever your work is, there is always work to do. There is the work of recovery. There is reading, writing, and praying. There is getting yourself to another 12-step meeting, therapy session, support group, mentor call, or book page, even if you have to drag yourself there.

There is the work of life—the work of going to school or your job, the work of taking care of yourself, the work of getting up in the morning, the work of remembering to take a deep breath now and again. It all counts. Doing your work can help accomplish many things. First, it can be a distraction from the noise in your head. Even though the noise does not want you to do your work, rest assured that you can always tune back in.

Second, doing your work registers in your psyche as one more accomplishment and victory over the disorder, and you need to rack these up.

And third, even if you want to or feel like it's your lot in life to stay one step out of society, work is a statement that you are part of the human race. Doing work means that you are, in fact, productive—just de facto, you are. And being productive helps move you along in life, even if you are under your own house arrest.

I know that in certain moods you do not want to be part of the human race. You would prefer to swaddle yourself in a cocoon and protest the futility of life. You do not want to affirm life in any way, let alone by doing your work. But there are many ways to protest while still doing your work. Stay tuned.

Even when the days seem like they run on forever and you cannot, just cannot imagine how to get through another minute, it is time to just do your work. What work? Any work that is your work.

I am not downplaying the overwhelming heaviness of depression or melancholy or the surge and buzz of big anger or fear, but I am saying that you can feel these feelings and still do whatever is next on your list—even if you don't have a list; even if your list for that day is just to brush your teeth. Brush them and give yourself a nod.

You can go to class—kicking and screaming or with your nose in the dirt—but you can still go. You can write one sentence of a term paper or an article. You can clean a closet. You can look over your shoulder at Mr. Depression and Ms. Anxiety all decked out in their dark cloaks telling you that they are here to stay and have come with more buckets of concrete to pour into your veins, and tell them that you will be working anyway today. Tired and deflated, you can push the truck uphill in the mud, show up, and do your work. On days when you do not know what to do with all the pain, still . . . do your work. It's a tool, and it counts, even if only you know about it.

A while back, when I worked in a county mental health agency, I overheard my boss on the phone in the front office. She was talking to her husband. She said, "Well then, just make him a peanut butter and jelly sandwich." Pause. And then, "Why not?" Pause. And then, "OK, then I will hang up." Then she looked over at me and said, "He cannot make my four-year-old son a peanut butter and jelly sandwich because he is talking to me on the phone. He cannot do both at the same time." And then she shook her head and her big red curls went wiggling all around. "I can write a memo, talk on the phone, and eat lunch all at the same time, and he cannot stay on the phone with me while he is making a PB and J." And she let out a jolly chortle, "Ha!" that made everyone in the front office jump.

Ever since that day I have understood that not everyone can do two things at once. And not everyone has to be upset when they can't. You can feel many feelings at the same time and still do whatever work you need to do while feeling those feelings—at least most of the time. When you feel your lowest, you can still do your work—something that counts. And you can count everything you do! You can feel torturously, awfully low and still take out the garbage. You can do it under deep protest with angry stomps or with a slow, muddy drag, but you can do it.

Here at the intersection of emotional pain and eating disorders, self-injury, and self-attack lies the common denominator of *refusal*.

"I can't. I just can't. I need to sleep. I need to cut. I need to be alone. I need it all to go away." OK. I know about giving in to this, about letting yourself slip under the truck and curl into a ball. But doing some or part of your work even when the pain meter is busting out of the gauge helps you move, part by part, forward out of the hurt.

Somewhere in the *Big Book* of AA, there is the idea of *acting* yourself into thinking instead of *thinking* yourself into acting. Sometimes we just have to act "as if." We have to go through the motions until the motions go through us. We have to go at it from both angles. Acting "as if" is not instant magic, but it works, and it goes a long way toward ushering in relief.

My friend Liz's idea about not having to feel grateful to be grateful can be stretched to mean that you don't have to feel brave to be brave, and you don't have to feel willing to be willing. You can act "as if." And that sometimes means doing your work when you don't want to or feel like it.

Just as important as it is to rest, it is important to do your work. Don't devalue it. Don't say, "It's just math class" or "It's just a counter job at the mall; it won't matter if I don't show up." It matters. It's your work. Getting busy with the tasks of the day can lead you out of the hole as long as you give yourself credit for doing it. We need credit. Denying this and depriving yourself of it only helps the cloaked ones carry out their plot.

At some point in your recovery you are going to have to agree to do your work so you can say that you have done, are doing, and can do it. Having meaningful work goes a long way toward holding you steady through painful times and feelings and propelling you out of death mode and into life.

The work of recovery is work, and anything you do counts. Anything.

The final part of doing your work is to think past the moment and consider what life might look like if you were not living in pain. You do not have to know; you just have to guess and dream a little about what you might like to do in the world—not what your parents want you to do; not what you have the potential to do; not what you could do if only you did not have the eating or self-injury disorder, problems in life, difficult parents, or depressive episodes but what you might like to spend your time doing and what you believe is valuable to do in the world. Not all work, by the way is *work*. Work can be easy, light, pleasurable, and fun. Just because it is work, does not mean you can't enjoy it.

When this subject comes up with my clients, I hear all about how nothing matters in the world anyway; there is no job worth doing. I have heard every kind of philosophical argument from the beginning of time, and I don't care. Any pervasive attempt to devalue every worker on earth from garbage collectors to the president is the right arm of Mr. Depression waving his flag.

As he's waving, do your work.

Your Personal Creed

Many of the young women I work with tell me that their intense focus—their obsession, their deep belief, their creed—gives them immunity from anything else bad happening in life. And their creed is this:

My worth equals my weight. As long as I am in my eating disorder I am immune from all the negative "what ifs"—the potential pitfalls and out-of-control life events that happen along the way. Controlling my food, my weight, my body, and my cutting the way I am doing it now (or trying to) equals safety. Hating my body is the best way to avoid hurt in life. It is also the best way to control my food compulsion. So is focusing on comparing myself to others and trying to get skinnier than my sister or my neighbor or my mother. Having the best body, the skinniest body, the flattest stomach is the goal of life. It is more important than love, friendships, charity, and clean drinking water. Needing food is one of life's evil tricks. And I don't need food. I don't deserve food. (Or I have to have all the food I want when it calls me—I cannot stop my binge- ing.) There is really nothing in life that is worth doing or that I can or want to do. There is no point in making any effort. I will only get better through deprivation and punishment, not love. Never self-love. There is no point in trying to find myself. I don't exist.

I asked one of my clients if she would be willing to teach this to a class of sixth-graders. Would she stand up in front of my daughter's class and present this creed as solid advice for going forward in life—as a blueprint for girls everywhere?

I am not saying that you should not strive to feel comfortable in your skin. You must. And I am not saying that on days when the voice is loud and pounding, or depression and emotional pain are searing, that you are aware that this is your creed. But is it? Would you walk into a class of little girls and teach this to them as a way of life, a way of thinking, a way of finding their healthy core and creating a good life?

Rewriting your creed is an ever-constant tool. Separating your creed from your disorder, your obsession, and your challenges in life is essential in coping with emotional pain and deciding to recover. You can tell me that you would not teach your creed to little girls, but for you it's true. You can tell me that for you it's too late, that you have no other creed, or that you are different. And I am telling you that if you are not willing to teach your creed, then it's not your creed, it's your disorder.

You don't have to know exactly what your creed is, but you can start by knowing what it is not.

Protectzia

Protectzia is my word for protecting yourself without hurting yourself. When you are hurt and hurting, you need someone who's got your back. You need to cultivate ways to help yourself through. Use the tools I am talking about to create a safety net, a plan, a way of thinking and helping yourself that will carry you through the rough spots. Part of protecting yourself is cultivating relationships with people who can serve from time to time as protectors. It can be one person or several people you can turn to and rely on for help when you need it.

Sometimes those people include your parents. Sometimes not. It is parents' job to protect their children. Some parents do it well and others less so. Sometimes the very people who are supposed to protect you are hurting you the most. Of course there are lots of different kinds and levels of hurt. Hurt and danger come from many places, not just parents.

We are not born with a script for how to best protect ourselves. Protection is something that we have to learn. And many of us who self-attack believe very deeply that attacking ourselves is the best way to protect ourselves, that attacking ourselves protects others, and that if we keep it to ourselves and take it out on ourselves, we are being noble and safe. We take the pain and anger out on ourselves rather than lashing out at our mother, father, or best friend. We are afraid of confrontation and of being rebuffed, rejected, or hurt further. We think we are safer in our own bubbles of self-attack. We know well how to isolate. We believe we are protecting others by taking our anger out on our own bodies and minds.

Feelings are often so unbelievably big and powerful. You can get so fearful of them, not realizing that they are just feelings. When the impulse to act on a feeling and get relief is so urgent and powerful that it is almost trancelike, uncontrollable, and robotic, you operate on the semiconscious assumption that you are better off hitting yourself in the head than screaming at someone else. Sometimes that's true, especially if you might get hurt in return. But there are other ways to protect yourself. You can protect yourself, and everyone else, without doing it through the eating or self-injury disorder.

When I bring up the topic of protectzia in therapy, I often hear, "How can I protect myself from my own thinking, my own hands? Cutting myself with the edge of a knife is protecting myself. It's a whole lot better than jumping out the window." I agree that it is, and I know this mantra well. You need new ways to protect yourself that leave room for the old ways to fade away. But believing that it's best to keep risking your life because there is no better way to protect yourself falls short of the truth. And believing that you are not really risking your life also falls short of the truth.

Even under the spell of obsession and compulsion, of overwhelming physical and mental craving, you can be honest about your belief system. It's not easy to decide that you should protect yourself from your own mind, or to believe that there actually is a better way to be and to live. If you have not experienced it, you don't believe it. Even if you see it in others, you don't believe it can be true for you. Part of protecting yourself is being dependent on others—sometimes new others—for this knowledge.

Dependency has gotten a bad name. You might think that being dependent on the eating or self-injury disorder is better than being dependent on a therapist, a 12-step group, friends, clergy, teachers, coaches, mentors, family, God, or yourself. When my clients feel too dependent on me, they sometimes want to miss sessions or come late. Sometimes they stop talking. Sometimes they tell me that everything is fine, that they feel great, and that they are not doing anything at all risky anymore. They love their body, their life, and their parents. Sometimes they ask me if I am sick of them, or if I am bored. Or they ask how I am doing. These are clues to me that there is some feeling not being talked about—maybe about our work together, maybe about their pain, maybe about me.

Sometimes it has to do with feeling dependent and thinking that there is something wrong with that.

———————◆———————

Not that these behaviors and sentiments are always indicators of bad feelings, but sometimes they are red flags. Being dependent on your therapist in a healthy way is a good thing. Your relationship with your therapist is something you should be able to count on. Sessions should be the time when you can say anything on your mind and talk through whatever you are feeling. Or just talk. You should be able to depend on your therapist to be there at the appointed time, to be appropriate, to be sincere, to maintain professional but warm boundaries, to listen to what you are saying, to understand, to help you understand yourself, to help you set goals if you want to, and to guide you toward them when you are ready.

———————◆———————

Your therapist is there to help you get ready to move forward if you are not ready, or help you wait until you are and study what might be in the way of progress if you are stuck. Your therapist can offer suggestions or feedback if you ask, or tell you that he or she is not sure what to do if he or she does not know. These are all good things to be dependent on your therapist for. Healthy dependency on a therapist means you can count on your therapist for support, for consistency, and to help you figure out who you are and what you want for yourself. This kind of dependency is wholesome and good. It does not mean that you have to be in therapy forever, or that you have to go all the time, or that you are somehow failing because you feel safest in your therapist's office. We all need consultants in life. This is also true for people who are resources for support and voices of recovery and wellness.

Occasionally someone skips a session with me because she wants to protect me. She is afraid she will hurt me with the force of her anger or with the truth of what she really does behind closed doors. If she is mad at me for some reason, she has an even bigger fear; she fears her own hurt, her own feelings, feeling abandoned by someone she trusts, causing a rift in our relationship, or disappointing me by just going along with my agenda if she thinks that I have one. A good therapist is well trained to deal with his or her feelings and yours, and to work them through with you. A good therapist is interested in protecting your relationship with him or her so that you can continue to depend on it, and in straightening things out in an emotionally safe, healthy, healing way. If that means talking through some difficult feelings sometimes, that's what he or she will help you do.

Depending on others who have generally proven to have a good ear and good suggestions when you ask is good dependency. You can depend on different people for different things. Young women are often dependent on many people for many things, both physically and emotionally. Healthy dependence is a way to protect yourself. Knowing where to turn for help, comfort, guidance, and a good ear is protectzia. Having other people around is like having your own personal mafia—in a good way!

There are also many kinds of *unhealthy* dependencies. When you look only to one person for all your good feelings, or to bail you out when you act irresponsibly or recklessly, it is a sign of unhealthy dependency—so, too, when you believe that your self-worth or self-esteem comes only from pleasing that person; or when you believe you cannot be happy without that person's attention or affection; or that that person must change some fundamental part of him- or herself or his or her attitude toward you. These are not only unhealthy dependencies but unreliable protectzia. When you believe you must make someone else well or happy or stable in order for you to be well or happy or stable, that is faulty dependency.

There are some dependencies that are healthy but that you should lighten up on, like financial dependency on parents, or a friend who always gives you a ride. It's not always easy to pull apart the healthy dependencies from the unhealthy ones, but protectzia means being aware of the difference as best you can. One way to sort it out is this: With healthy dependency, the relationship can be deeply meaningful to you, and it can disappoint you sometimes, but you have a mutual respect for each other's thoughts, feelings, and ideas. You are able to be honest, authentic, and not manipulative. You generally feel good about yourself in the relationship, and you don't feel like you are desperate, urgent, or at its mercy.

One day, I get an e-mail from Marla asking me to please swoop down and save her. She is really feeling the urge to cut and is particularly angry with her psychiatrist who, instead of validating Marla's feelings, told her that she had *seasonal affective disorder* on top of her depression and that she should buy a sunlamp. The psychiatrist does not really get how Marla is feeling, or how much Marla does not want more diagnoses and advice at the moment, but just some support, and this makes Marla furious. She wants me to protect her from hurting herself.

This is the junction of dependency and protectzia. And I am glad to swoop in for the save when I can, if the save means helping you get in touch with yourself and ground yourself again; if the save means listening well enough so that you know you are not alone and that this is not how it will forever be and that you can stop yourself from picking up the razor. You can find, name, feel, and relieve your feelings with the help of good dependency and healthy protectzia. You can call someone who will swoop in and hear you. This is an ongoing human need and a truth for all of us, always.

Protectzia means that when your brain is on rev, you take out your list of emergency protectzia people (which you can now make) and make a call or two.

It stinks to have to be your own knight in shining armor sometimes. We often wish people would just intuit what we need, especially when it necessitates calling for help—helping yourself by reaching out for help. But you can protect yourself by calling in your troops. Not everyone will say the right thing or help you the right way all the time, but healthy dependency means that most of the time you get something you need. And you will see, as your recovery moves along, that you will have a growing and healthy dependency on yourself, one that you can trust and feel good about.

When Marla's mother nags her about her food in the name of trying to help and comments in ways that drive Marla crazy in spite of how many times she has been asked not to, it makes Marla feel out of control. Her mom watches her eating and asks if Marla is sure it's enough, or if it's what she is supposed to have, or if she wants something else. Sometimes she does not let up. Even when she is not actually talking, Marla can feel her mother's eyes on her.

Marla tells me that every time this happens she wants to shove her fingers down her throat and throw her guts up. I feel a knot in my midsection. I start to imagine Marla telling her mother to shut up and back off (not that I think this is exactly what Marla ought to do). But I don't say anything for a while. I just listen to Marla talk about how she knows her mother means well and how hard her mother is trying to help her.

I think we must be a million miles away from the rest of the truth—the truth of Marla's feelings—because the knot in my stomach is growing into a boulder and my shoulders are beginning to feel tingly. I recognize this as anger, and I know then that Marla wants to rattle her mother in the worst way but is so frightened of this that she would rather stick her fingers down her own throat a million times than get furious toward her mother.

In my mind I am begging her, "Tell me, Marla! Tell me how angry you are with her! Tell me that you are afraid you might haul up and smack her silly. A thousand times! I know she loves you. I know you don't want to feel this way. If we don't get to your anger—the anger you are so deeply afraid of—and if we don't get to how ashamed you are of your own feelings and your own force and of what you think you are capable of feeling and doing, you will forever be jamming your fingers down your throat."

So I say, "Tell me. Tell me how you really feel." And she tells me that she is afraid her anger will kill her mother, if not physically, then emotionally. She is dreadfully frightened of this. She has no idea what real words will do to her mother or what kind of response she will get back. The fingers down her throat are keeping everyone safe from everyone.

And I nod. Because I believe that all this good talking is the best medicine right now. It is the best antidote for anger, pain, shame, fear, and doubt. Hearing all of Marla's thoughts, and keeping quiet with that boulder growing in my own gut, is how Marla and I can let the monster out of her head and shake hands with it. We can welcome it, shrink it, and eventually send it on its way. And we can figure out what the next right possibilities are. She can depend on me for that.

And that is protectzia at its best.

Gratitudes and Victories

Gratitudes and victories are what you can hold on to when you are in the pain. Sometimes they offer perspective, but they do not mean that your pain is not valid. Listing them and being very aware of them is a way to loosen your brain's grip on you and find relief.

A gratitude is when you are grateful for, or you know you can eventually feel thankful for—what you have. You do not have to *feel* grateful to *be* grateful, and you do not have to conquer fear to declare victory. You just have to agree to keep a list (even if it's in your head) of gratitudes and ponder it for a few real minutes each day. Having a bed and teeth to brush and shoes to wear count as gratitudes.

A victory is when you succeed in doing something you thought you could not, or which is very, very difficult. When you are depressed, getting out of bed and brushing your teeth count as victories. And it's the same with victories as it is with gratitudes—you must note them.

A victory is also when you are aware of your own internal challenges, at least to some degree—your character defects, shortcomings, fears, and faulty beliefs. You should not use this awareness as an excuse to keep swimming in addiction or disorder or to assure hopelessness, despair, and failure. A victory is when you use this awareness about yourself as a stepping-stone, not a stumbling block, to progress; when you know what it is in your psyche that trips you up and you make a different choice, take a new tack, or follow an alternative path. When you appreciate progress over perfection, you can declare victory. There is no relief from emotional pain and no progress in recovery without gratitudes and victories.

Victory is also about identifying with others rather than comparing yourself to them, though it's so human to compare. Gratitudes and victories are not benchmarks for being better or worse off than anyone else, but rather routes to inner peace, confidence, faith, and balance.

Here is what a victory is not: It is not getting through another day without eating more than 200 calories. It is not hiding your scars so no one notices them. It is not drinking enough water to get the number on the scale high enough to fool your doctor. It is not feeling safer because no one noticed that you threw up dinner.

And a gratitude is not being grateful that you were able to run extra miles, down extra laxatives, or skip lunch. Sometimes it seems like it is, but then you know that your disordered voice is calling signals.

---◆---

I used to think that life was a seesaw. When I was up, someone else had to be down. And when I was down, someone else had to be up. I did not know, for a very long time, that lots of people can be up or down at the same time; that my upness does not affect anyone else's upness, and my downness does not mean that I must bring someone down to get back up, or stay down to get the things I need like love and care and attention. I can get those things when I am either up or down or floating around in the middle.

When you know this in your heart, you will have one more big victory and something to put at the top of your gratitude list.

---◆---

Nourish Yourself and Others

When I was thinking about writing this book, I knew that I had a few inherent challenges. The most important was that I wanted to write to young women who did not want to get better, and to young women who did want to get better but were stuck, which to me meant that part of them did not want to get better. I wanted to write about what it takes to want to get better and how to deal with overwhelming emotional pain. The problem was that someone who did not want to get better or have a better life was not going to be interested in reading my book; she would just be out there still doing what she was doing, miserable in a cocoon of obsession, frustration, fear, isolation, and unwillingness.

I wrote it anyway. I've not a clue how I will interest someone in reading it who does not want to get better, except to say that everyone in some way really does want to eat. On some level everyone is hungry, and everyone deserves to be fed—physically, emotionally, and spiritually. So maybe that hunger will lead those who might be helped by my book to find it. I wrote it anyway also because it is nourishing to me. And I hope that it is nourishing to you.

Since nourishing yourself can be nourishing to others (the better you feel, the better you feel toward others), and since nourishing others can be nourishing to yourself (the 12-step folks say that you can't give it away if you don't have it, and you can't keep it if you don't give it away), then nourishment is a win-win proposition. Nourishment in this case includes recovery, goodness, strength, hope, and the willingness and ability to push through the pain.

I know that when you are feeling your worst—when the voices are shouting so loud you cannot hear them except to feel the din of the rage or worthlessness or loneliness—you do not want to nourish yourself and you do not want to go out and do someone a good turn. But if we are talking about how to have a better life and not be in the yada yada of awfulness all the time, then you must do it. Shoulder shrug. You must. Smile at someone old. Or young. Say something nice to anyone. Anyone at all. It does not have to be untrue or fancy. It can just be a simple "Pretty dress" or "Thank you for talking with me, I appreciate your time." You don't have to wait for some lovely phrase to come to you, or to come back at you, or for any response at all. Listen to someone else's story. Ask someone about his or her day. Buy someone a flower. Put kindness and good vibes out there in the world—even if you feel like garbage.

Nourishing others does not mean taking responsibility for their feelings or circumstances. It does not mean doing things that could harm you or that are too strenuous or demanding or unreasonable. Nourishing can be done no matter how low or crazy you feel.

Here are some ways to nourish yourself: take your vitamins; get a massage; take a walk; take a deep breath; rest on a comfy pillow; listen to some good tunes; brush your hair; put on lotion; get a mani or a pedi, or both; play with a pet; buy yourself a flower; go to a garden center and walk up and down through the flowers, plants, and shrubs.

It can get corny, I know, but it matters. And it counts. And it's part of getting out of the muck and making a better life. It's part of going from can't to won't to "OK, I will."

And because that line between can't and won't is so blurry that it's hard to know where you fall at any given time, nourishment helps you get clear and get moving. I think it comes down to two things: The first is believing that if you do all these things you will have a good result. That does not mean that magic snow and happiness will fall all around you, but it does mean you will feel better, you will find your voice, and you will be able to walk around most of the time without feeling like you are from Pluto.

The second is that if you are waiting to believe or to act "as if," nourish yourself along the way because it will send a tiny but powerful message to your unconscious that even if you are stuck you can do something kind for yourself and others. Wait and pray and nourish until willingness knocks on the door and kicks out skepticism, cynicism, and doubt.

Sometimes nourishment means good, appropriate touch. You need healthy touch—hugs, an arm around you, a hand squeeze. I know that touch is a touchy subject, but safe touch is a basic form of nourishment. Along your healing journey you might find this to be true.

Sometimes the nourishment that brings hope and relief comes in the form of anticipation, of looking forward to something, even if that means you are just going to *think* about walking around the corner to check out the bird's nest you saw yesterday on your way to school, or that you will watch your favorite show later tonight, or Google how to crochet and dream about what kind of comfy socks you could learn to make (and maybe actually go buy some yarn and start fooling around with it).

Nourishment infuses us while it gives us something to look forward to, one inch at a time. And it makes us generous. It shapes us out of our own self-focused world of pain and gives us a broader purpose. It outsmarts the worthlessness and squashes the self-attack.

Nourishment is to emotional pain like gauze is to a burn. It helps wrap up the rawness until real healing sets in. It is also like water flowing through the cracks and openings and filling up the emptiness and soothing over the hurts.

We do need to be careful not to mistreat nourishment by devaluing it or by thinking it needs to be grand in order to satisfy us. As far as nourishment goes, small is the new big, because nourishment is not only a means to an end, it is an end itself. We cultivate kindness and we are instantly kind. We feed ourselves and we are fed. We give a dollar to charity and we are a giver. We hold open a door for someone and we are considerate of others. We end the selfishness in that moment. We end the uselessness. We end the worthlessness. We end the belief that we are not capable, that we are all good or all bad. We end the hemming and hawing in our brains about what we ate for lunch or what was said to us at work or how awful someone is. We are instantly transformed into our best self, even if it is for one split second when you visit KindSpring.org or doonenicething.com. Being kind to animals counts, too. And being kind to yourself—well, that's the point of the story, isn't it? Because kindness begets kindness. So yes, that counts, too. Big time.

Boot Camp

OK, here is the worst part (mostly, except maybe for the dealing with your parents part). I am totally the grim reaper now, except that this is where the good stuff really starts to happen, where you begin to heal and grow. This is the one part where no one can swoop in and save you. And no one should, because it's where you find yourself and learn to be with yourself in a way that is true and good and reliable.

Though we are together now, you have to get the hang of this part on your own. Don't worry, it will only take a hundred years or so. (Not really, but it might feel like it at times.) This is the part where you feel your feelings and practice the ability to bear discomfort; where you know that there is always going to be a deep part of you that is alone. But once you make friends with yourself, this aloneness will not feel so bad anymore. It will not be a dark place but rather a place that is clear and peaceful. Feeling your feelings and bearing your discomfort is not shaped around anyone else; it is you-shaped. It is where you can be OK with what you feel and who you are—no matter what. It does not mean you will always like how you are feeling or agree with yourself, but it means you can be with yourself.

Practicing the ability to bear discomfort does not mean that you should learn to slice deeper and sit with the blood longer. It does not mean that you should commend yourself on your trained ability to seemingly get through the day on a pack of Trident and a handful of baby carrots. It means learning the ability to feel awful and not hack away at yourself or push dizziness to a new level.

My version of boot camp is the "letting yourself feel emotional pain and not hurting yourself" part of getting out of pain. I know I am telling you that you have to get used to tolerating emotional pain without the help of the disorder in order to make progress, and that's the heart of it. All the other tools come in handy and will help you do this, but this is the center of the quake. Feel your feelings. And communicate with everyone else in a way that does not pummel your body or waste your mind and soul.

The resistance to just feeling feelings is so great that I think we are sometimes willing to do anything not to feel. This is especially true of those who come from addictive homes and verbally or physically abusive homes, those who have been abused or neglected, and those who have witnessed a lot of conflict in their parents' marriages.

It's basically true of most humans in one way or another. Few people grow up being taught to identify their feelings. Fewer still are taught how to communicate them effectively. And fewer still know how to instinctively accept them and release them, or how to tolerate them in healthy ways.

Since many adults are not practiced at knowing how they feel and communicating feelings in healthy ways, many kids are not helped to do it well, either. If you think for a minute about how anger was handled in your family, or what your earliest memory is of a parent being sad, frustrated, or frightened and how he or she reacted, you will start to get some clues about how your emotional education took shape.

Not many of us had parents who when angry would say, "I am angry now, and I am going to go for a run to blow off some steam." Or "I am sad about [whatever], so I am going to cry for a while, take a long walk, write in my journal, and call a friend."

Drama, in many cases, rules the day. My clients can usually cite lots of examples of name-calling, yelling, hitting, guilting, shaming, or denial of feelings altogether. While we can feel many feelings on many levels and with varying degrees of intensity, feelings pass. They do. Sometimes it takes a long, long time, and sometimes not, but they pass.

If ever you doubt this, get up half an hour before dawn and watch the sun come up. And go outside half an hour before sunset and watch it set again. This happens every single day, whether you are there to witness it or not. And even if you are stuck in your pain, when you know what you are feeling and are willing to feel it you will witness the rise and fall inside yourself as well. You will start to realize in a most visceral way, inside your gut, that time passes and feelings don't stay forever as sharp and bright as the midday sun.

Unfortunately, this goes for the good feelings, too. They also time out. But lots of folks who have trouble feeling the bad feelings have just as much trouble feeling the good feelings. Maybe more. We are so afraid that the good feelings will take us high and then drop us out of a thirty-story window. We are so afraid that we don't deserve the good feeling, that it's not real, or that we are being disloyal to all our pain if we let some joy, delight, or excitement sneak in. Or that once we have felt it, we have used up our ticket and can't have any more. Or that feeling our feelings, good or bad, means we are giving in. It's like joining that part of the human race that we shun; that does not deserve us, understand our pain, or is altogether too common.

Feeling our feelings means we are getting better. If we refuse to sit and feel and be with ourselves, we are deciding to hold on to our self-harming behaviors. We are deciding that what others feel—or what we think they feel or want them to feel—is more important than our recovery. When we think that by getting better and dealing with our feelings in ways that are productive, healthy, and maybe even superior to their ways we are letting them win, we are sacrificing ourselves to a false god.

Many who suffer from eating or self-injury disorders do not want to have to lead the way to sanity. You can get comfortable being the sick one and thinking that others should be the well ones. Feeling feelings can seem disrespectful to all the rebellion that lives in the part of you that is unhealthy and unwilling. But I am telling you that it is the highest form of self-respect. Feeling your feelings means you are getting better. If you practice it, you will develop a six-pack set of abs in your psyche, and it will serve you well for the rest of your life.

Sitting Still

Believe it or not, the day will come when it does not occur to you to binge or cut or restrict. The idea that time passes and takes feelings along with it will settle into your soul like a feather in your hand, and you will be able to sit quietly and feel your feelings. You will be able to be with yourself without hating yourself or anyone else; without running or raging or itching to get up; without wishing you could die or disappear or jump—or eat or starve or slice into your body. You will no longer stare at yourself with disgust and focus on how fat your thighs are. The number on the scale will just be a number, and it won't send you into a panic, a frenzy, or a nosedive into feeling like a worthless failure. You won't focus on these things because you will be more able, inch by inch, to sit and just be.

While it feels good to walk when you are hurting, and to move when you are in pain, feeling feelings, or your brain is on rev, it is equally good to practice peacefulness, sitting quietly and still and just being with yourself as you allow all of your feelings to exist. You can practice this by trying it out when you are not in any especially acute, immediate pain. You can just pick a quiet, comfortable place to sit and do so. You can breathe in and out, listen for birds, focus inward, focus outward, or practice meditation. You can let the feelings come and go and focus on where in your body you feel them, what color they might be, or how intense they are. You can pick a phrase or mantra or prayer and visualize it or say it over and over slowly in your mind. Or you can just sit and see what comes up inside you. The more you do this, the easier it will be to keep doing it, the easier it will be to be with yourself in an easy way, and the better you will feel.

You will find that just sitting still in your own skin is not only not so bad, but actually quite delicious. You can feel yourself being alive and not having to slice to do it or to get away from it. You don't have to sink into melancholy or tantrum into fits, you can just breathe. You will come to believe somewhere deep in your psyche that all your thoughts and feelings are allowed; that having them does not obligate you, define you, or command you. If you let yourself sit still, even for a second, through the worst of compulsions—the worst of feelings, your life will start to shift, and moments will turn into minutes, which will turn into longer moments. The moments will add up, and you will begin to like just sitting with yourself. Keep at it, and you will see.

Part Four

A BETTER PLACE TO BE

CHAPTER 14

Good God, Really?

Whoever wants to reach a distant goal must take small steps.

—SAUL BELLOW

"I'M HUGE," Rachel, in her normal-sized body and long blond hair, tells me. She is curled up in a ball on my couch with her black down coat covering everything but her eyes, which are staring down at the floor.

It's been a while since Rachel has cut herself, and while she has stopped throwing up, she is still at war with her body, which, through my loving eyes, does not seem huge at all. The huge I think she is really referring to is her frustration. I don't doubt that she feels uncomfortable in her own skin or that she feels physically huge. I know the experience of physical hugeness is real. And we have talked and will talk again about all things body—and all things emotion that come out as all things body.

But something about her hugeness has me thinking about God. When things seem so stuck, so huge, so despondent, I get the idea that it's time for something bigger. Something like God.

When You Feel Huge

I know that here we are toward the end of the book, and all of the sudden I am springing God on you. So I just want to let you know that this chapter is not about religion, theology, denomination, or ritual practice. It's not about going to your (or any) house of worship or telling you what to believe. It's about being open to some kind of faith, some deeper meaning, deeper wisdom, some help, from something bigger than your pain and your disorder. Something that is huger than your huge.

God is the elephant in my office. If talk of God makes you uncomfortable, hang in there with me. I am not about to start preaching. I just want to spend a little space talking about how helpful and calming it can be to have a Higher Power of your own understanding, especially when you are in emotional pain, stuck in recovery, or struggling with life. (And if you'd rather not walk through this one with me, or you feel like you've got God already, feel free to jump ahead to the next chapter.)

It seems to me that there is a lot of confusion about God these days, especially when it comes to recovery; to wanting recovery; to God's role in recovery. Maybe we don't need God. Maybe nature, meditation, spiritual awareness, and mindfulness are enough.

But I don't think so. I think we need God. We might need nature and meditation and spiritual awareness and mindfulness, too, but God is God. No substitutes. I am not suggesting a definition of God to you, just the idea of God. You should have your own definition of God.

I am also not suggesting how to find God, though for me, the closest that I get is when I sit quietly. (My friend Rose says she feels closest to God when she is running.) I also used to think that I would find God by looking outward. Somehow I was always straining toward the sky. But lately I find that even though there is beauty and inspiration from the world around us, God, for me, comes from the inside out. I believe that my healthy self and my healthy thoughts reflect the quiet whisper of God's wisdom and guidance. My connection to Him does not come from trumpets on a mountaintop, but rather the gentle idea that I can tune in if I want to.

When we come to the realization that our addiction, disorder, and obsessions have been our guides, our go-tos, and our safety zones, and that in some real way we know we are dying a slow death because of them, we need to find a new guide. We need to face the vast emptiness inside us with something that is durable. This durability can be, for you, a spirituality of your own finding. It can come from within you as you begin a recovery journey in earnest. It can come from the guidance and ideas of others who believe in a power greater than themselves and who will help you find your own.

I have always thought that when things were not working the way I wanted them to, that I needed to do more, be more, have more. Make more effort. And sometimes that's the case. But I've come to believe now that sometimes the effort I need to make is to have more faith.

My own spirituality, though not limited to, begins with my own ideas, ever-evolving as they are, about God. I am writing about God with that in mind. Whatever that Higher Power is or will be to you, there will most likely be some vines growing over your path to finding God. To clear the vines is to be creating for yourself a new wholeness, a new internal universe that is not directed by the ultimately empty offerings of your eating disorder.

There is much to be learned about ourselves and our own spirituality in that space between the end of the disorder and the beginning of something new. When we can no longer turn to the disorder to relieve us of the pain of our eating disorder and the intensity of life, we need something new.

Belief in a Higher Power cannot be forced or pushed. We sometimes have to live in the void for a bit before we begin to discover our own path to a Higher Power. But rather than turning back again to the struggle of our disorders, we can turn to, be awake to, and be interested in an ultimate wisdom, a life force—a Presence that both is—and leads us toward wholeness.

In her book *Women, Food and God*, Geneen Roth says that there is something better than endlessly pushing the boulder of obsession up the mountain: putting it down. And I think that it's a big boulder. And even with a stockpile of great tools and good help, we need something much bigger, especially since we often need help to even want to put the boulder down, and help believing that putting it down is actually better than continuing to push it.

When you live in your own head, with hatred for your own body, with the craving of food or the urge of starvation, you are pushing the boulder. When you hedge and hesitate and give in to the overwhelming pull of the obsession, you are pushing the boulder. When you turn to the food—or away from it—when you know you could reach out for help, you are pushing the boulder. When you hear the voice saying, "Screw it, forget it, you'll figure it out later, skip dinner, eat, eat, eat until your stomach hurts," and you can't *not*, and you obey because you feel defeated and overpowered, you are pushing the boulder. When obeying and giving in seems easier than all the options in the pull and heat of the moment, you are still pushing the boulder.

It is in those moments that you need something bigger than the boulder to help you put down the boulder. You might still have to find out who you are and what you really believe. You might still have to learn how to feel your feelings, find your passions, be in your own life, and get comfortable in your own skin. You might still have to talk back to the negative voice, loosen the grip of fear and resentment, and learn how to sit still.

We are always learning. It's a lot harder to learn without a working faith in something greater. People do recover without active inclusion of a Higher Power, but I believe that including a Higher Power in whatever way you can goes a long way toward helping you sustain your recovery and live well.

I once took an informal survey asking a bunch of my old addict pals who have had long-term successful recoveries and are living healthy, meaningful lives what they thought the trick was. "How," I asked them, "do you turn this ocean back with a spoon?" An overwhelming majority (OK, everyone) answered, "God, Melissa. God."

"OK," I answered back. "But how did you get willing to get better? It's such a long haul, such a big boulder. There's so much pain in life. The food is so *it*. The self-hate is so real. So is the uselessness. I mean, sometimes it's just so *bad!*"

"Go to God, Honey," they all said. "Go to God."

And from one friend of mine who is undergoing radiation treatment for breast cancer: "When they put me in the treatment room, set me up, and tell me not to move, all the technicians run out of the room. But God stays. God always stays." (Thank you, Pam.)

But I am the queen of *but*. But this. But that. And I've been in good company—lots of people are But Queens, too. Often that's a good thing. Seeing many sides of an issue or situation can yield good results, just like understanding other people's motives can help you get along better. *But* has an upside. And you can find God if you are just a wee bit open to it and to unpacking the buts.

I have come up with my very own list of things that get in the way of going to God. It's my own But List. But with some answers back. Perhaps it will help you start clearing away some of the vines. (I refer to God as He or Him, but again, this is just my angle and shorthand. You can of course shift it to *She* or another reference.) Following the But List items are buts to the buts.

But List

I would turn to God for help or believe in God . . . but . . .

- **I hated my place of worship growing up. I felt forced. It was never meaningful to me.** God does not live only in places of worship. You can learn about God as being independent from your childhood memories of people and places.
- **My parents don't believe. (So I don't either.)** You can think about and learn about the God of your own understanding. Though your parents do help shape your ideas about God, you can separate your ideas from theirs and adopt your own. Doing so is part of creating your own spiritual life.
- **My parents do believe. (So I am not buying into it, too.)** You can find many ways to rebel and differentiate yourself. You do not have to deprive yourself of God to spite your parents. If believing in God will satisfy them and you don't want to give them the satisfaction, don't tell them. You can have your own private personal relationship with Him.
- **I'm already religious, so that's good enough.** No it's not. Turning to God in a personal and spiritually connective way might be a given if you are religious. But only you truly know if you are bringing God into your life in a quiet and personal way. Doing so can go hand in hand with religious observance, but observance alone is not enough.
- **God does not have time for my silly problems. Especially food stuff or how fat my thighs are.** You do not know what God does or does not have time for. Usually this line of reasoning is just a projection of your own self-attack and resistance to being nourished. Besides, you have the ability to create good vibrations (or bad ones) in the world with your words and deeds. If you are tuned in and willing to use this power, you can take part in creating a better world. If you

treat your problems with respect and not demean them, you
can get unstuck and move forward.

◆ **There are some pretty awful things happening in the world,
so maybe that means He does not exist. And if He does exist,
how can I reconcile these?** Yes, there are some pretty awful
things happening in the world, but they are not proof that
He does not exist. They are just proof that there are things
beyond our comprehension. There are plenty of inexplicable
good things happening in the world, too, like the more than
10,000 different species of flowers, or exactly how the heart-
beat starts in a fetus, or what is beyond the last star that the
most powerful man-made telescope can see. Radio waves
exist, and you can't see them. But if you turn on a radio, you
hear the music. You don't have to understand radio waves to
listen in.

◆ **If God loved me, He would not have given me this problem
to begin with.** I have learned a lot about God from my children, especially when they were small and wanted to run into
the street. From their perspective catching them and holding
on to them seemed the worst thing I could ever do. The ball,
the friends, the fun were on the other side of the street! But
I saw the bigger picture. I saw the car careening down the
block. I saw what they could not. I think this is what God
does for us. You want what you want, and it makes so much
sense to you, but you cannot see the bigger picture sometimes.
Protection can seem like punishment if your faith is shaky or
you are hurting too much. And again, you can't always know
what is meant for you on your journey.

◆ **I cannot trust or rely on something I can't see or touch.**
Trusting and relying on God when you cannot see or touch
Him can feel like free-falling in air. Many of us think if we
worry enough or think enough or try hard enough, we can
really control the outcome. We have been so frightened by life

or disappointed that we want to believe it really is up to us, especially since we can't see God.

Choosing to trust and rely on God and learning to listen for His inspiration and love amid your own pain and self-attack takes practice. Sometimes resiliency and relief come from letting go, not holding on. If this is a stumbling block for you, try being open to the idea of just *turning* to Him.

◆ **If there is a God, then I will have to follow religious doctrine.** Some folks believe that if they believe in God they will be obligated to all kinds of religious rituals or doctrine. Finding a God of your understanding can lead you to or back to your religious institution, practices, or traditions, or even toward new ones. But finding God to help you in recovery and life does not mean you are suddenly bound to take on the disciplines of religious practice. You can choose whether or not to do so at any point, but to stay away from God because of your confusion about an established religious practice is to gyp yourself out of some much-needed comfort and relief.

◆ **If I believe in God, people will think I'm a nut job.** Some folks do think that believing in God is crazy. Others struggle with finding and feeling a connection. But at some point in life and in recovery, you have to take your own unique stance and figure out what you are willing to believe and what you would like to believe so that you can open up spiritually. You can survey people whose lifestyle and spiritual approach you respect or find appealing to glean some ideas. Remember, though, just because someone is emphatic or insistent does not mean he or she has the answers or the answers that are right for you.

◆ **God is fine for other people, but not for me.** Most people find that if they are open to the idea of a God of their understanding, something starts to shift. Excluding yourself by saying that God is fine for others means you are bowing out of taking a look at something you really might benefit from. You can be part of the human community, no better or worse than anyone else, and just as entitled to God as the next guy.

◆ **If He does exist, why would He pay attention to someone like me?** Lots of people believe that God exists but does not pay attention to them. This is up to you. If you begin to be open to God, you will see that you can dispute this one for yourself. You might see God's *absence* in your life because you are not looking for His *presence*. Try shifting your focus.

Many people have semiconscious ideas about how God feels about them based on how they believe or experience their parents' feeling for them. If you have felt unloved or neglected by a parent, you might attribute that idea to God. And just because you feel unworthy at the moment does not mean that God thinks you are unworthy.

◆ **I'm too miserable to find God. I need something faster.** God does not always work as fast as I'd like Him to. When we are miserable, we want something fast, but sometimes God says no, or not yet. And sometimes He sends us the solution but we don't want it yet, even if we know somewhere deep down it seems right. Many of the God folks I know from across all recovery programs and religions say that instant relief can be found when you practice turning things over to Him. They say there is a heaviness that gets lifted and you get unburdened just by asking Him for what you need and letting go. They find that relief often comes right away from believing something is bigger than you; bigger than the problem at hand; larger than your disorder, your intense feelings, and your hopelessness.

Relief also comes from knowing, or attempting to know, that you are truly doing all you can and the outcome is not, ultimately, up to you. You are in charge of taking the right action to the best of your ability and leaving the rest to God, even when you don't like the immediate picture as you see it. Fast relief can come by just being willing to believe that He does, in fact, have your best interests in mind, that all your thoughts and feelings are welcome with Him, and that He is protecting and guiding you, especially when you are most lost and alone. Part of doing your part is to try this idea out until it takes more of a hold in your psyche.

◆ **I'm not really so bad off. I know God is around if I want him.** It is hard to know what is your human effort—your own right action to take—and when you should stop and say, "OK, God, it's up to you now. I've done all I can." Things don't have to be utterly awful before you turn to God. You can turn to God in gratitude, in happiness, in just plain blah. You don't have to be living in the gutter to ask Him for help.

◆ **I like my misery on some level. I don't want Him interfering.** If on some level you like your misery and don't want Him interfering, you can tell Him that. Maybe He will let you keep it. Or if He takes it away anyway, you won't mind at that point. You can be unsure about what you want, need, wish for, or hope to get from God and still include Him in your search for something better.

There is no exact script for how to bring God in. You don't have to do anything about it if you don't want to. I know it's strange to say that you want your misery, but sometimes it seems like it's all you have, or it's your only way to be, or it's the way to get through to those around you, or it's just who you are. Sometimes your misery keeps you feeling right, or safe, or in familiar territory, or connected to those around you. Or it's your unconscious mind's way of trying to help you work something out, survive, or protect yourself. These are all good things to study in therapy. But they don't have to preclude you from talking to God. And sometimes it is the misery itself that is the path to God.

◆ **If He does exist, He hates me. Clearly.** Most all the God-believing folks I know believe that God loves us unconditionally. Thinking God hates you based on your circumstances and pain is certainly understandable. It's very hard to believe that He loves you when you are suffering so much. But believing that God hates you is yet another projection of your own self-hate or your ideas about how other people feel about you. It's also presumptuous. You can be baffled about what God gave you to deal with in your life and which parts of your life are your own doing—this may be an ongoing study for your entire life—but deciding that He hates you is professing to know something that is unknowable.

You can make the same case for His loving you just based on the fact that you can see a sunrise, feel fresh snow on your face, breathe clear air, drink cool water, walk, hear, read, and listen to music. When you focus on the hate, the case for hate gets bigger. When you focus on the gifts, the love, and that all things and circumstances have a reason even if you don't know it at the time, the grace and serenity get bigger. So does the relief. And the hope.

Shifting from viewing God as being punishing or distant or nonexistent to an evolving sense of a loving presence—no matter how long this might take—can be part of developing a new and loving sense of self—of your own presence and the existence and goodness of your mind and body.

◆ **If I ask for help, I'll also have to do everything else I think He might want from me.** If you are hard on yourself, you assume that God is hard on you also. If you experienced your parents as demanding—as always wanting more and more and more from you—you might transpose your fear of not doing enough or being enough onto God. You don't have to start (or finish) by saving the world, or understanding the mysteries of the universe, or taking on all the commandments.

You can ask for help with the word *softness* in your mind. And if at some point you decide that there is meaning for you in figuring out if you believe God wants something from you, and if so, what that might be, you can endeavor to find out.

◆ **I do believe, but I don't really think talking to God or asking Him for help will make a difference.** Many people believe in God but don't really think talking to God or asking Him for help will make a difference. But you won't know unless and until you try. And repeat. And then try and then repeat again. And again and again and again. Sometimes you have to look for God in order to find him. You have to be willing to take that one step that is really a leap of faith. You have to be willing to believe that you can get relief just from the asking. Because the asking itself is relieving. Because it means that you know you are not ultimately alone or in charge. Because asking for help does not mean you are helpless, it means you are humble. And it means that hope lives. When you are all kinds of lost or frustrated, sad or stubborn, turning to God takes you out of your own charge and sets you on the journey to a better way to be.

And you don't always have to be serious and heavy about going to God. I know a clergywoman who tells people that it's OK to pray for new appliances. My friend Marcy believes this is how she got her new dishwasher.

You will find that developing a sense of God and a relationship with Him can carry you forward toward willingness in new and unexpected ways. It doesn't happen overnight, but you will find your heart softening and your life getting better if you can get warm to the idea of God and to the idea of His help with your pain and your struggle.

When I ask Rachel what she thinks about God, I get a shrug in response. And then, "If I did believe in Him, I would tell him not to help me." And then, "Maybe I just want to be alone in my loneliness. I don't need any intruders."

And you know, I respect that. But when the despair outweighs your stubbornness, and when there is nowhere else to go, you can go to God. Even when there is everywhere else to go, you can still go to God. When you are fed up, hung up, messed up, have given up, and want to throw up, go to God. When you really truly are all alone and out of ideas, and your suffering is so great that even the softest words of love, wisdom, and hope will not take up residence in your soul, you can still go to God.

You can ask God to quiet the catcall of food. You can ask God to smooth the spiky edge of pain caused by your best friend looking better in Levi's than you do. You can tell him anything, anytime, anywhere.

If you have the idea that this God stuff is really some ruse to knock you off your game so that the rest of the herd can stampede over you and win, you are operating under fear and the unhealthy old idea that while you would like some protectzia from above, you know better than to let your guard down.

It takes a bit of openness and reflection, but being curious about what you really think about God, and why you think it, is a great beginning.

Out of the blue one day, not too long after I brought up the idea of God, Rachel tells me that she has actually been giving the idea of God some thought. She tells me that her friend Debra is a real God freak. She says that what bothers her about Debra's God stuff is not so much how much she preaches it, but that she feels Debra has cornered the market on all things God. Debra takes up so much room and is so vocal, so emphatic, and so very sure of her relationship with God that Rachel feels like she is on the outside looking in. The image in her mind is that Debra and

God (whom she pictures as a soft, warm, divine presence—sort of a luminous glow) are sitting in a comfortable room surrounded by pillows and having tea. And Rachel is standing outside in the frosty air with her nose pressed up against cold glass looking in. Rachel thinks in some vague sort of way that God belongs to Debra, and even if that's not the case, He is so busy being close to Debra that there is no real room for Rachael, so why bother?

We discover that it reminds Rachel of how she feels when her father yells and she cannot eat. It's like all his anger and words suck out all the space inside of her that could contain nourishment or food. His anger is so huge that it presses out room for anything else.

Rachel and I talk about this for a bit, and we come up with the thought that Debra seems huge, too. We consider the idea that Rachel has suffered a lot already in her life, and maybe—just like she might not have to give over her body as a battleground for dealing with her father's anger—she might not have to give up on God because of Debra. We decide that Rachel can duck under Debra's hugeness and create a quiet, genuine, private place of her own with God that is big enough for Rachel and way too small for Debra. Underneath all her food compulsions and body-hate is a deep longing for something that has so far been indefinable. And huge. And we decide that if Rachel can put down her weapons, even for just a trial, there will be room to find out what it is.

Prayer

Prayer is the best way I know to find God. It is the best way I know to get the feeling that God has found you. You don't have to believe, you just have to pray. You don't have to feel God to have God. You don't have to have proof, you have to have prayer. The right feeling will come.

Prayer comes in many forms. I prefer the direct route: words—simple, easy, and sincere. Say anything to God. If you seriously object to prayer and to God, pray that it be less objectionable. But begin. Say, "OK, God, I'm doing this prayer thing because Melissa says it will open up new possibilities. So here I am."

Prayer teaches you about yourself. It teaches you that you are the most important person in the world. It also teaches you that you are not. You need both. Prayer is when you get to remember that you don't have to run the show. That there is both human effort and divine power in the world and your humble part is the human effort. Prayer is when you get to tell God about the pain you are in and the people who drive you crazy. You can talk to God about your parents, your body, your brain, your boyfriend, and your path in life. It doesn't really matter what you pray about or how, as long as you pray.

Prayer is also about paying attention to your deepest longings. If you have no idea what your deepest longings are, pray to find out. Prayer helps you formulate what you think, what you feel, what you need, and what you want. It gives you the space to safely say what is so private and so personal. In your prayers you can work out what you believe and what you fear. Prayer helps you organize your ideas, priorities, and opinions. It helps you find out what they are if you don't know.

You can pray to have the food stop calling you. Pray to get your parents off your back. Pray to fit into the new green dress in time for the wedding. Pray for help bearing the unbearable. Pray for love and kindness and peace and direction and good guides in life. Pray for others. Pray for your best friend from your residential program who just went back in for the fourth time.

Pray to say, "Thank You," "I need You," and "Where are You?" Pray out loud. Pray quietly. Pray in the car, in line at the store, and in bed at night. Pray when you are happy, hungry, scared, stubborn, full of hate, tired, wired, or weary—it doesn't matter. Just talk.

Just talk to God. Say anything you want, and don't stop until you know for the moment that you've said what you needed to say.

I do not believe that God is clueless about the trouble you are in, or the pain. He wants a connection. I think we have just got to believe this. Mostly, I think because there are times when the loneliness is so profoundly awful that there can only be one solution: God Himself. You know the loneliness I am talking about— the kind that gives you that hollow feeling in your chest; when the world looks watery; when there seems to be an echo in your mind; when no one in the world could possibly understand you; when you feel like you are on the moon. That kind of loneliness is for God. When you are dark, desperate, and totally deserted, and there is nowhere to go, pray. When you don't know what to do or where to go: pray. Wait and pray. Wait and pray. Wait and Pray.

God brings recovery. God brings willingness. My friend Lori tells me over and over and over again: Trust and rely on God. Trust and rely on God. I fight her on this with every fiber in my body. And then I don't. I know that this is the bottom line. I know that when it comes down to it, really giving up and surrendering it all to God is the beginning of possibility and hope. It is the beginning of knowing that you have choices in life but that all that control you are after is just a bunch of thick smoke. And on some level, that's actually a huge relief. And mostly it does not matter how you approach God. It matters that you acknowledge on some level that you are not, ultimately, the boss of things.

CHAPTER 15

Everlasting Starting Points

*God, grant me the serenity to accept the things
I cannot change, the courage to change the things
I can, and the wisdom to know the difference.*

—THE SERENITY PRAYER

I USED to think acceptance was the end. Now I know it's the beginning. I thought that acceptance meant defeat, despair, disconnect. I thought that when I accepted something I was giving up hope of ever feeling or having something better and resigning myself to badness.

Today I know that acceptance is the starting point. It is where I humbly admit once again that there is an ultimate force of life and it is not me. And while I have to look at my role and my responsibilities, I am not the sole cause or the sole cure for anything or anyone. I used to think that when life presented me with difficult people or situations I needed to come out swinging. Fight the fight. And now, after all these years of swinging and missing, I finally know that acceptance means pausing and nodding and saying OK, this is how it is, how it is supposed to be. Now what?

Fish Is Fish

There is a wonderful children's story by Leo Lionni about a frog and a fish who are friends. The frog leaves the pond and goes about the earth discovering wonderful things and comes back to tell the fish all about it. The fish of course wants to see these things for himself. You can guess what happens. The fish propels himself out of the pond and almost dies, if not for the frog coming along to push him back in. And the moral is (drum roll, please) . . . the book's title . . . *Fish Is Fish*.

You cannot be who you cannot be. And you are who you are. You are in your skin, with your bones. You have your eyes, your hair, and your knees. You have unquestionably unique talents, character traits, hang-ups, and tendencies.

Sometimes it's really good to know that you cannot be the girl across the room with the perfect stomach, or the one with the really rich parents, or the sober one, or the one with the easygoing nature or the natural athletic ability.

There will always be things in life that you can't be, can't have, and don't like. You will have things you don't want, and you will want things you don't have. But fish is fish. And you will probably find this to be true of other people as well. Your mother might always be critical. Your father might always have a temper. Your sister might always be skinnier than you are. Your best friend might always have a hard time not flirting with boys and stealing attention. Fish is fish.

Accepting that you and everyone else—*everyone*—has a character with some good stuff and some bothersome stuff will help you breathe easier. Having a good life means working on your character so you can deal better with other people's characters without hurting or getting hurt too deeply too often. Our characters exist for a reason. They are God-given, biological, genetic, based on nurture, environment, et cetera. You are not to blame or brag for having them (and again remember that character flaws are just survival instincts that worked well for us and helped us to survive when we were younger but now as we grow do not serve us the same way), but it is up to you to tend to your character and keep growing, fast or slow, and without fanfare or self-attack.

First comes acceptance; then you can decide what to do about things. Twisting yourself into a pretzel and straining, beating, and pummeling your way into looking, acting, feeling, thinking, or being other than who you naturally are is about as effective as the fish jumping out of the water and attempting to hop around on land like the frog. Better to learn about your own scales and gills and where and how you can breathe best and swim free.

Maybe the best part of the story is that the fish gets a little glimpse of the stuff that the frog was talking about, just enough to know that it's not really as amazing as the frog made it seem, or at any rate not any better than what the fish already had. Different does not necessarily mean better.

At the end of the book, by the way, the fish is glad that he did not die on land trying to live like the frog, and he really sees the beauty of the pond and is grateful for the water washing through his gills. He can have lots of good stuff just being a fish.

When your work includes recovering, feeling your feelings, forgiving, or learning to live with difficult people, acceptance is the gentle shore from which to set sail. You start by sitting quietly and letting the idea take hold that you can feel all your feelings without dying and without eating or cutting or sticking your fingers down your throat. You can ask God for help. You can ask God for the willingness not to go it alone all the time. You can ask God to help you have the ability to bear discomfort. You can say the serenity prayer over and over and over again. And you can let yourself believe that He will answer you.

You can survive being hurt. You can survive ocean waves of pain washing over you, knocking you out, and leaving you tossed onto the rocks. You can survive being bruised and banged up and sore and broken. You can heal and move and dance and find the parts of you that still work—that are whole and strong and open to a better life. Sometimes we try to be something we are not in order to find out who we are. But if you spend too much energy on that, you begin to lose oxygen.

I know this because I have done it, seen it, and helped others get up and walk on. Your journey to find out about yourself does not have to involve forcing yourself into being something or someone you are not. You can let your mangled insides heal and go forward and build a life for yourself.

And Rachel, who felt so huge, tells me after a while that she has gotten comfortable in her own misery; that maybe acceptance means accepting that she will always be this way—sullen, angry, and huge; that she will always be obsessed with what other people think of her even though she cannot really ever know or control it; that she will always have a difficult time with her food and her body.

I think that *always* isn't always what it seems. And some many moons into therapy, after allowing a few more feelings to poke through the hugeness, Rachel is willing to accept that she has certain qualities that are smooth and soft; that she is not, actually, only or always the rough edges or the sum total of her character quirks. We have also been talking about Rachel's internal wisdom and her sense of humor, grace, and compassion and have come to recognize that most of what Rachel does, she does to survive; that while those things, those patterns, have served her well until now, it might be time to think about doing things differently; that there are other ways to survive. These realizations are pivot points along the way. And there will be pivot points, when you turn a new corner in your mind, and you will know that something, *something*, ever so slightly has shifted for the better.

Rachel tells me with a sigh that she has been eating more mindfully lately and has taken to saying a few prayers here and there.

She wants my help to learn more about her character, and her mother's, since they seem to clash so much. She has the idea that maybe life does not have to be lived on the tip of a pin dodging her feelings because everything is always so sharp.

Forgiveness

Rachael also talks about forgiveness, though it's difficult because she still lives at home and her frustration with her parents seems like a never-ending story. She is often caught in the crossfire of their fighting and their dissatisfaction with parts of their own lives. Though they are loving and supportive in some ways, they are overly focused on how Rachel is doing and what they want from her and for her. She seems to be a good distraction from their own lives; they are focused on her food and not theirs, even though her mother's diabetes is getting worse and her father's weight keeps climbing.

She wants her mom to be less critical and her father to stop punching walls and her sister to respect her privacy. And because not one of these things seems to be happening at the moment, Rachel and I marvel at the characters of those around her and wonder about how to forgive them, because the resentment and the frustration seem to spin Rachel into not wanting anything for herself. They keep her from moving forward. We think that forgiveness and acceptance have a lot to do with the desire to recover.

I am a big fan of forgiveness because I have tasted it, and it is delicious. And it is no coincidence that forgiveness follows the God chapter. I don't really know if it's possible to forgive without divine help and a spiritual life. I think we even need help *deciding* to forgive before we get to the forgiveness part.

One of the biggest problems with forgiveness is that it deflates the rebel in you. When you forgive, or at least decide to, you lose all that rebel fuel that you might not even know you have. Forgiveness implies that you forgo your right to be right and your right to soldier on in quiet fury; that you drop your end of the rope—even though when you do, it can seem like you have nothing to struggle with or hold on to or pull for.

I used to be afraid of forgiveness the same way that some of my clients are afraid of giving up their eating disorders, cutting rituals, or body-hate—the same way I was afraid of letting go of acute, pinching, heart-bending grief. I was afraid that if the grief went away I would lose the person I was grieving all over again. I thought my grief was the only connection I had to that person.

It was the same with the anger. I was afraid that if the anger was gone there would be nothing—no feeling at all—a gigantic, huge, flat, never-ending field of nothing. And I thought that feeling nothing would be even worse than all the bad feelings put together. Even though I thought that all the things I did to escape and manage and control my pain were about achieving a blissful state of nothingness, I really did fear that deep, wide void.

Then one day I saw the person whom I had once been very close to and very angry with—the one I spoke about earlier. I had held on to that anger for a long, long time. I might have even liked being angry with her—it made me feel right and strong and better about myself. I liked knowing I had been wronged and I was right. I liked stalking about in my own knowingness. I thought that as long as I was angry, I was safe. As long as I could remember the anger, I was protected from ever getting hurt in that way again. And I was afraid of the big, flat, never-ending nothing.

When I passed by her that day, I felt . . . nothing. And you know what? It wasn't so bad. If anything, it was a little disappointing.

Being angry with her really gave me a charge. But I realized that forgiveness does not mean "forgetness." It just means that I don't have to hold in all those hot feelings, that they can go. It occurred to me that the absence of that anger might leave a hole, but it also might stop eclipsing the possibilities of other feelings—good ones maybe—and good ones not necessarily connected with that person; that I can get my rev some other way. Forgiveness, too, comes with pivot points.

I am not going to forget that being close friends with her would most likely result in more hurt. Deciding to forgive her does not mean that she is not who she is or that her character has changed. Maybe it has. People grow. I don't know. Forgiveness means that I have decided to let go. Even if it does not come fast or easy, I have decided that forgiveness is the path I am going to take and that even if I am not there just yet, I can see the calm blue sky at the end of the lane up ahead. And it's better than what I've got now.

Perhaps being right is not so important anymore. And being revved up is overrated—calmer waters are actually pretty good. At the time of the initial wronging, I wanted to drag her before the Supreme Court with full press coverage. But I think it's OK now that I am either right and no one knows it but me and God, or that I am not so right and I lose. I don't care about losing so much anymore because there are other things for me to do in life.

When it comes to people close to you, or who live with you, forgiveness is a tall order. Resentment and anger shape you—and not for the better—just like *mean* does. Anger does not set and give rise to the soft moon of forgiveness just because you decide it should, but deciding is a good start.

Forgiveness, ultimately, is an act of kindness to yourself most of all, and a step forward in going on with your life and not being caged in by the doings of others. I am not saying they deserve it (though they might); I am saying that *you* do.

You do not, by the way, always have to tell the person you are forgiving that you are forgiving him or her. You just have to tell yourself. If you can forgive the people in your life who have or are hurting you, you are a giant step closer to a free and better life.

Forgiveness is both a decision and a process. It's like a sunset. At some point in life your anger just starts to sink slowly down past the horizon, and then a clear blue night appears and you are calm. If you believe that forgiveness will bring you relief, you are right. If your anger has not started to sink yet, you can decide to help it along. Either way, you will win.

The act of forgiving has two parts. The first part is looking at your own role in things—not to blame yourself or let the other guy off the hook, but to see your side of the street. Sometimes you really have contributed to the problem in some way, even if only by your reactions or choices. But looking at your own role is not about blaming yourself, it's about understanding your motives and actions, owning up to your stuff, and acknowledging that there are times when you desire the forgiveness of others. Asking for forgiveness and being forgiven is part of an emotionally healthy life.

The second part is looking at things from the other person's point of view. This does not mean the other person was right; it just acknowledges that he or she is human, with a character, personality, and angle of his or her own. Other people have their own set of problems, limitations, fears, frustrations, and work to do. It might hurt to know that you have to accept this sometimes in order to be with those you love, but it helps in tolerating the losses you suffer along the way and staying steady for the greater benefit of the relationships you value.

Looking at your role and theirs neither lets them off the hook nor puts you on it; it just allows you to make progress.

So what about abuse? What about forgiving abusers? Clearly, children who have been abused, sexually or otherwise, are in no way to blame for the abuse. Clearly, as Mary Anne Cohen writes in her recovery book *French Toast for Breakfast*, "the truth is that children are *never* the seducers—they are always the victims. The only thing a child is guilty of is the innocent wish to be loved."

Forgiveness and understanding of perpetrators of abuse is in its own category. There is no side of your street to clean up. There is only the process of healing with all that it encompasses. Is healing a vital part of recovering from self-harm? Yes, but in the right place, at the right pace, with the gentle movement of time. For some, forgiveness is part of that process, and for others it is not. Only you can come to that decision, without rush, without pressure, and within the safety net of loving support around you.

In some cases we forgive in order to restore or maintain relationships. In others we seek to forgive in order to release ourselves and heal. Forgiveness does not have to mean, by any means, returning to or staying in a relationship that is harmful or destructive. Sometimes forgiveness is the gateway to getting out.

Self-Forgiveness

Forgiving *yourself* is the gold medal of the emotional Olympics. It's a true victory over all the voices that want you to feel shame, fear, worthlessness, and self-pity. It's pulling up to a stop at the end of the rainbow and finding the pot of gold.

Self-forgiveness doesn't mean not caring about or not taking responsibility for your actions, or giving yourself permission to carry on as if there are no rules in life, or that you have no self-respect. It doesn't mean not saying you are sorry or making amends when you can. It doesn't mean being cocky or placating or self-pitying. It doesn't mean you are free to go about acting like an idiot on purpose, or that you are an idiot to begin with. It doesn't mean that you should feel free to down whatever toxic substances you like or take the iron to your hips. That's not true self-forgiveness;

that's just doing what you always did and getting what you always got—burned.

Forgiving yourself means breathing deep, fresh, cool air, letting it fill your lungs, linger for a minute, and then gently seep back out. It means continuing on the path of honor, dignity, grace, humility, kindness, and acceptance of the most basic of facts: you are human. It means saying "I'm sorry" to yourself and asking God to help you accept your own apology.

Self-forgiveness means that you are not the prosecutor of your own sins. You are not the jury or the judge, either. It means that you will not decide to rest on the idea that whatever you have done is so beyond the realm of legal, acceptable, and OK that you must hold yourself under water for it forever.

Self-forgiveness means that you accept that you are not perfect and are not expected to be; that on some level you know that perfect is the enemy of good; that you have made mistakes and will make them again; that you can have regret and sadness but you can sprinkle them with faith and kindness and growth.

You can start the process of self-forgiveness in any number of ways. You can write down the thing or things you have done to harm yourself. You can write down the things you have done to others. You can list the fears that have been part of the picture.

You can write, "I am sorry and I forgive myself." You can practice saying to the mirror, "Darling, I forgive you for _____. It's OK. You're all right. You're growing toward better."

You can write a list of your mistakes or grievances about yourself and put them in a "God box," or flush them down the toilet, or rip them up. You can talk things out with your therapist, sponsor, best friend, mentor, spiritual advisor, or God.

Self-forgiveness is not a choice between punishing yourself and letting yourself off the hook. It's being open to practicing a kinder, gentler, more accountable life.

If you think cutting, starving, or holding on to your self-hate is punishing yourself or atoning for your shortcomings or mistakes, it's time to rethink. Self-punishment doesn't atone for anything. It might provide temporary relief—some way of being alone again in the private universe of your pain and suffering. It might provide a diversion from the chaos around you and the chaos within you. It might provide a feeling of familiarity and an escape back into your disorder. But it won't provide atonement.

There are times when you need to make real amends. But amends are not about self-punishment, they are about freedom, responsibility, and rightful living. When real amends are necessary—and they are at some point for everyone—it's a good idea to talk it over with someone whose spiritual fitness you trust.

I used to think that to forgive would mean some kind of disloyalty to myself and my pain. I thought, "Gee, you know, I spent a lot of time and energy being angry and being devoted to the eating disorder, and if I stop now all that powerful righteousness will have been in vain, like some sort of faithful guard dog I am now sending away." That might even be true. But other protectors can materialize. You don't have to regard your judgments of others and yourself as permanent fixtures. You can allow for some flexibility. You can agree to set yourself free. First there is acknowledgment, next comes acceptance, and then comes understanding, apology, and freedom.

Rachel tells me that she thinks she and her mistakes are unforgivable—that's how huge they are—and that no matter how much she accepts her parents for who they are and forgives herself for not being able to fix their problems (and for wanting to, even though she knows it's not really up to her), she will always feel the heat of anger and the heaviness of despair in her chest. She thinks that believing this might be just another way to hang on to the eating disorder and depression and stay stuck. She thinks this, too, is unforgivable.

We toy with the idea that even when we do decide to forgive, we might have to remind ourselves about it over and over again. Forgiveness might in fact need to be repeated again and again. Rachel fears that once she forgives her parents and herself for the many things on her list of resentments, more demands will come her way; the expectations and problems will continue on. They seem endless and huge.

So together we wonder about waiting for God. We talk more about the great discipline that is needed to move forward in recovery and in life; how even prayer and forgiveness and food require discipline of some sort; how recovery means having to hear the right messages over and over and over again and doing the next right thing over and over and over again.

That seems huge and hard to do. When you repeat what you know works, get help when you need it, push back against the pull of isolation, and ride the swell of emotion, you can put the boulder down. Accepting yourself and opening yourself up to forgiveness means you can leave your post at the cold window and walk through the door and sit with God.

Rachel says that maybe allowing acceptance and forgiveness and God to all have tea in the room together, along with her stubborn self, is possible; maybe there is hope. She says she is feeling more ready to forgive herself and a few others in her life. When she thinks about it she gets the sensation of free-falling in space. It's not actually a bad feeling, though. There might be something to it.

CHAPTER 16

Hope Forward

The knowledge that you have emerged wiser and stronger from setbacks means that you are, ever after, secure in your ability to survive. You will never truly know yourself, or the strength of your relationships, until both have been tested by adversity. Such knowledge is a true gift, for all that it is painfully won, and it has been worth more than any qualification I ever have earned.

—J. K. ROWLING

HERE AGAIN at the intersection of emotional pain, self-harm, and eating disorders, where the willingness and readiness to recover hover uncertainly and progress comes in slow, quiet steps, also exists the need—the absolute necessity—for fun.

Taking Fun Seriously

Fun can be a foreign concept to us when we have grown used to suffering. When you have been floating for so long in the sea of body wars, self-hate, identity issues, emotional pain, and family stuff, it's hard to imagine having fun or to even really know what fun is or how to have some.

But fun is a part of recovery. It is crucial to wanting recovery. It is crucial to living a life that is better. We need to incorporate fun into our psyches in ways that will work going forward. In the depth of our anguish, we might believe that having fun is a betrayal of sorts to our suffering and to our recovery. We might not believe that fun helps both recovery and the willingness to recover and that it helps heal our pain, but it does, and in so many different ways.

Fun puts us in touch with parts of ourselves that can be expansive, uninhibited, light, and in the moment. It helps make grooves in our brain that usher in good feelings, distract from the pain, and allow us the experience of freedom.

For a lot of young women who are caught up in eating or self-injury disorders, fun is a complicated concept because it usually involves other people; since isolation is often the central component of eating disorders, cutting issues, and emotional suffering, that's a problem. It's also hard to enjoy yourself when you are busy hating yourself, comparing yourself, reeling from bad feelings, starving, bingeing, or obsessing about your weight.

Deep inside you might have fundamental objections to fun. Having fun can be as frightening as putting down your weapons, eating according to your food plan, or not obeying your compulsions. Many of the young women I work with think they don't deserve fun, or that if they let their guard down and have fun they will get clobbered once again. They think maybe it's safer to stay in the same old, same old.

What is fun anyway? Fun is anything that brings enjoyment, amusement, or lighthearted pleasure—simple, uncomplicated, safe, easy stuff—at least that's the official definition. Fun can also be anything that safely lifts you to a better feeling. Fun is going on rides at the amusement park. It is a quiet night with a movie and a soft blanket. It is a long walk in the park, a good old-fashioned board game, a concert, a museum, a bike ride.

You can have fun alone—and I really believe this—but since the pull of isolation that comes with emotional pain can lead us away from others, we have to be careful not to have fun only when we're

alone. We have to be willing to reach past our fears and isolation-
ism into safe friendships and activities. Though it's not easy to say
yes when you are hurting, or no when you know it's best for your
recovery, being open to fun is part of helping yourself move forward. It's not always easy to know when to push yourself and when
to rest, but if you listen to your true voice—your healthy self—you
will know what to do.

One of the biggest issues that many young women in recovery
bump into is that it's often hard to find friends to have fun with.
Much of what is considered fun these days involves food or alcohol
or drugs, so hanging out with the girls when they are barhopping,
smoking, or going for dinner can present real challenges.

But fun can usher in happiness, relief, diversion, and serenity.
To a hurt mind and heart, these can feel unfamiliar and even scary.
They can make us feel like we are not who or what we said we
were. Just like forgiveness, feeling relief and peace—and having
fun—does not let those who have harmed us off the hook. Having
fun does not mean we have cleared anything up. When we agree
to have fun, we are not only landing on the side of recovery, but
we are saying yes to creating and discovering our sense of self. Our
willingness to have fun is a nod toward doing something different,
something better, something good. It is saying yes to life.

When you are hurting, having fun is a signal to yourself that you
are willing to live, that you *can* live, and that it is, in fact, OK to live
outside of your pain or with your pain. This can be both appealing
and appalling, depending on how you are feeling and how you want
to or are able to look at it. Having fun can help you cope with your
pain, get relief, and move forward. But you must believe that you
are not turning your back on your hurt by letting some levity into
your life. You can have both.

Be brave and try it. It can help you want relief. Just know,
though, that sometimes you may feel letdown afterward. The voice
might tell you that you should steer clear so you don't end up

disappointed one way or another. The voice may tell you that you will have had fun, but it will be over, returning you to the same nightmare of bad feelings you had before, as if having a reprieve only serves to make you feel worse when you return to or remember your pain—only sharper for having had a break. The reentry may indeed be painful. But if you keep this in mind, that there is a before, a during, and an after to fun, and that there are feelings that come along with each part, you can be more aware and more OK with the transitions. It will get easier the more you do it.

Fun can also be too stimulating. It can rev you up, and when you are revved up you have to take extra care not to calm yourself down by using old behaviors or hurtful relief valves. Again, just your awareness of this can help you relax and enjoy new experiences.

Fun can turn out to be disappointing, too, so much so that you have to redefine how you view fun. It does not have to be dangerous or wild; it can be sweet and slow and simple. Don't confuse fun with thrills and excitement. You don't have to get too much of a rev out of it, just pleasure, joy, and light. As with most things, keeping our expectations reasonable helps keep our serenity intact.

When it comes to fun, even the most routine kinds of fun can help you move forward. I'm not suggesting that you settle for boring and blah. I'm suggesting that when you demand or expect so much from fun and the people you're having it with, you set yourself up for a letdown. Think of fun as something that brings easy pleasure, safe distraction for your mind, and good feelings. Work toward accepting fun as pockets of good times sprinkled through your life, not as once and done or something you have to strain to accomplish.

If you go in knowing that you are going in a different direction now and letting light in—that it's OK to be OK—you can let yourself feel the good feelings without shying away. If fun catches you off guard, you can call for help; you won't be washed away if you have fun and let go of your vigilance bit by bit, moment by moment.

It takes time to learn to enjoy fun, so go gently with yourself. Sometimes the good feelings are as hard or harder to bear than the bad ones you are so used to.

When your pain is high and your mood is low—when you don't feel that you have the words or the social capacity to put yourself out there—fun with others seems like a distant, undesirable concept. And you don't want to have to lead the way or make the plans or initiate the calls. The effort seems like it is too much, the fear of rejection is too much, the responsibility of having to ask is too much. I know that it can feel dangerous to put yourself out there, even when you know how. Sometimes just picking up the phone can seem like picking up a truck.

Making the right call can be confusing. It may not make sense to hang out with friends who are still involved in the culture of hurting themselves, or who are into stuff that does not bode well for your progress. And if it causes you shame, then it's not fun. I have heard many stories of supposed fun that is not really fun at all.

You might have to tell yourself again and again that fun is necessary. Fun is good. Fun is part of living. Fun can help your recovery. You need relief, release, and pleasure. We all do.

Relapse, Retrauma, and Remembering

I know you know this: The road is neither straight nor smooth. There will be slips and bumps and fits and starts and restarts. Despair will not disappear. It will pop over now and again for a visit. There will be triggers and times when you'll wonder if you've made any progress at all, or why you even bother. You can chalk it up to the disorder's voice getting loud again, or to some old pain knocking on the door again, or to a new pain—because life will be life. Sometimes new pain is a *retrauma*—new and present feelings and circumstances remind you of old or difficult feelings, opening them up to you again, clouding or adding to the situation at hand. When you trip or when something difficult happens, it can trigger your hypervigilance, your fears, and your old bad feelings.

You will fall short, fall off, fall apart, and not be able to figure it all out. Relapse is part of recovery. But relapse brings you new ideas, deeper meaning, and more curiosity about life. If you look at setbacks as stepping-stones, you will find your way forward again. And you will continue to discover new ideas and new depths of love and grace and perseverance.

You will, more and more, be able to tell the difference between feelings and obsession. You will know in your heart that you can keep growing and keep going. You will feel better. You will believe more and more in the value of balance, serenity, and gratitude. And in the vital importance of a good and healthy inner life. You will come to trust that your inner world can be and is a safe place. It is a place where you feel at home.

You will feel your efforts drip softly down from your head to your heart. And sometimes even better—from your heart to your head. You will get the subtle difference between self-reflection and self-attack. The phrase "easy does it" will become part of your inner psyche.

We need to continuously expose ourselves to healthy voices, recovery voices, and loving voices. Not all the time will these messages be perfect or the messenger spot-on, but you will know how to consider things differently and how to go gently and take in what you need. You will come to view people's foibles as reassurance that we all have them, that not one of us has a perfect character. And this will, over time, become a welcome fact, not a call to battle or a trip to loneliness.

We are in a lifetime process, and you can always keep a list of safe comforts and releases nearby—reminders of what to do when you need solace and relief. There are endless sources of wisdom and insight in literature, online, and from folks who have walked before you through the hurt. They are not perfect either, or the last and truest word, but they can offer guidance, grist for the mill, and hope.

It is never selfish to be focused on self-care, so be careful not to confuse selfishness with care or use it as an excuse to avoid the work of recovery or to punish yourself. You will feel better the more you hang on to the idea of being committed to giving back in some way. Maybe you will mentor, or volunteer, or give a good ear to a friend in need. You can do this without sacrificing your own care or shooting it all down under the false self-attack of selfishness.

It might be that the size of your stomach will always matter to you, but it can lose its power as the most fundamentally important thing in life. When this happens, you will be OK with it. It will flare up every now and again, but it will pass.

When we work gently and continuously on creating and revealing a self that is not a reaction to other people's moods and thoughts and feelings, or only to the pain that we have gone through, or to the disordered part of our minds, we can keep going forward to create a life worth living. We can continuously give ourselves permission to bypass the negativity even when we are in the pain, and to know, name, and feel our feelings without bringing harm upon ourselves.

When we come to know, hesitantly at first, then with more certainty that taking care of ourselves does not mean forfeiting our right to receive love and care from others, but actually enhances it, we begin to soar. We begin to trust truly that we do not have to perpetuate a stance of helplessness or self-pity by depriving ourselves of true nourishment, and while we may not have control over our feelings or impulses, we have a choice about how we respond. And a combination of working on our responses as well as unpacking our pain and our beliefs does yield us a different kind of relief than we could ever have imagined.

When we are suffering it is always hard to believe that it won't always be the way it is—that it won't always feel how it feels.

Painful feelings can feel so permanent when we are in them. We will be tempted to give in and say "forget it" just like in early recovery. But this, too, is part of our ongoing journey. When we hear something that enrages us or seems to limit us, we can remember that there really is no hurry. Sometimes we can push ourselves, and sometimes we can't; our honesty with ourselves is the key.

In the back-and-forth between rebellion and rage, between recklessness and resiliency, the decision to move forward remains yours alone. As deeply as you might want and need to be cared for and tended to by others, you must face the fact that you have to participate in your own care. You need to receive from others, but that does not replace what you need to give to and do for yourself.

Recovery can mean growing past friends emotionally, and past parents. Your progress can feel frustrating to others around you, even those who seemingly want you to get well. Change is difficult, and you might have to persevere even if it means doing better, feeling better, and knowing better than certain people in your life. This is not arrogance or cockiness, but rather a humble acceptance and acknowledgment of the fact that recovery efforts deepen us, and those who are not working on themselves the way you are do not have the experience, benefit, insight, and knowledge that those who are walking the path do. You can neither fault them for it nor point it out to them, and you cannot let it hinder your forward motion. You might see others around you start to change as well; that is one of the miracles of recovery.

Many young women tell me that they are afraid to find out what happens next. They believe that they are not supposed to be waiting for something to happen but are supposed to take the lead. So when they are expected to follow, they rebel, and at the end of the day they become their own enemy.

Others tell me that they see empty spaces instead of dead ends, but the idea of opportunity fills them with dread. Some say that the fear is more the problem than the problem. Others say they are both the problem, in equal measure.

And some tell me that they feel stuck; that once they have started, they are obligated to go forward; they know now what is in fact possible, and they sometimes wish for the stubborn blackness of refusal and ignorance to come back.

It is normal to have doubts, to grieve parts of yourself, and to feel daunted about what lies ahead. It's OK to feel uncertain about feeling better. It's just a feeling, after all. Or just a thought, and sometimes we really are just one thought away from feeling better. Those old parts of you that rear up now and again are only the echoes of old ways of self-protection and survival. And perhaps now, dread is really interest, excitement, and hope. If you are open to this, it can be true.

Empty spaces don't mean black holes. Relapse does not mean failure. And regret is a doorway to creativity. You don't have to squash the rebel in you in order to be willing to keep getting better. You can put the rebel to good use. Redirect her energy and her passion and let her rip—but not rip you apart.

Passionate About Life

The truth is that we don't always know what the truth is. Sometimes there is more than one truth. You can't always know the right thing to do or whether you are acting on your own behalf or doing what is right. You can't know if or when you should sacrifice what you believe you need in order to be giving to or respectful of someone else. You can't even know what it is you really need or what would be best for you in all situations. But you can ask God for help. You can consult with trusted advisors. You can write, sit quietly, and pray for clarity and relief. But you cannot always know.

You will make mistakes, give in to compulsions, and slip up along the way. You might even do so knowingly at times. But when you do, you will slowly and surely, over the course of your recovery, be able to let go of self-punishment and favor self-respect and graciousness. There will be no point in hurting yourself any longer, but only in continuing your quest for a peaceful and passionate life, admitting your mistakes, making amends where you can—including to yourself, and going forward.

More and more you will learn to pause and be open to new ways to tap into and direct your passion, even if you don't yet know what your passion is or how to access it. Anyone who has suffered from an eating or self-injury disorder is full of a lot of passion. Until now, under the cyclone of the disorder, that passion has been directed at your body, or at survival, or at dealing with the pain. But now, hand in hand with a willingness to take steps toward recovery, you can find and redirect that passion in so many different ways.

Passion often gets confused with urgency, which often leads to impulsivity, especially when anger or fear is on high volume. One of the best parts of a more sane and centered life is the ability to wait. When you feel most urgent about something is when it's most important to wait. Wait and write. Wait and pray. Wait and talk. The discipline of waiting through urgent feelings, riding their wave, and not rushing forth into action opens the door to true passion. It allows you to decode the difference between intense emotional reactions and deep, abiding dreams and desires. It helps you focus on your accomplishments and achievements and not get too caught up in comparing yourself to others. You can then tap into your heart and create a life that you hardly dared think possible.

If you close your eyes and sit quietly for a while, maybe many times over, the ideas will come. You do not have to commit to them, but just be open to hearing them emerge from the part of you that dreams, the part of you that loves and wants and feels, and the part of you that is open to beauty and grace. Being passionate does not mean that if you do one thing you will always have to do another, or that you will have to live on the drive of continuous achievement as defined by others. Living passionately has meaning, credibility, and credence in its own right and on your own terms.

For a long time I was passionate about writing this book. Many times I felt a quiet tugging inside my chest. I knew I wanted to write it. I also wondered if it would be enough. Maybe if I wrote one book, I would have to write two. If I only wrote one, I might be a one-book wonder—if the book was even half good. But still, there was the pull. And even though the pull hid itself often (like a lunar eclipse it would hide behind fear, doubt, the size of my thighs, and the idea that it would not appeal to everyone or solve everyone's problems), I still knew it was there.

That pull is part of being passionate about life. That pull is about feeling alive—not just being alive—and liking it most of the time. And it is somewhere inside of you as well. It is the idea that even though life is sometimes difficult and people can still hurt or disappoint you, or you them, you can still be part of it. You can be in the stream of life in your own unique, self-defined, peaceful, and passionate way.

Passion is not a constant. It is consciousness. It is the ever-deepening notion that you are glad to be alive, to be interested, and to be you.

Comfortable in Your Skin

So this is what it all comes down to: being comfortable in your own skin, free in your own mind, and at ease with yourself. Not always; that's probably not possible. There are, after all, hormones, moods, cloudy days, and people who say awful things. But there is also a certain kind of freedom that comes to you as you grow and wade through recovery. It does come. There is progress, and there are new levels of awareness and joy—but not a final destination. When you keep doing the work and using the tools for life, you will find grace, and grace will find you.

It is not the thrill really that we are after; it is knowing that it's OK to just be OK in the moment. We don't always have to know the answers. We can practice gentleness with ourselves and give ourselves permission to be comfortable in our skin. We can let go of self-punishment and move more easily through our lives. The idea that we alone are responsible for ourselves, our recovery, our emotional resiliency—no matter how much support we have or need—now becomes a gift of knowledge and deep joy that we can in fact accomplish, achieve, and claim ourselves.

You might still have a body whose shape you do not embrace, but you do not have to be at war with it to distract you from matters of the heart and soul. You can survive without having to hurt yourself.

So what is recovery, really? It's the willingness to treat yourself well. It's the willingness to feel your feelings, use your tools, get back up when you fall, and admit it when you blow it. Recovery is reaching out for support and help when you need it and not expecting any one person to be the only one to take care of you. It's accepting that though you did not consciously cause your pain, you are the one who is responsible for tending to it; that though you might desperately want someone else to take care of you, it is ultimately up to you to do the work.

Recovery means having healthy dependency on others. Recovery means having reasonable expectations and practicing the ability to bear both discomfort *and* comfort. There is so much love in the world, and while gratitude for the things you have does not erase your pain, it does serve as a reminder that you are not only in pain—that life is a mix and you can find your own personal balance.

I no longer view my own pain as meaningless, nor do I view it as inevitable or as my own doing, though sometimes it is. I take responsibility for my mistakes and my character, and I know that my actions have consequences. What those consequences are I cannot always predict. But I can pause before I act (and know that God is in the pause) and seek forgiveness when I make a mistake. There is no longer an endless battle with a punishing baseball bat to my psyche. This is one of the most valuable parts of being further along on the road to recovery.

My pain has opened me up to an abundance of love and joy and to both giving and receiving it in many forms, from many people. In understanding and knowing both emotional pain and recovery, I have experienced a contrast in life that has helped true compassion, serenity, and goodness dwell in me. It is a better place for me to be. You will find this place too, if you are willing to look.

Many times over the years young women have told me that they had no idea what they wanted or if they wanted anything at all. They've told me they were not sure whether they really didn't want anything in life or they just didn't know what to want. Some have told me they didn't believe they deserved anything; it was all so unclear. My clients and I have discovered and rediscovered the idea that in order to want to get better you have to feel that you are worth it; that you matter; that what you want will open up before you like spreading arms as you begin to heal and recover. And even though there may be a pull toward living in the negative parts of our story, more and more we can live in the positive parts, in the progress, safety, and the happiness too.

Little by little, we have to be collectors of evidence of our own value. You have to be brave enough outside and inside of all your emotional pain to believe that you are worth it, even if you do not yet feel it. You were born wanting and needing. This is the human condition, and you are no different. You were born needing food and comfort and safety and light and love. You need these things in order to grow. Without them, you wither. The degree to which you have gotten them, have them now, and have been able to receive them is different from that of anyone else. Being comfortable in your own skin means you can accept that you are human, and that when you do not have what you need you must valiantly and appropriately seek to get what is missing.

You cannot demand it, but you can *create* it and you can access it. And then step by small step, you can turn to give a hand to others as well.

When you are comfortable in your skin, you no longer have to fight the wanting. You do not have to be afraid of your wantings or afraid of not knowing what your wantings really are. You no longer have to believe that anything good will never be good enough, or that you cannot survive being scared or overwhelmed. Your emotions can still seem intolerable at times. You might feel the urge to harm yourself or believe once again that you deserve to be punished or that it's OK to take your feelings out on yourself. You might lapse into confusion and occasionally get lost in the enmeshment of your food and body issues. But somehow, as you grow, and grow more comfortable in your skin, you will know what's happening and you will pause, center yourself, and go forward gently.

You can then finally ask yourself, "Why me?" without asking it from pity or fear, or with self-attack or urgency. Rather you ask it with love, curiosity, and patience. The ability to talk, to consider new ideas and points of view, to study yourself without lashing out at yourself or others, and to release pressure in productive rather than impulsively hurtful ways is not only the hallmark of resiliency and maturity but the outcome of good relationships, good therapy, good reading, good attention to life, and your own personal truth and persistence.

Time often works for you, soothing the rough edges, dulling the sharp pangs, and moving you along even when you don't see your way clear. If you let yourself be open to the idea that your feelings are not always facts, that you don't always have to act on them, and that they are not the enemy but how you know who and what matters to you, then you can allow them to be windows into the deeper parts of yourself and your consciousness. You will find that your feelings don't have to be and won't always be so intense. The world will seem lighter.

When you bring grace to yourself and to others, you begin to understand that healing yourself is part of healing the world. When you decide to recover, you are deciding to become part of the quiet, powerful, collective voice of recovery. Your effort—each and every next right step you take, no matter how small—matters. Your steps build your resiliency and fortify you so you can endure, create, and thrive through life's ups and downs. Recovery is all at once self-serving and selfless. It is as generous to others as it is to yourself. And you will want to be generous. You can trust that in looking to be of service to others and finding ways of being of service in the world brings its own private and powerful reward.

At the beginning of your recovery journey, or even along the way, there is no way to know how good you will feel further on. You have to go on faith. But you can go on faith.

Somewhere inside you there is a part of you that knows that you can, and when you are ready, you will; that perhaps, in fact, you want to; that your story is worth telling, worth writing, and worth hearing; that you need not know exactly where you are headed in order to start.

And that your recovery is profoundly and uniquely yours, and it's good.

RESOURCES

www.recoveryhopeandhealing.com
www.oa.org
www.eatingdisordersanonymous.org
www.nationaleatingdisorders.org
www.something-fishy.org
www.mentorconnect-ed.org
www.anad.org
www.selfinjury.com

ABOUT THE AUTHOR

MELISSA GROMAN, LCSW, is a psychotherapist specializing in eating disorders, relationships, and healing emotional pain. A graduate of the University of California, Davis, and Yeshiva University's Wurzweiler School of Social Work, Melissa has more than twenty-five years of experience helping people live healthy, satisfying lives. In addition to maintaining a busy private practice, Melissa provides clinical supervision and training to therapists across the country. She is the founder of www.recoveryhopeandhealing.com, an inspirational audio library of interviews with experts on recovery and emotional health.

Melissa's trademark warmth, sensitivity, and profound understanding of human nature permeate her work. She believes that talking and being understood are a vital part of the healing process. Her expertise in helping people to move from fear, frustration, and self-attack to self-reflection and self-compassion has helped many to uncover their creative, joyful, and authentic selves.

Melissa has written for a variety of magazines, websites, and blogs including www.hopeforward.blogspot.com. She lives in New Jersey with her husband and five children, where she cultivates an organic garden. For more information, please visit www.melissagroman.com.